ORIENTAL CARPETS

From the Tents, Cottages and Workshops of Asia

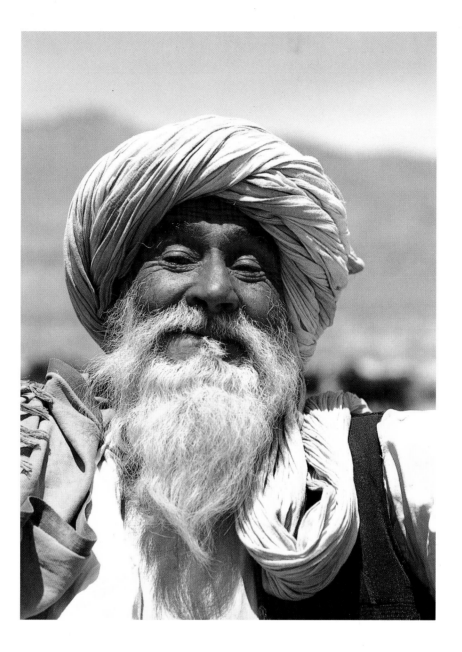

JON THOMPSON

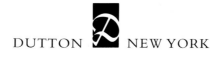

DUTTON NEW YORK

A Note on the Text

Irrespective of the shape or design, the length in the warp
direction is given first.

NAMES AND PLACES

Spellings of names generally agree with the rules of the
Permanent Committee on Geographical Names. The main
departures are where the rules demand a character not present on
my typewriter. The Turkish c is used for the rarer Turkish names,
whereas names familiar in western literature, for example Mujur, have been
retained because the more correct Mucur seems
pedantic and confusing. Iran is usually called Persia, the name
familiar to English speakers through centuries of usage, except
where a specific political entity is referred to. The conflicting
claims of transliteration systems compatible with Arabic, Roman
and Cyrillic characters, and the different rules of spelling
generated by the logic of Arabic, Turkish, Persian and the Turkic
dialects, cause fruitless and unending arguments. As this is a text
for the general reader, diacritical marks have been omitted
altogether.

Under the title *Carpet Magic*, this book was first published in the UK in
association with the Barbican Art Gallery, London, 1983

This revised edition
first published in the United States, 1988.
by Dutton Studio Books,
an imprint of Penguin Books USA Inc.,
375 Hudson Street, New York, N.Y. 10014.

Library of Congress Catalog Card Number: 88-71012

ISBN: 0-525-24697-5 (cloth)
ISBN: 0-525-48426-4 (DP)

This book was produced by
JOHN CALMANN AND KING LTD, LONDON

Designed by Trilokesh Mukherjee and Roy Trevelion
Typeset by Balding + Mansell Ltd, UK
Printed in Hong Kong produced by Mandarin Offset

10 9 8 7 6 5 4 3 2

This page: A shepherd couple, Chamba valley, India.
Title page: A Pathan from Afghanistan.

CONTENTS

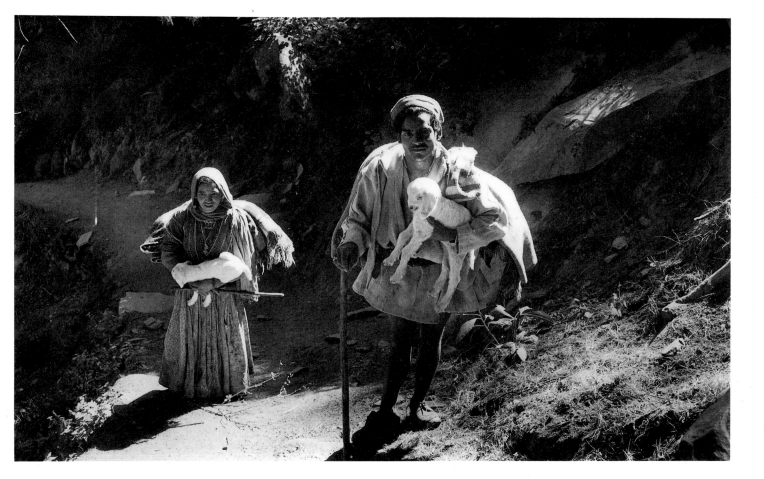

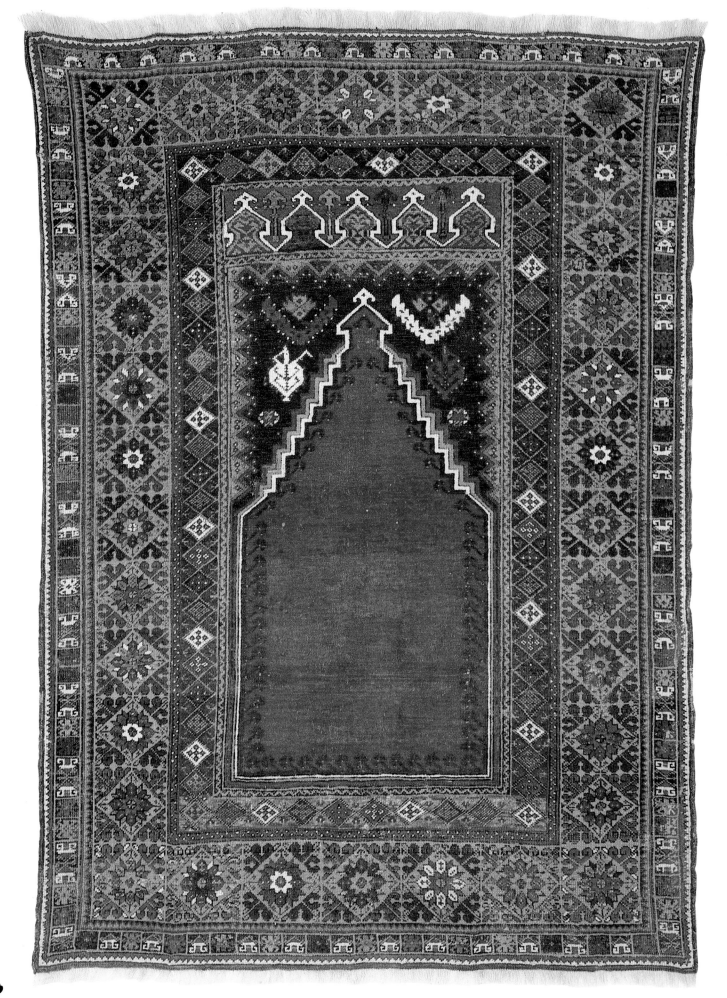

Introduction

A new way of thinking about carpets

In recent years there has been a growing interest in carpets. Many books have appeared including catalogues, introductory texts and more specialised works covering new ground. Yet in spite of all the effort put into these publications the subject of carpets still bewilders and confuses most people. What seems to be needed is a basic framework of ideas that can be used in approaching this huge and perplexing field. The scheme set out here aims to provide this framework. Normally carpets are classified according to their country of origin, but the types produced within any one country are so dissimilar that grouping them together merely causes confusion. As a result many people are discouraged from following the subject any further. Here the geographical classification is abandoned and instead carpets are arranged in four groups according to the circumstances in which they were made. This is a new way of looking at carpets, and their division into four main categories is the underlying and unifying theme of this book. The four categories are: tribal weavings; products of the cottage industries; carpets manufactured in town or city workshops; and court carpets.

LEFT: *The cottage industry is supplied by women working at home to increase their family income. Because they are weaving to sell, cottage weavers are less conservative than tribal weavers, are always on the look-out for new ideas, and are sensitive to what is in fashion. In common with tribal weavers they enjoy bold primary colours and use unsophisticated equipment. The form and layout of this rug from Mujur, central Turkey, derives from the design of a prayer rug made for the Ottoman court in the sixteenth century (p.149). The same design exists in many rural versions (pp.126 and 129). Its strong colours and bold angularity are typical of cottage industry production. Nineteenth century.* 183 × 130 cm/ 72 × 51 in.

BELOW: *The tribal weaver cannot retain in her memory the large complex patterns found in workshop carpets. Expressive power is achieved through the use of colour, space and proportion. This outstanding example of Turkmen tribal work illustrates the use of small, easily remembered patterns set in a perfectly balanced arrangement. It was woven by a member of the Salor tribe of Turkestan before 1850.* 47 × 111 cm/ 18½ × 43½ in.

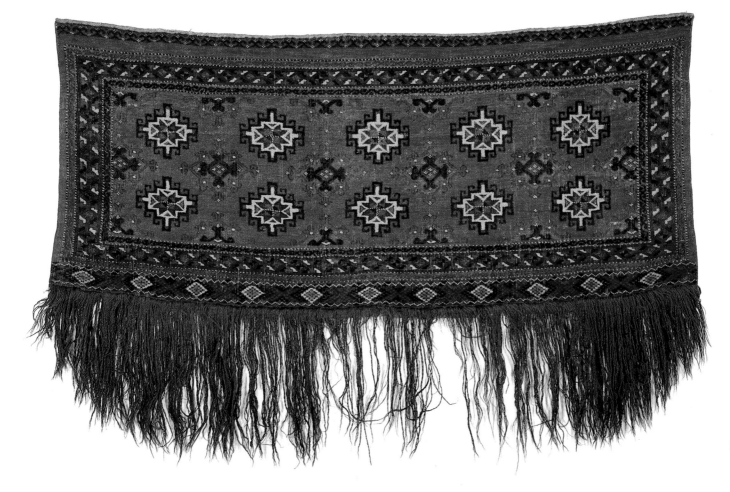

The four groups are arranged in order of increasing technical achievement. Our interest is centred on the carpets of the first three groups made between the seventeenth century and the present. Most were made in the nineteenth and early twentieth centuries. The fourth group, which is not covered in detail in this work, consists mainly of carpets made for the Islamic courts in the sixteenth and seventeenth centuries. They probably account for less than a tenth of one per cent of all surviving carpets made before 1900 and are mentioned for the sake of completeness and because they had an enormous influence on the design of later carpets belonging to the three other groups.

Those with expert knowledge will be quick to point out that the proposed divisions are not exact, so let me do it first by saying that to be concerned with exactness or lack of it is to miss the point. The classification is intended to provide a way of looking at carpets, an intellectual framework to be used as an aid in learning about them. As soon as a person acquires sufficient information of his own and has built up a store of his own observations then he can abandon the classification and devise one for himself. Part of the value of having such a scheme is that it obliges the user to search carefully for clues that will tell him what sort of carpet he is looking at. It is the effort made in trying to decide which category a carpet belongs to that is important and not how well it fits it. A lot can be learned in the process and things may be discovered which would otherwise have passed unnoticed. As a help towards this end the approach throughout this work is deliberately general, technical discussion is limited, jargon avoided, and no attempt is made to cover new ground in terms of attribution or to provide detailed information on classification. The aim is to take a bird's eye view of the whole field of carpets with the non-specialised reader in mind and examples of the different categories have been selected to give an idea of the great range of taste encompassed within the field.

One effect of the lack of a satisfactory working classification of carpets is that many museums with collections of carpets do not know what to do with them. The fact that they originate in an Islamic country is often sufficient to ensure that they end up in the department of Islamic art, where the great majority, since they have little to do with Islamic art, are treated as unwelcome clutter and put into storage. They might be in better company in a museum of anthropology, but I know of no major primitive or ethnographic art collection that has taken more than a passing interest in tribal carpets. The usual reason given is that there is no point in gathering a mass of unclassified material because objects, to have any value, must be collected directly from the producers and documented at the time. But since the tribal way of life is fast disappearing I believe it is shortsighted not to acquire carpets for collections on these grounds. After all, lack of knowledge concerning the source has not prevented European museums from building up spectacular collections of pre-Columbian textiles, pottery, metalwork and so on which as archaeological artefacts are completely unsatisfactory since their source is often unknown. It could take just one curator of a primitive art collection with an interest in the field to change the outlook of others and start a phase of serious scholarship in tribal carpets.

It was mentioned that the four categories are arranged in order of increasing technical development. Perhaps the main value of the classification is that it also describes four different artistic categories, though it must be emphasised that no judgement on the merit of each is implied. A progression in the artistic sense is present but only in that it mirrors the increasing technical elaboration. In the art of carpet weaving the progression is from those executed entirely from memory to those resulting from exact written-down instructions. I believe that the greatest source of confusion in carpets is a lack of understanding of the artistic differences between them which the classification should help to make clearer. Put very simply tribal carpets can be thought of as 'primitive art' (in the best sense of the word), and workshop carpets as 'decorative art'. As each has its own aesthetic logic, comparisons between carpets in different categories is meaningless.

To introduce such ideas is to tread on dangerous ground so perhaps I should explain a little more and at the same time define the categories in more detail.

Tribal carpets are not designed as such but woven directly from memory. They are primarily made for use, not sale, and, in addition to their practical role as grain sacks or pannier bags, have an important place in tribal life. They were and are used for when guests come, for weddings, as gifts, for picnics, prayer, the decoration of animals, the tent, the home and for every important aspect of life. Traditional and sacred patterns are woven into the rugs making them part of the very fabric of tribal life and identity, and the borders protect and enclose a space decorated with devices for the promotion of good fortune, fertility and for warding off evil influences. Some designs are used only by a particular tribe or on a special kind of object. All these patterns, charged with significance, can only be understood by reference to the culture of those that use them. Regrettably much tribal weaving found in the market place is little more than ethnographic junk, equivalent to the grass skirts and assagais of the ethnographic art market, and much that passes for tribal weaving has been made by weavers no longer constrained by the traditions and demands of tribal life. Among the tribal weavings of the nineteenth century are objects of surpassing beauty and a few have been selected to represent the best of tribal work in this book. Leaving aside the aspect of decay in tribal life, which is not peculiar to the carpet weaving communities, the best tribal carpets bear comparison with the best examples of the art of Africa, Oceania and the north-west coast of America, which are now widely acknowledged as art of a high order. Curiously the art of the north-west Pacific coast, based on certain design principles which were forgotten during the last century and recently 'rediscovered' by Holm,[1] has many parallels

RIGHT: *Workshop carpets are produced for commerce by an organised team of specialists. Artists design the patterns, dyers match the colours, and weavers work from detailed cartoons which make possible the precise execution of large curvilinear designs. This carpet, with its sophisticated colour palette, intricate pattern and faultless workmanship, is a fine example of the classical Persian workshop style. Sarraf Mamoury workshop, Esfahan, 1970s. 240 × 148 cm/94½ × 58 in.*

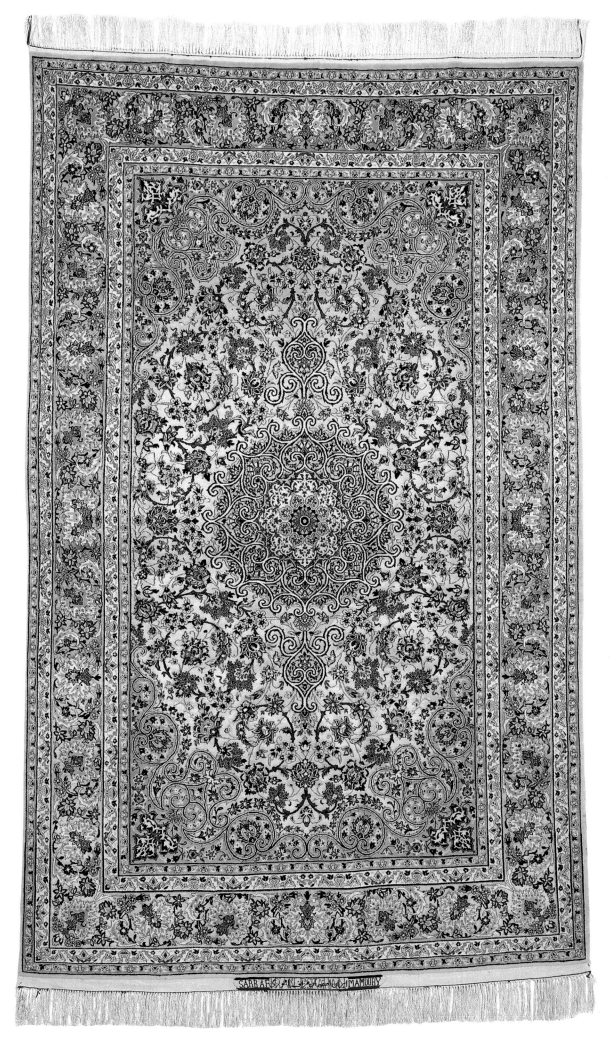

BELOW: *In essence tribal weaving is functional as well as decorative. This type of horse cover, woven by the Yomut Turkmen of north Persia, is used at race meetings and on other festive occasions. Its striped pattern, worked in knotted pile, imitates the appearance of their more common flatwoven covers. Twentieth century. 109 × 102 cm/43 × 40 in.*

RIGHT: *A typical item made for domestic use is the salt bag. This delicately patterned tribal weaving is the work of Aimaqs or Baluchis in eastern Persia. Though not very old, it shows no sign of the decline in standards so common in later tribal work. Mid twentieth century. 58 × 38 cm/23 × 15 in.*

BELOW RIGHT: *A horse in Kordestan, north-west Persia, models a flatwoven cover acquired for the Royal Scottish Museum, Edinburgh.*

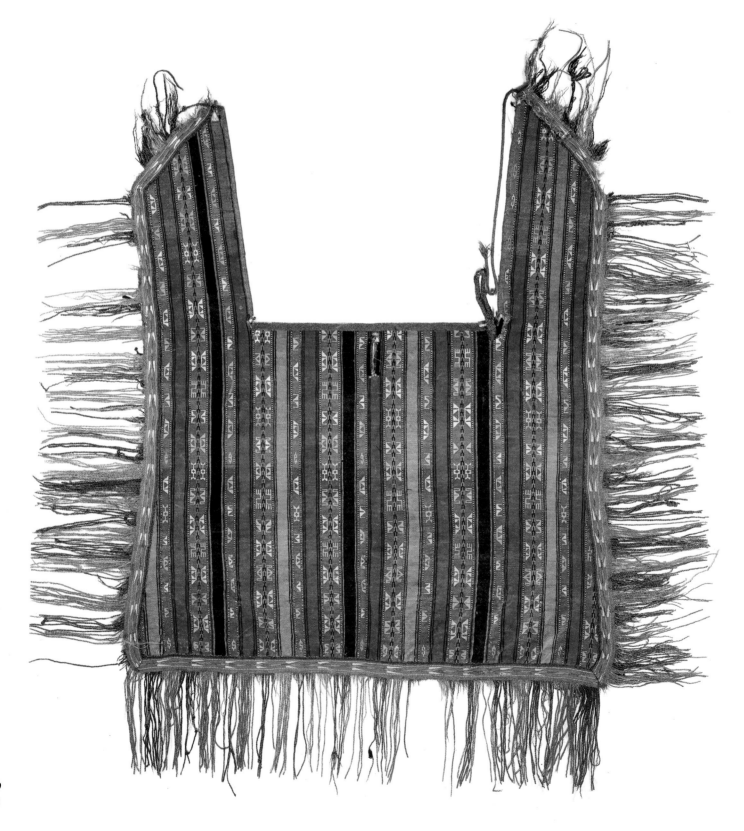

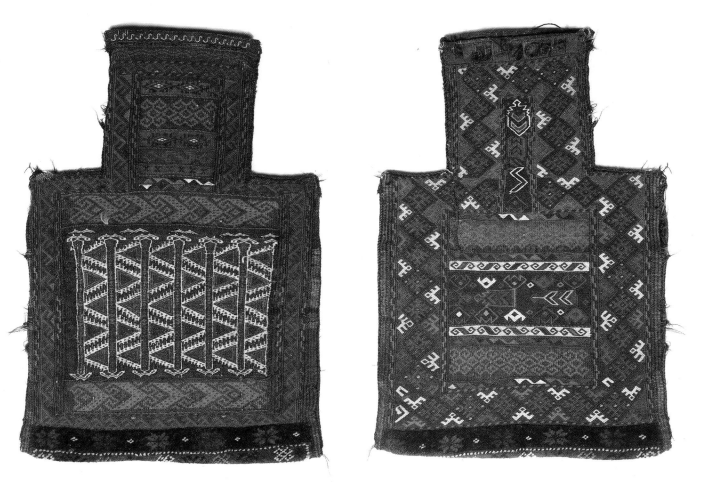

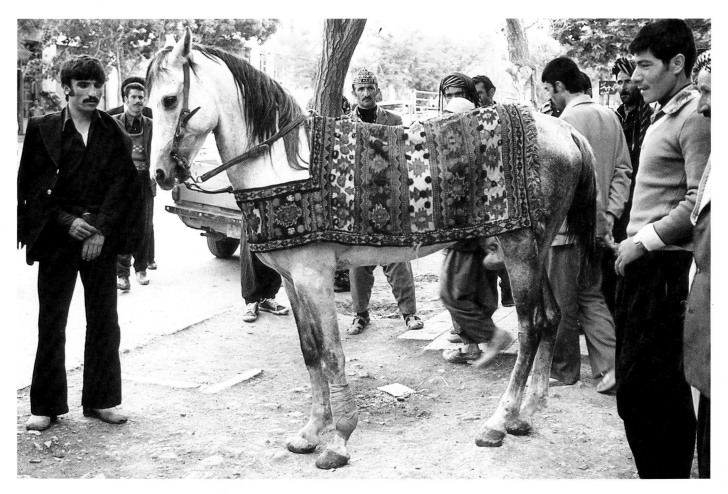

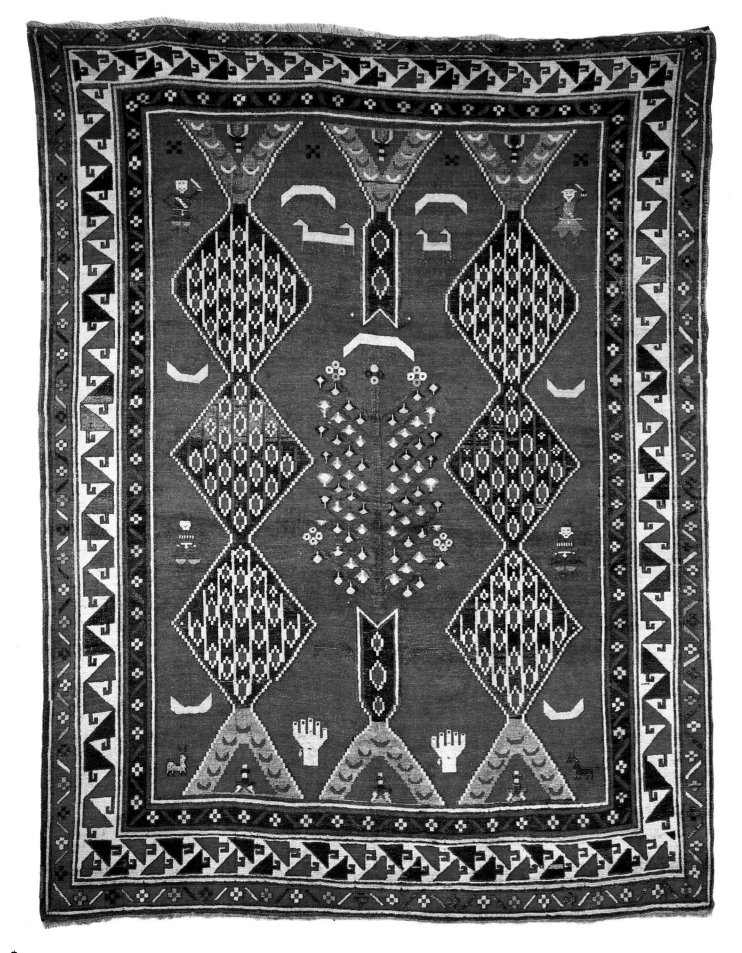

LEFT: *In the Caucasus during the second half of the nineteenth century growing demand for carpets caused a huge increase in the output of the cottage industry. Many new patterns were invented at this time. This Kazak carpet from the Karabagh district of the south Caucasus uses a design borrowed from a tie-dyed textile and combines it with a tree, stylised animals and little human figures in a highly individual composition. The two hands convey the idea of protection. Nineteenth century. 240 × 183 cm/94½ × 72 in.*

RIGHT: *The severely abstract design of this carpet makes an interesting comparison with the work of some modern painters. Its shaggy surface resembles an animal pelt, which some historians believe was the inspiration for the making of the first knotted pile carpets. It is unusual in that it was made in strips on a narrow loom using undyed wool, The strips were dyed in one piece and then sewn together. Though often ascribed to the Uzbegs, who also make coarse long-piled carpets, these rugs are the work of a nomadic Arab tribe migrating between Qataghan and Badakhshan in north Afghanistan. Their appearance in the Kabul bazaar in the 1970s coincided with rapid changes in local social and economic conditions that caused a sharp reduction in the number of families making the migration. After 1950. 305 × 107 cm/120 × 42 in.*

with the art of one of the most outstanding groups of tribal weavers, the Turkmen (Turkoman) of central Asia. I believe that the design-power, primal abstraction and profound character of some tribal and cottage-made weavings, a tradition maintained exclusively by women, will come as a surprise to many people who have never seen this type of work before. Likewise I shall be interested to learn what impression they make on people who have never considered carpets as art, and particularly lovers of twentieth-century abstract painting who should find much to excite them.

The cottage industry is sustained by the weaver working at home in her spare time. In character her work has some of the primordial quality of tribal weaving. But, unfettered by the traditions of tribal life and with a customer to satisfy, she can modify her work to suit the buyer. The character of the cottage-made carpet is moulded on the one hand by the weaver's preference for bright strong colours, and on the other by her desire to make something up-to-date, fashionable and saleable, which is expressed in a readiness to copy town carpets or even to devise entirely new patterns. In the Caucasus during the second half of the nineteenth century cottage weavers became extraordinarily inventive and created a whole new repertoire of rug designs using elements of traditional patterns and reworking them in an original way. These are now much in demand with collectors. Most cottage rugs are woven from memory or with the aid of a drawing. Sometimes a cartoon is used but not with the same exactitude as is demanded in the commercial workshops. They are distinguished from the tribal carpets by their more cosmopolitan designs and adaptability to the demands of the market. In character they occupy a middle place somewhere between tribal and workshop carpets.

The town and city workshops make carpets for

BELOW: *This small rug from the Shirvan district in the south Caucasus, a product of the cottage industry, shows great originality in its pure abstract design and use of colour. Nineteenth century.* 122 × 91 cm/48 × 36 in.

RIGHT: *Silk dyed in brilliant colours gives force to the powerful abstract design of this striking rug, a product of the cottage industry in the Heriz district of north-west Persia. Nineteenth century.* 144 × 92 cm/56½ × 36 in.

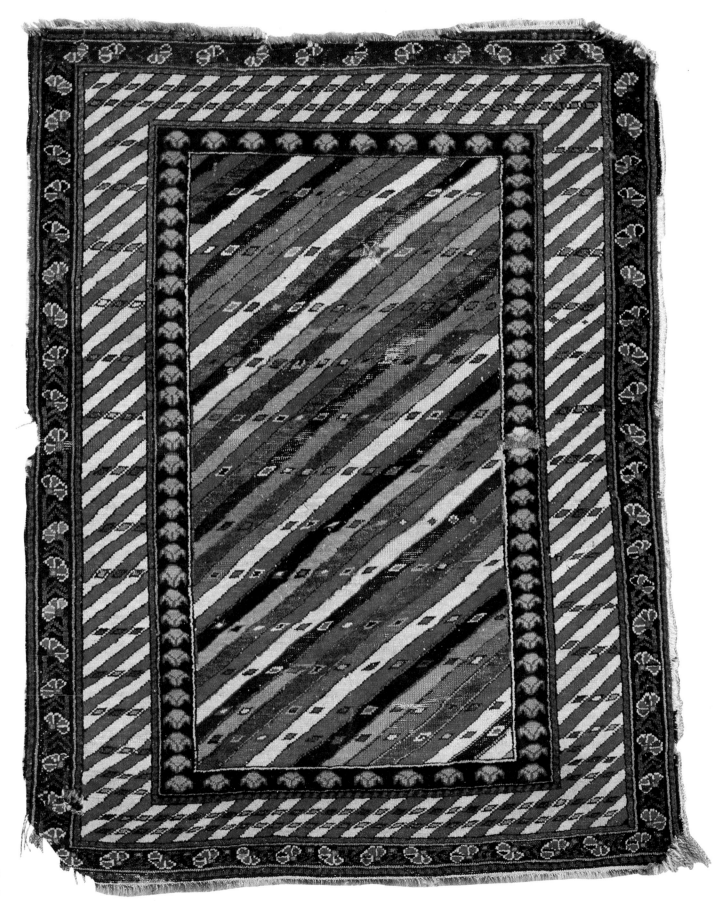

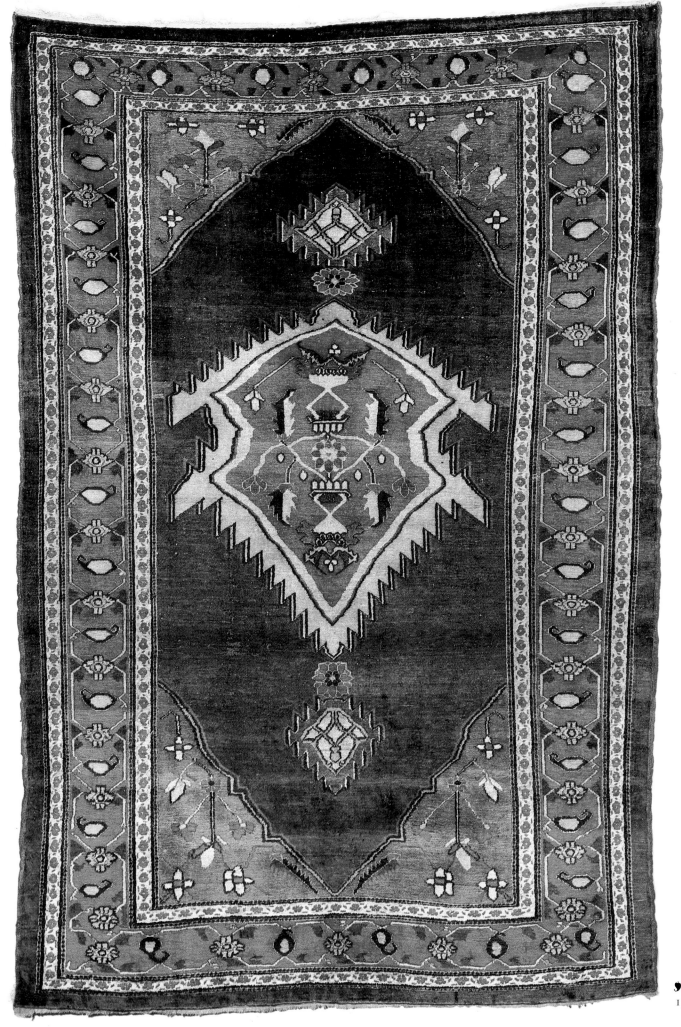

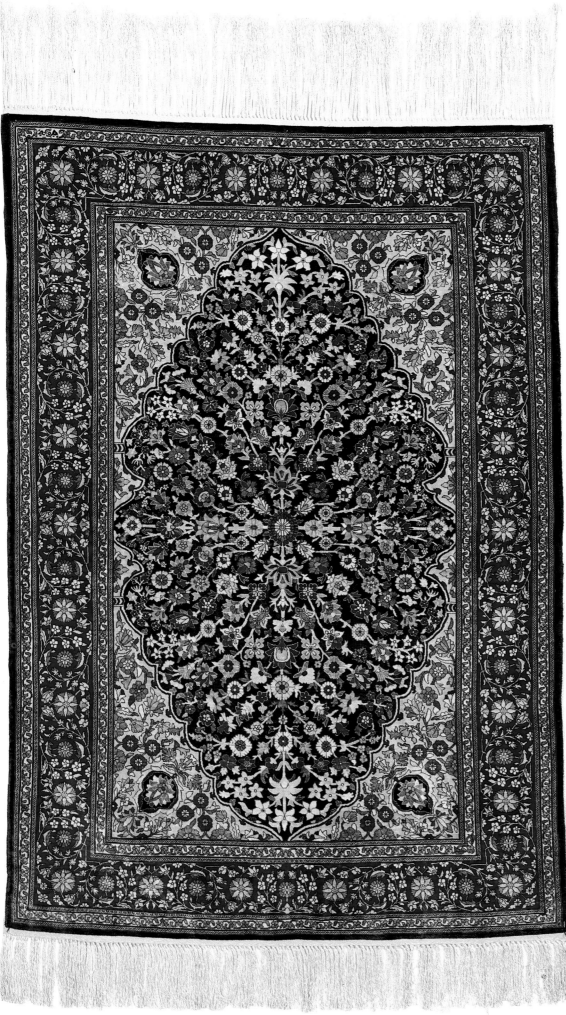

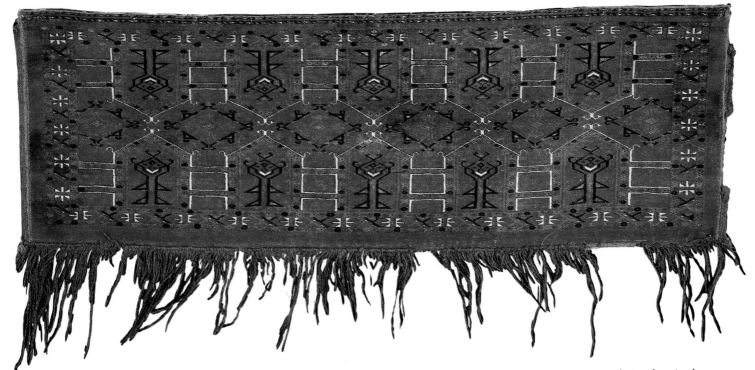

LEFT: *The art of the workshop carpet is the art of the designer. This modern silk rug from the Hereke workshop, the source of Turkey's most refined carpets, has a pattern based on an eighteenth-century Indian design. 145 × 99 cm/57 × 39 in.*

BELOW: *Goat hair tents in the Engizek mountains. Atmali village, Marash province, Turkey, 1981.*

ABOVE: *In nomadic tribal society great pride is taken in the appearance of the tent which is always ready to receive guests. This bridal camel trapping would have been used after the wedding to decorate the tent (felt type, p.77). Saryk Turkmen. Nineteenth century. 45 × 129 cm/17½ × 51 in.*

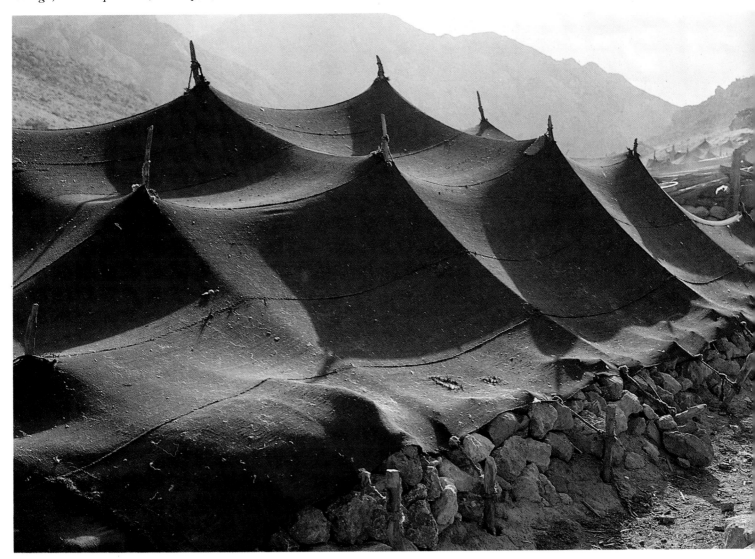

A. U. Pope, one of the greatest scholars in the field of Persian art, wrote in 1926: 'The elements of the design are like notes in a melody or words in a poem.' Rhythmical repetition, inversion and the varying combination of patterns give carpets a quality akin to that of music. This beautifully made rug from the nomadic Qashqai tribe of southern Persia uses a floral cluster pattern, or boteh in a simple alternating rhythm, where the use of different colours creates a secondary diagonal design. Nineteenth century. 237 × 137 cm/93½ × 54 in.

commerce by a production process. Instead of one person doing everything, production is split up into a number of specialised crafts. A designer makes an exact drawing in the form of a cartoon and the weavers follow it exactly, reproducing knot for knot the specified pattern. For them there is no question of any particular attachment to the carpet other than as a means of earning a living. Workshop carpets are thus designed in the same way as wallpaper or curtain fabric and in the modern home have a similar function. It is in this sense that the term 'decorative art' was used. After a long period of disfavour that began with Ruskin and lasted until recently, 'decorative art' has been reinstated and is now the subject of renewed interest. The tendency to deny it the status of genuine art is no longer tenable. Furthermore the twentieth-century exploration of all aspects of abstract art has, by way of reaction, brought back into focus problems of special interest to the designer, such as the use of pattern to order the space on a plane surface. With hostility to 'mere decoration' a thing of the past, ornament no longer a dirty word, and the designer acknowledged as an artist in his own right, designed carpets should be assured of a fair assessment. They will, I hope, be judged as art objects by the quality of their design and not compared to carpets of fundamentally dissimilar character such as those woven from memory.

Carpets and music
In trying to think and talk about carpets I find myself constantly comparing them with music. The warp and weft of their underlying structure are, like the musical stave, the vehicle for the pattern and impose upon it a basic order. Their visible surface is covered with thousands, sometimes millions, of tufts of wool and the resulting minute points of colour are arranged like the individual notes of a melody into motifs and patterns. There is a musical quality in the combination, inversion, repetition and rhythm of their patterns, and in their colour harmony and texture. Like music, the art of carpets is poorly supplied with terms capable of conveying the flavour of the experience they evoke. The achievement of an aesthetic effect by using space, colour, proportion and pattern gives some carpets a completely abstract quality which I find only in music. Musical comparisons are a recurring theme throughout this review so it may help to think of the four main streams of carpet production and design in terms of a musical analogy.

Carpets made by the nomads and tribeswomen have the character of folk music. The pattern, like a folk song, is learned by girls from their mothers as soon as they are old enough to help. It is not written down anywhere and is kept alive by direct transmission from person to person. A number of tunes or patterns known within a community resemble in a general way those of neighbouring communities while retaining a distinct and individual character. The communal repertoire is never static, new things are being absorbed and others forgotten all the time, but at a slow rate.

The cottage-made carpet is like the performance of a solo entertainer with a repertoire of popular and traditional songs.

In contrast the workshop carpet, especially the court carpet, resembles a concerto such as those Bach composed

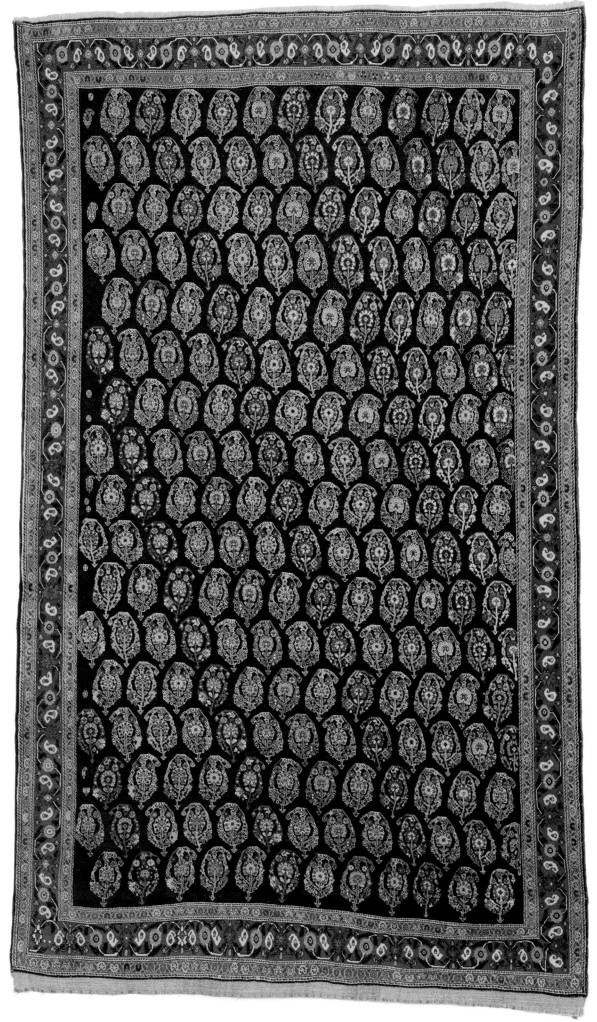

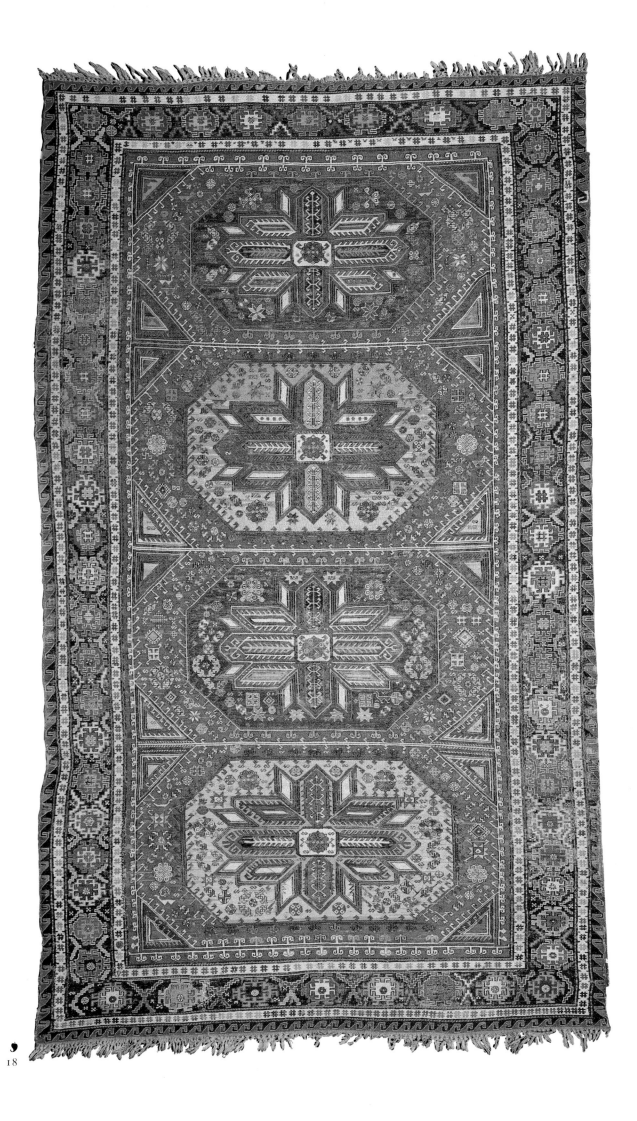

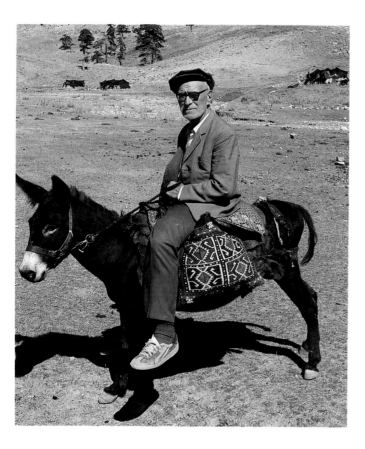

FAR LEFT: *For centuries weavers in the east Caucasus (Dagestan and Azerbayjan) have been making pileless carpets using a weft wrapping (Soumak) technique. Their patterns, transmitted within the community from one generation to the next, are conservative and contain motifs which are often quite archaic. This example has a design that appears in a carpet painted by Carlo Crivelli in the late fifteenth century. In the nineteenth century many were sold abroad, but the demands of the market place seem to have had little effect on their patterns, for beautifully worked examples are still being made and used in many homes to this day. Nineteenth century.* 321 × 185 cm/ 126½ × 73 in.

LEFT: *A man of the Karakoyunlu tribe. Summer pasture in the central Taurus mountains, Beyshehir region, Turkey, 1985.*

BELOW LEFT: *Weavings made and used by the nomadic Karakoyunlu tribe. Summer pasture in the Taurus mountains near Ulukishla, Turkey, early 1980s.*

BELOW: *One member of a Turkish nomad, or Yuruk, family on migration. The child is well strapped in and held in place by a large, elaborately decorated storage bag. Sarikechili tribe, Marash province.*

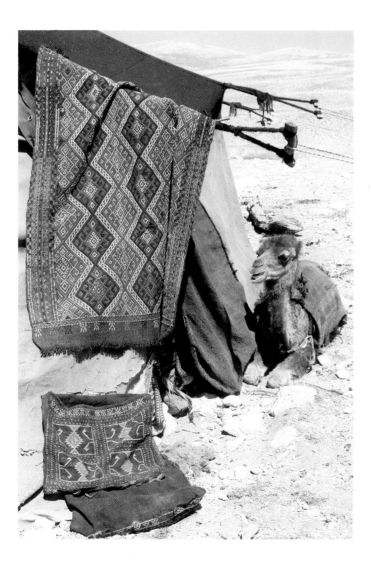

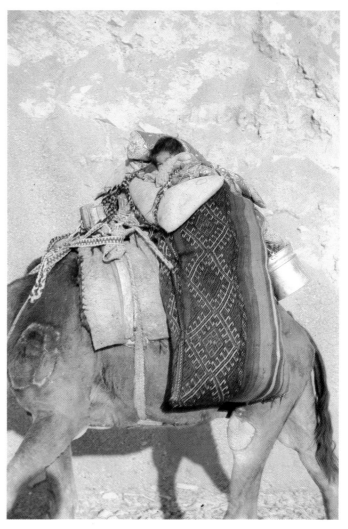

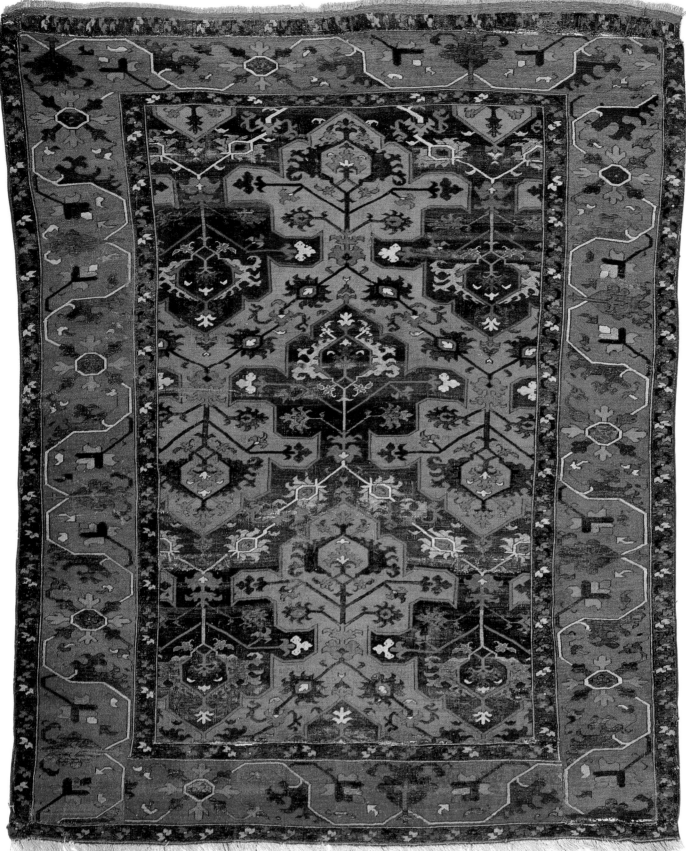

ABOVE: *In this (incomplete) seventeenth-century carpet Turkish weavers in a cottage industry have translated the design of a luxury velvet into that of a carpet. This is how designs emanating from the court found their way into village weavings. Some, such as the Ottoman prayer design, lived on for centuries; others, such as this one, had a shorter life.* 281 × 218 cm/110½ × 86 in.

RIGHT: *The closest villagers could get to the luxurious velvets and silks made for the court was to copy them in the materials they had to hand. Through the ages luxury textiles have been an important source of designs for the embroiderer and carpet weaver. The design of this carpet fragment, a cottage-made product from seventeenth-century Turkey, has been copied from that of a contemporary velvet or brocade.* 278 × 108 cm/ 109½ × 42½ in.

for the Duke of Brandenburg or Haydn for the court of Esterhazy. The concerto has a style, character and musical form created by the composer. Every note is exactly scored and the musicians give expression to the composition by playing precisely what is written down. Similarly the court carpet is 'composed' by a designer in a style compatible with his training, current fashion and the expectations of the patron. Every knot is specified in the pattern and the weavers, using all the skills acquired in a long training, convert signs on a piece of paper, knot by knot, into a carpet.

The history of carpet design has parallels in the history of music. Traditional dance forms, rhythms and melodies were a starting point for the elaborations of much European court music during the seventeenth and eighteenth centuries. Likewise the corpus of ideas and patterns constituting the tribal or folk tradition has acted as a sort of prime substance for the periodic development of the court carpets. Many of the basic ideas and forms of court carpets derive from earlier traditional forms. The movement of ideas in the opposite direction is more obvious. Designs emanating from the court workshops had a powerful and sustained influence on the patterns woven in the cottage industries and were even taken up by the less isolated tribes. They have also been the biggest single influence on the design of commercial carpets and remain so even today. Visual patterns, like ideas and musical melodies, have no real frontiers. They spread far beyond their point of origin and are kept alive by a vital series of communications, so difficult to follow that the pathway from person to person or place to place may never be known. There is a constant two-way flow towards and away from the two 'poles' of influence, the court circle and the rustic community.

The question of taste

Before dealing with each of the four weaving categories in more detail, some attempt must be made to address the problems of taste and aesthetic preference. Part of the reason for dividing carpets into the four streams is that they mirror the great divisions of taste. It was an education for me to witness the amazement and disbelief of an educated and successful Persian dealer, a recent refugee from Iran, when he saw the price paid at auction for a Kazak, a coarsely woven, crude looking Caucasian village carpet with a bold pattern and strong colours. 'They are so coarse and ugly,' he said. 'How can they pay so much money?' He was genuinely distressed. For him the ideal of beauty and desirability was a rug with a perfectly ordered, detailed pattern, finely and exquisitely worked in evenly balanced colours without any mistakes.

In contrast for many lovers of tribal and village rugs the typical Persian city-style carpet, with its fussy scrolls and plethora of minute ornaments covering the whole field, has no appeal. Their preference is for powerful designs, empty space and primary colours – 'The rug has gotta have guts,' as one American collector put it. The coarseness or fineness of weave is for them irrelevant, and inaccuracies or mistakes in the weaving, unless they are so gross as to be disfiguring, are regarded as pleasing irregularities – a feature of the hand-woven item. This idea of 'pleasing irregularities' is a target for intellectual jokes among anthropologists and for cynical amusement among others who feel that tolerance of 'irregularities' in

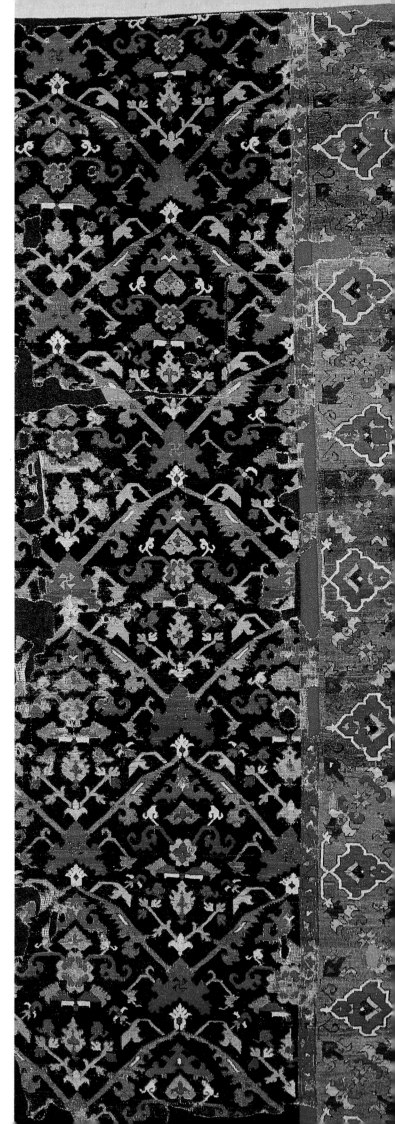

BELOW: *One reason for dividing carpets into four streams is that they mirror the great divisions of taste. At one extreme people prefer powerful designs, empty space and primary colours. Coarseness of weave is irrelevant and mistakes or inaccuracies, unless they are so gross as to be disfiguring, are regarded as pleasing irregularities. This Kazak rug, the product of a cottage industry in a south Caucasian village, is in the typical 'primitive' style of many tribal and village carpets. Nineteenth century.* 141 × 125 cm/55½ × 49 in.

RIGHT: *At the other extreme of taste is the preference for a perfectly ordered, detailed pattern, finely and exquisitely worked in evenly balanced colours without any mistakes. This attractive Tabriz carpet with its original design based on classical themes is in the best Persian workshop tradition. Early twentieth century.* 452 × 305 cm/178 × 120 in.

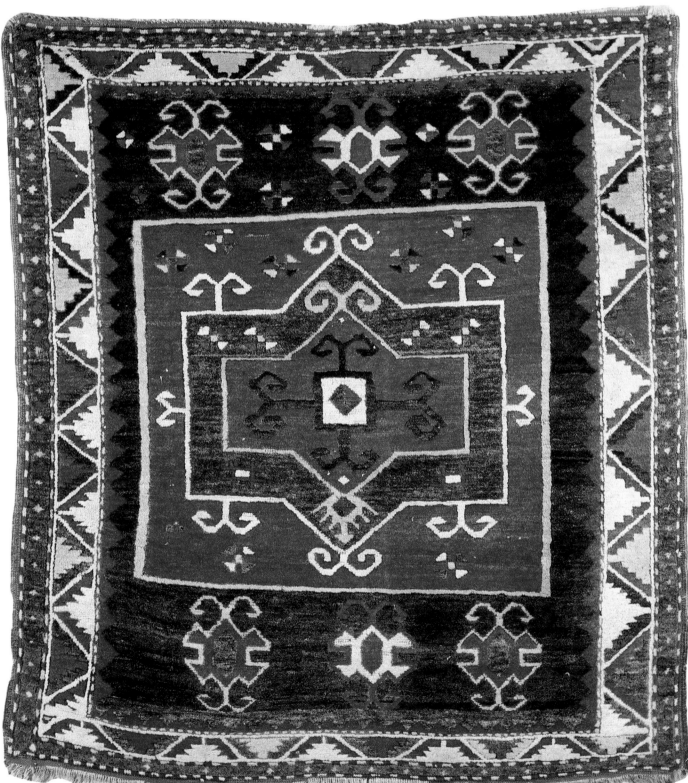

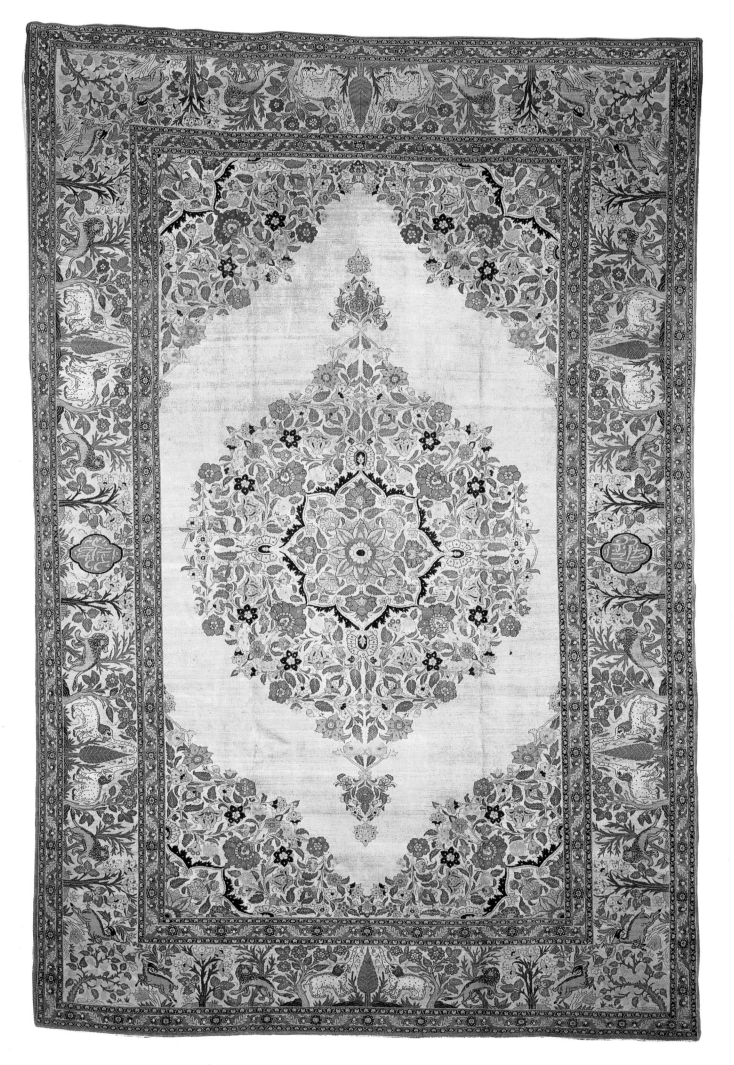

23

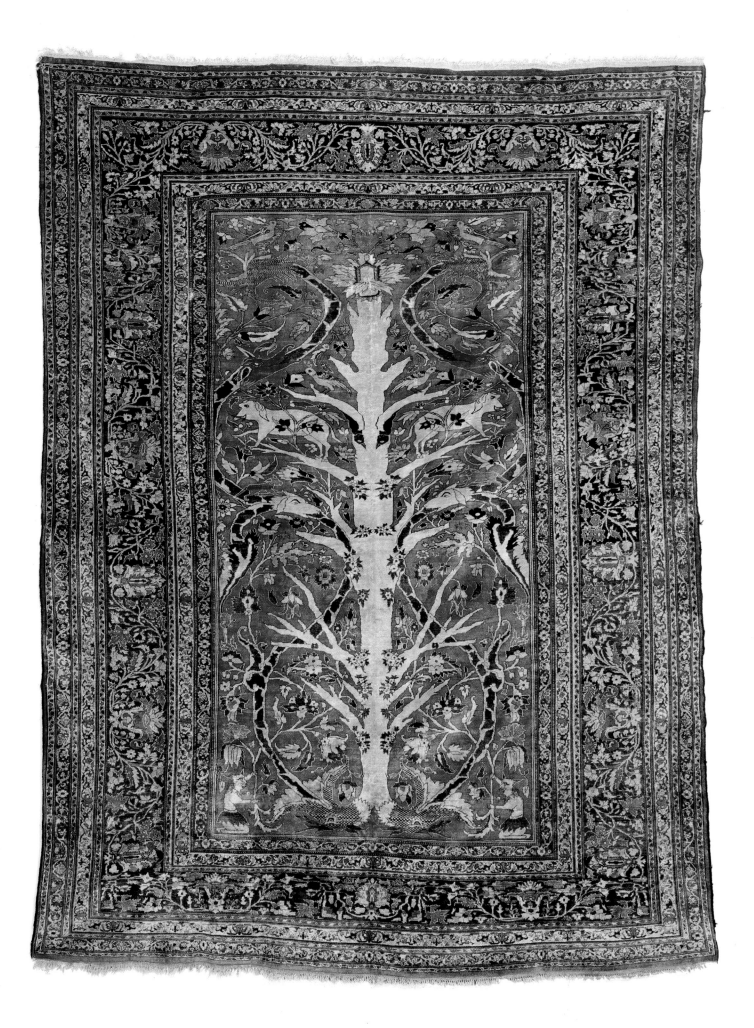

an object is the same as the inability to see its faults. This of course may be true but let someone with this view be fitted with a set of dentures of perfect regularity and he will not smile so readily. If uniformity and standardisation are so desirable, why is it that manufacturers of mass-produced, factory-made goods in the west like to give the impression that their products are actually home made? Is it the quality of wholesome freshness, the unspoiled honesty of the ingredients and the individual care in making something intended for personal use that appeals so much to us? For the lover of the 'home made' carpet, however, the perfectly made, regularised, commercial carpet has as much individuality as wallpaper. But in case the comparison to wallpaper appears pejorative, and before I wander too far from my theme, I must stress again that the division of carpets into categories carries no suggestion of one being better than the other. Let me illustrate the absurdity of comparing the divisions with one another by yet another example – when the claim is made that a coarse peasant rug from Loristan is 'better' or 'worse' than an elegantly designed and finely worked rug from Qom.

Let us consider first the Loristan rug made by a young bride to celebrate her wedding. Woven into the design are her name and that of her future husband, the date, and a variety of special charms, amulets and protective designs which she learned from her grandmother. It is to be used in her future home and will always have a special place in her affections. Somehow or other the rug passes out of the family and into a western household. Even in its new situation the rug conveys something of the feelings of the young weaver so many years ago. The colours are bright, strong and unsophisticated. The patterns have a naivety of execution which gives the rug an enduring freshness.

In contrast the Qom rug has a pattern drawn by an experienced designer, a popular one based on a classical prototype first used in Persia during the sixteenth century. The carpet was woven by a skilled weaver with fifteen years' experience, using the best woollen yarn for the pile. The final clipping and finishing was also carried out by a highly skilled craftsman. The end product seems to recapture something of the elegance of court life in former times, a perfect addition to the furnishings of a wealthy home.

So which is better? Arguments about the merits and shortcomings of art objects are pointless when the things being compared have so little in common. If you look for quality and refinement the Loristan rug is a crude whimsical contraption altogether lacking in merit. If the appeal lies in a sense of the weaver's presence, the charm, directness and childlike lack of sophistication with all the little mistakes and irregularities, then the Qom rug is contrived, mechanical, sterile and over-refined.

If there are some people with fixed ideas about what they like, there seem to be many more 'floating voters' influenced by what other people think and say. Fashions of taste exist in the field of carpets as much as any other and are a fascinating side of the art world. It is astonishing how the rare and valuable objects, collected at such expense in the face of fierce competition by our fathers and grandfathers, can be ignored by the fashionable mainstream of today. Succeeding generations overturn

LEFT: *Weavers in the Heriz district of north-west Persia, the centre of a large cottage industry, are noted for their ability to weave complex designs from a drawing without the use of a cartoon. This example, with its design of a mythological tree, was probably worked from an illustration in a book. Their silk carpets have an unusual and pleasing colour tonality with red-brown, light blue and a silvery ivory, which, together with the rustic interpretation of the complex curvilinear design, give them a character unlike any other Persian carpet. Nineteenth century.* 235×185 cm/$92\frac{1}{2} \times 73$ in.

BELOW: *In the 1920s 'oriental' rugs changed hands for huge sums of money. Fashionable demand was for the pastel coloured rugs from Ghiordes and Kula which were considered exotic rarities. Today they are not so highly regarded and sell for much less in real terms than in the 1920s. Ghiordes (Gordes), western Turkey, nineteenth century.* 180×137 cm/ 71×54 in.

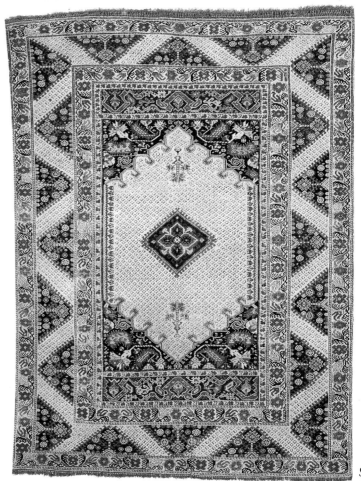

: *The design of this Persian silk prayer rug from Kashan is based on an earlier Mughal original which it resembles in its exquisite workmanship and minute attention to detail. The first Indian carpets were designed by Persian artists in the sixteenth century and only took on a uniquely Indian character in the seventeenth. The two artistic cultures remain closely connected. Nineteenth century. 216 × 137 cm/85 × 54 in.*

: *Interesting tribal carpets are still being made today. This little prayer rug, worked mainly in plainweave and partly in knotted pile, has a delightful simplicity in the imagination of its design. Baluchi, western Afghanistan, 1970s. 125 × 76 cm/ 49 × 30 in.*

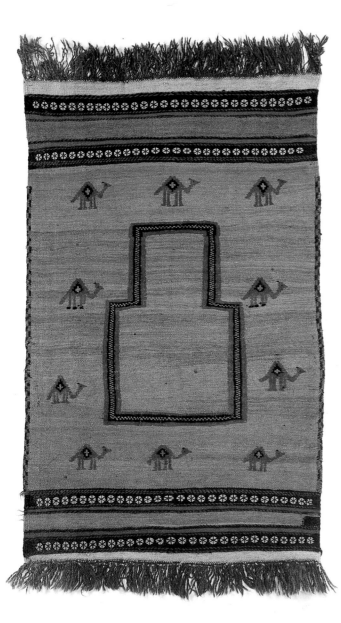

received opinions; old ideas are dropped and replaced by new criteria of judgement. Sixty years ago the carpets most popular in Europe were cottage-made Turkish rugs of the eighteenth and early nineteenth century. In the eighteenth century there was a vogue in Turkish high society for French architecture and decoration and, true to form, rugs made in the cottage industry at the time incorporated features of the new fashionable style. Their refinement, soft colours and tendency towards elaboration had a sympathy with the Louis XV gilt and ormolu style favoured since the eighteenth century by the wealthy of Europe, so they fitted well with prevailing ideas of good taste in the west. Today, in keeping with the spirit of our times, there is an adventurousness in taste, a willingness to accept the unfamiliar and to enjoy the abstract. The derivative is rejected in favour of the primal, the elemental is preferred to the elaborate, the austere to the cosy. The rugs in fashion sixty years ago are no longer thought of, and in real terms have fallen to between a half and a tenth of their value in the 1920s.

The time is ripe, I believe, for a renewed public interest in carpets. For those experienced in other fields of art, such as painting, the division of carpets into four categories should provide a short cut to their aesthetic appreciation. For those who have never seen carpets as anything other than floor covering I hope it will be the beginning of a new awareness. If my hope is realised and this view of carpets brings people to the point of wishing to buy carpets because they love them, it is as well to point out that court carpets are too rare to be worth collecting without considerable knowledge and means. There are however plenty of possibilities in cottage rugs, and interesting inexpensive tribal rugs are still being made today (illus. p.29). There is even an elite band of collectors, often people who have lived in Persia and acquired a taste for the subtleties of Persian design, who buy and keep only the finest and most outstanding workshop carpets.

I have often wondered if it is possible to look at the taste and opinions of today with the eyes of a historian living a hundred years in the future. Can those works of art destined to be acknowledged as masterpieces in time to come be recognised today? I do not claim that all or even half the examples of the categories shown here are masterpieces of the art of carpets. They have been selected to give an idea of the great range of taste encompassed in the field of carpets. But there are enough outstanding examples for the person with artistic awareness but no previous experience to have the pleasure and excitement of seeing if he can discover them for himself.

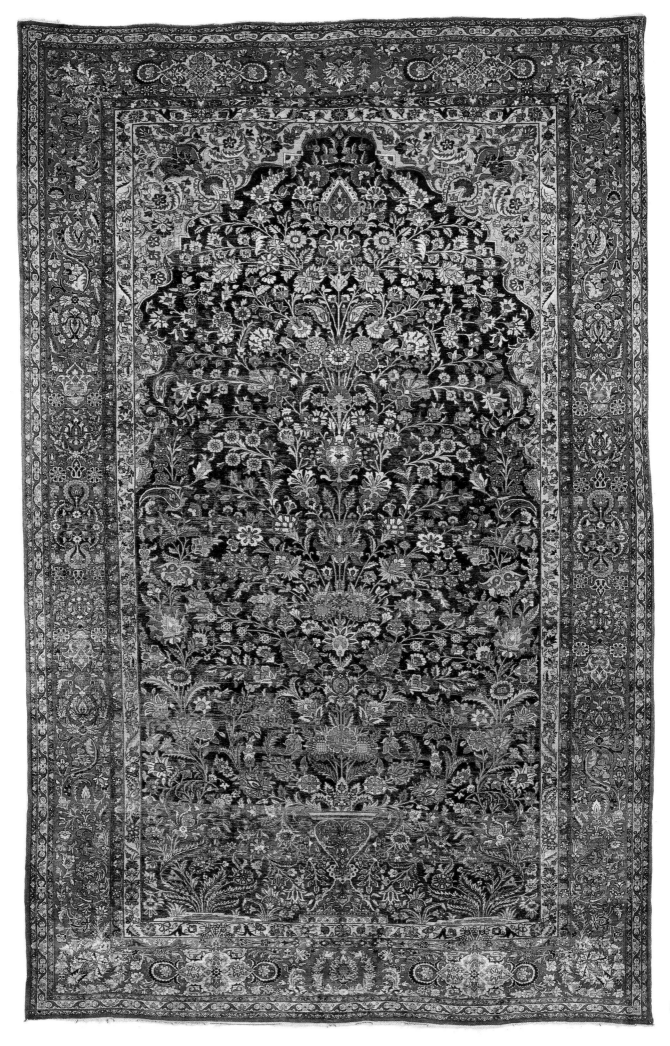

BELOW: *In recent years many books on all aspects of carpets have been published, and buyers today are much better informed than they were in the 1920s. Tribal weavings have been 'discovered' and the best examples are much in demand. For someone wishing to explore new territory the most exciting discoveries are to be made among cottage industry weavings. The powerful abstraction of this Heriz carpet is perfectly in keeping with today's taste. In the 1920s it would hardly have attracted a second glance. Nineteenth century. 190 × 175 cm/ 75 × 69 in.*

RIGHT: *Some of the most appealing modern tribal weavings are those made by nomadic people in the Fars district of south Persia and known as 'Gabeh', a Lori word applied to a type of coarse rug woven for use rather than for sale. They display in their designs an unclouded vision and directness of expression like that of children which gives them an exhilarating freshness and vitality. They are inexpensive and deserve greater recognition. Mid twentieth century.* 183 × 100 cm/ 72 × 39½ in.

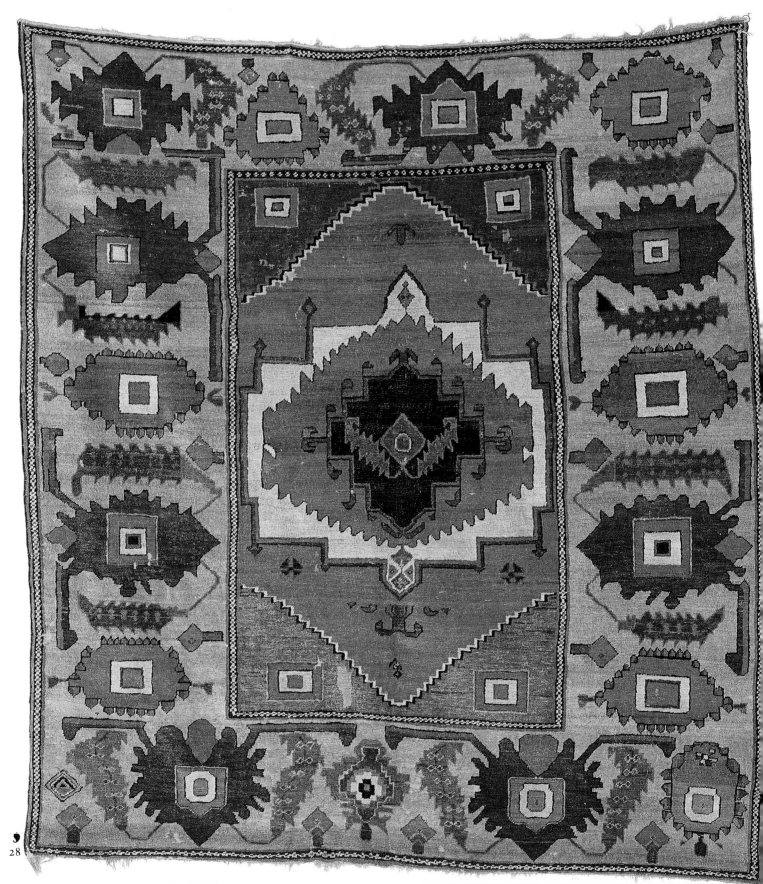

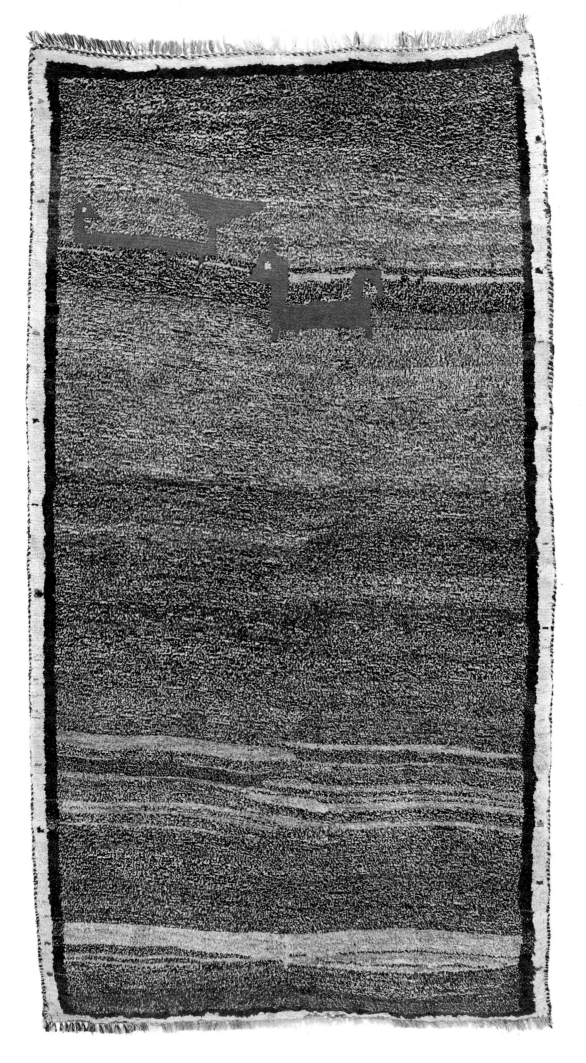

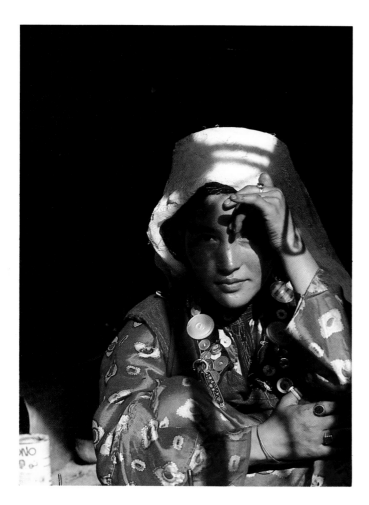

RIGHT: *This carpet is a rare survival of a vanished tradition. It was used to cover the entrance to a Turkmen tent and a magnificent spectacle it must have been. It is some time since piled rugs have been used for this purpose and, although their use is remembered by the Turkmen, no photograph of a piled door rug in use has ever been published. Furthermore the tribal group which made this piece was virtually extinguished in the mid nineteenth century. Few museums own tribal carpets of this quality and it is all too common for them to be kept in the deep storage of their Islamic art departments, whereas it would be more appropriate for them to be held in a museum of ethnology or primitive art. Salor tribe, nineteenth century.* 182×129 cm/$71\frac{1}{2} \times 51$ in.

LEFT: *A Kirghiz woman, Afghan Pamir, 1975.*

BELOW: *In Turkmen society a woman's status and respect depended to some extent on her skill as a weaver. The first and most important test of her accomplishments came on her wedding day when the bridal camel was decorated with the weavings she had made for her trousseau. Great care was therefore taken to reserve the best materials and workmanship for such pieces as this rare trapping, one of a pair draped around the bride's litter. Salor tribe, nineteenth century.* 75×170 cm/$29\frac{1}{2} \times 67$ in.

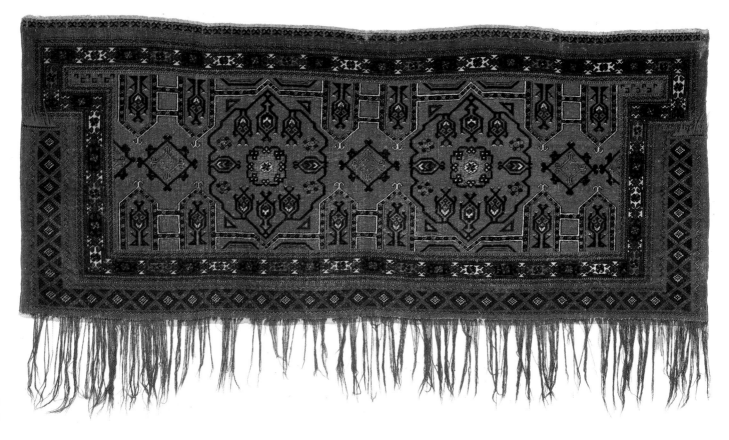

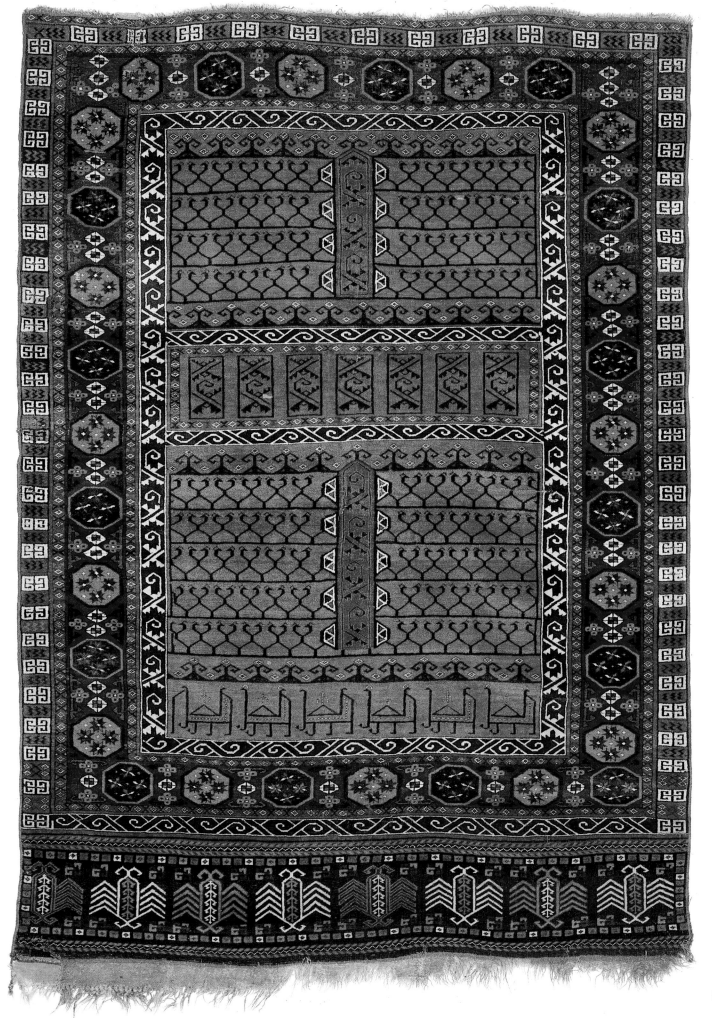

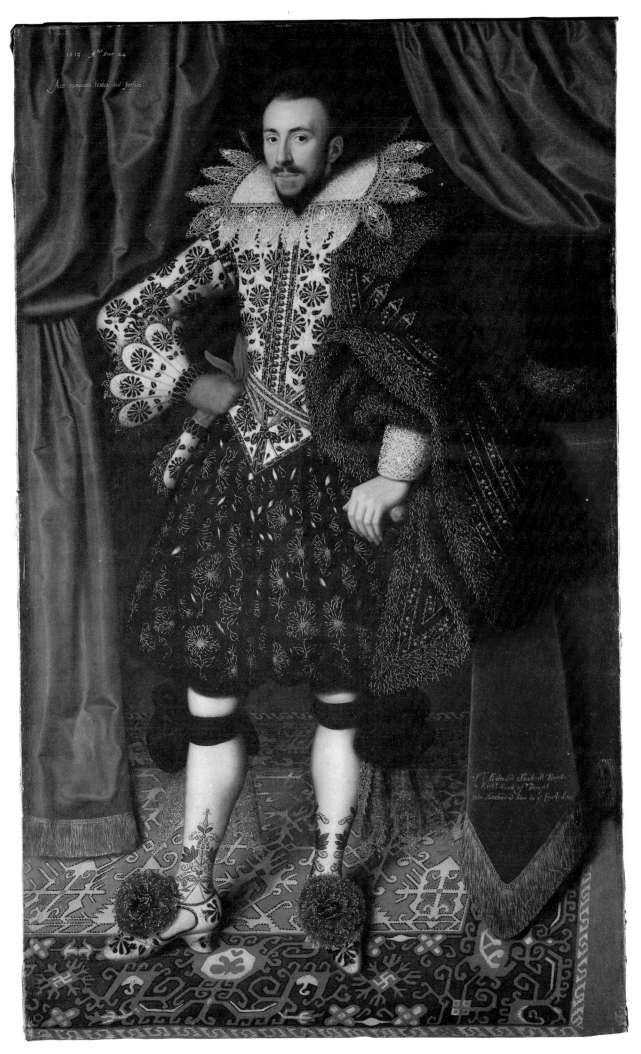

Chapter one

Western interest in the eastern carpet

Early interest

You may be treading on a work of art without knowing it. If you think this is an over-dramatic statement you should know that remarkable treasures are being sold from homes and estates all the time, and that the owners may have little idea of their importance before the sale. So if you have a rug at home bought more than fifty years ago there is a chance that it could be something exciting. It is not only the public who have difficulty in understanding carpets. Of all the objects circulating on the art market carpets are probably the least understood, so let us look at how these carpets came to the west and see how this state of affairs came about.

Carpets came to the west throughout the sixteenth and seventeenth centuries as objects of value which conferred dignity and status on their owners, as many paintings of the period reveal (illus. p.32). King Henry VIII had a sizeable collection of carpets and must have had an important influence on their popularity. Portraits showing him standing on recognisable Turkish carpets,

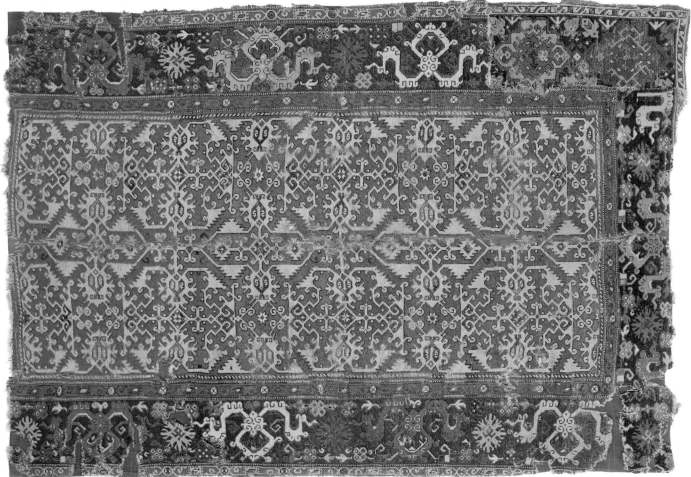

'A Nubian model reclining' by Roger Fenton, a photograph taken in the late 1850s, which, in common with the orientalist painters, seeks to capture the flavour of the Middle East. She is lying on a rug from Megri, western Turkey.

or seated on a carpet-covered podium, bear witness to their importance; so much so that copies of Turkish carpets were made in sixteenth-century England during the reign of Queen Elizabeth I. Turkey seems to have been the main supplier to the west through Venice and as a result all hand-knotted carpets, whether from Persia or Egypt, were called at the time 'Turkey carpets'. Some idea of the different types of carpet imported to the west can be gained from a study of contemporary European painting.

In the seventeenth century interest in carpets grew to include Persian, Egyptian and Indian products but already in the first decade of the century a new style of European carpet, destined to displace the oriental carpet from fashion, had made its appearance in France. Later, during the reign of Louis XIV, a workshop making carpets for the court was established in an old soap factory on the outskirts of Paris. The name '*Savonnerie*' became famous and the French decorative style was adopted as the norm of taste throughout Europe.

By the eighteenth century a designer commissioned to design an interior would include the floor covering in the overall scheme. It is known that the Adam brothers made their own carpet designs and had them executed in workshops in London and Axminster. Several other workshops are recorded as having been established in England and Scotland at this time to make hand-made pile carpets in European designs. The new décor made oriental carpets look unfashionable and demand for them faded away. It was at this time that the factories at Axminster and Wilton, now famous for machine-made carpets, began.

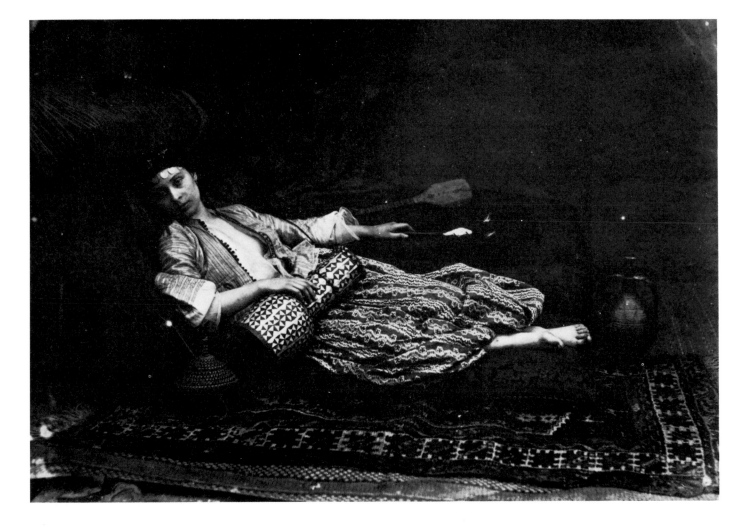

The rediscovery of carpets

In the nineteenth century 'oriental' or 'Persian' carpets as they came to be known again aroused interest. Paintings of nineteenth-century western interiors often include a rug or carpet, usually a tribal or village weaving from the Middle East (illus. p.36). Some of these were bought in the local bazaars and brought home by those tireless Victorian travellers, while others were imported by merchants from Turkey, which became the centre of the carpet trade.

The resurgence of interest in carpets was stimulated by the so-called orientalist painters, artists working in the Middle East, who presented to the European public a romantic and dramatised view of local life. This type of painting, typified by the work of J. F. Lewis, became extremely popular. The subjects are meticulously drawn and frequently include representations of carpets that are on the whole accurate, just as they were in the sixteenth century, so that various types of piled carpet and flatweave can be identified without difficulty (illus. p.36). Research into European painting prior to 1700 has yielded important information on the dating of early carpets, and, in view of the difficulty of obtaining accurate data on the dating of tribal and village carpets, a similar approach could be used for later paintings. Nineteenth-century painting, potentially a rich source of information, has yet to be explored.

A few early photographs also include recognisable carpets, notably the work of Roger Fenton in the 1850s (illus. p.34). He, like the orientalist painters, attempted to capture something of the flavour of the Middle East.

One result of the increasing awareness of oriental carpets was the interest taken in them by William Morris.

Interest in carpets during the nineteenth century is mirrored in the work of William Morris who set up a commercial workshop in 1879 at Hammersmith. His designs were influenced by those of Persian carpets. Carpets made at Hammersmith by the River Thames between 1879 and 1881 are signed with his device consisting of an M, hammer and double wavy line signifying water. 180 × 120 cm/71 × 47 in.

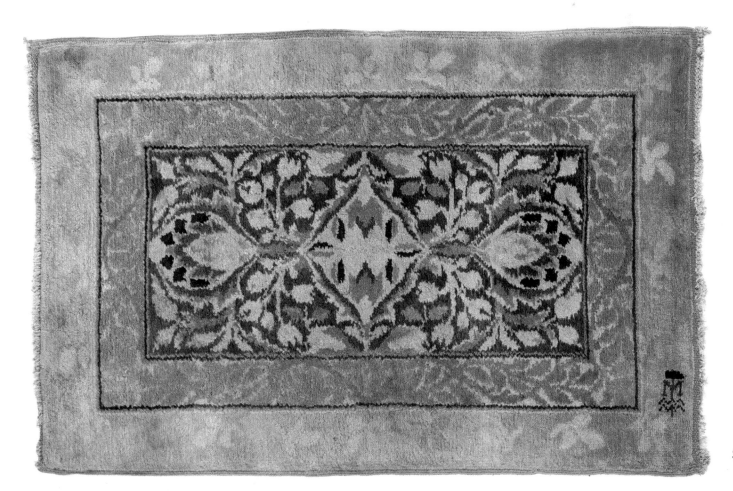

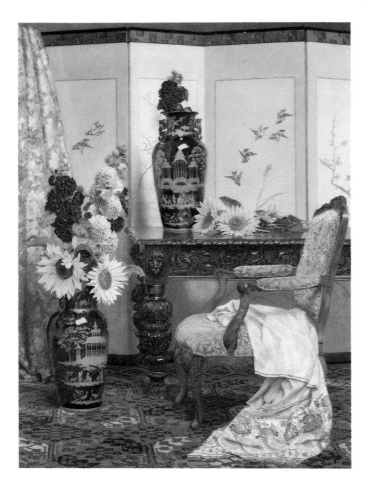

LEFT: *Nineteenth-century paintings often include identifiable carpets and are potentially a rich source of information on the dating of tribal and village products. In 'Sunflowers and Hollyhocks' by Kate Hayllar, 1889, the carpet on the floor is a Turkmen tribal weaving, made probably by the Ersari tribe in Turkestan.*

RIGHT: *A Turkmen tribal carpet made by the Ersari tribe in Turkestan. In the late nineteenth century many Turkmen tribespeople, including those who wove this type of design, fled to northern Afghanistan and settled in tribal villages, living in tents during the summer and in mud brick houses in the winter. Carpets such as this, made before the migration, have a wide range of colours and are the ancestors of innumerable later 'Afghan' carpets. Nineteenth century. 275 × 206 cm/ $108\frac{1}{2}$ × 81 in.*

BELOW: *The so-called orientalist painters presented to the European public a romantic view of local life. In 'A Carpet Sale in Cairo', Charles Robertson RWS (1844–91) portrays a number of identifiable carpets, including three Caucasian, a Turkish flatwoven prayer rug and an Uzbeg embroidery hanging over the balcony. An amusing feature, also found in other orientalist paintings, is the heightening of sense of drama by drawing the human figures to a scale much smaller than they would be in life.*

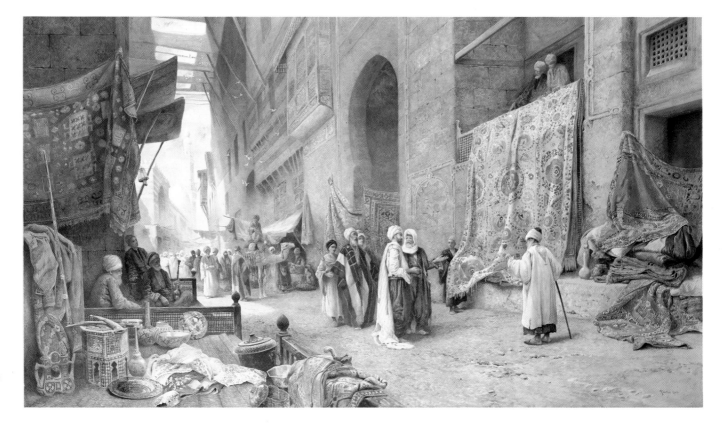

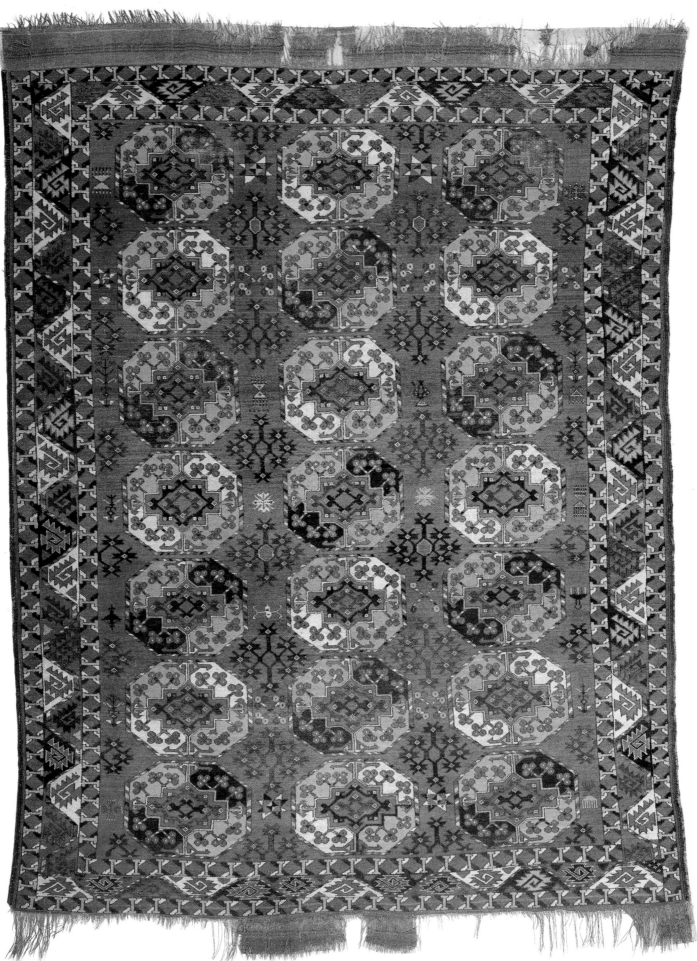

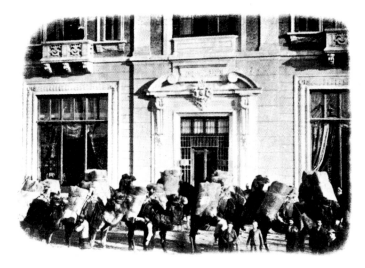

Goods arriving by camel train at the OCM warehouse at Smyrna (Izmir). After 1902.

RIGHT: *This is the type of rug that came to the west from a remote village a hundred or more years ago. It has a delightful 'primitive' quality and is probably the work of a Kurdish tribe in north-west Persia. Nineteenth century. 287 × 142 cm/ 113 × 56 in.*

BELOW: *So few tribal artefacts reached the west in complete condition that many people are unaware that these wide strips were shallow bags with an integral back. They were hung on the wall of the tent and used for personal belongings. This bag is missing its tassels and hanging straps. The remains of both are still visible. The colour, style and design are typical of the work of the Turkmen Tekke tribe before the penetration of western influence (see also p.64). 46 × 126 cm/18 × 49½ in.*

His indebtedness to eastern, especially Persian, design is well known, but he appears to have been particularly interested in carpets and set up a workshop for their commercial production in 1879 at Hammersmith. His designs, while original and distinctive, draw heavily on Persian carpets for their inspiration. Those made in his workshop between 1879 and 1881 are signed with his device consisting of an M, hammer and double wavy line, signifying water (illus. p.35).

In the second half of the century demand for these exotic imports increased enormously and the carpet, formerly a curio, became an accepted article of furniture in the respectable home. The response to this demand had far-reaching social and economic consequences for the carpet producing countries. The whole pattern of production gradually changed, as did the carpets themselves.

The growth in demand increased steadily and it became apparent to the more far-sighted merchants that tribal and cottage weavers would not be able to supply the requirements of the market for much longer, and that some additional source of supply was needed. In the 1870s the first of a new wave of carpet producing workshops was set up in Tabriz in north-west Persia. Others soon followed, and from these small beginnings grew Persia's huge commercial carpet manufacturing industry which has since been successfully copied in many other countries. We will look at this important development in more detail later. First we must look at how the carpet producing countries responded to increased demand prior to the great expansion of commercial production.

Exporters, hungry for goods, prompted enterprising local traders to visit the nomadic encampments, tribal areas and villages, and buy wherever the ancient craft was to be found, usually on a price per unit area basis. They then brought their wares to the trading centres such as Bukhara, Shiraz, Mashhad, Tabriz and Tiflis, from where they were transported in bales by camel, mostly to Constantinople, as it was called at the time, and then shipped to the west, having passed through several hands on the way.

As well as carpets and rugs the traders bought many items made for everyday use in tribal life, such as saddle bags, pouches and animal trappings. But what began as a basically functional object was not necessarily what

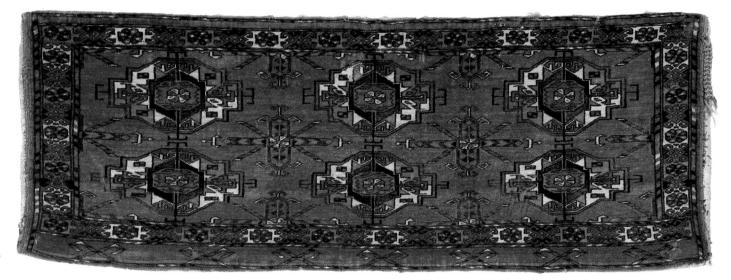

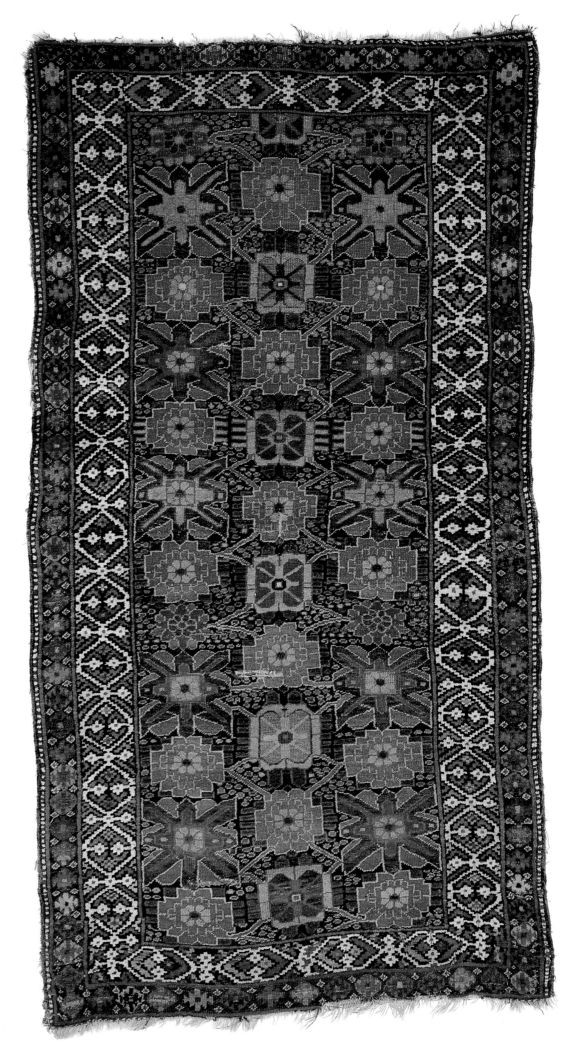

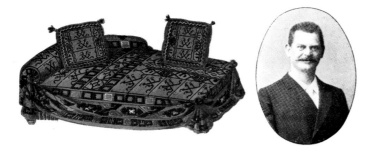

ABOVE: *Mohair divan, no.801 from the brochure of Koch and te Kock, 1906. The use of tribal rug patterns for machine-made upholstery material was prompted by the vogue for cutting up tribal rugs for the purpose. The portrait is of Carl Wilhelm Koch, born 1855, proud inventor of the tribal-style upholstery fabric.*

BELOW: *In the 1870s and 1880s there was a fashion for cutting up tribal carpets and using them as upholstery material. Paradoxically, this destructive practice has caused a few old tribal weavings to survive, which might have been destroyed if used on the floor. Here bits of two carpets made by the Turkmen Tekke tribe have been used.*

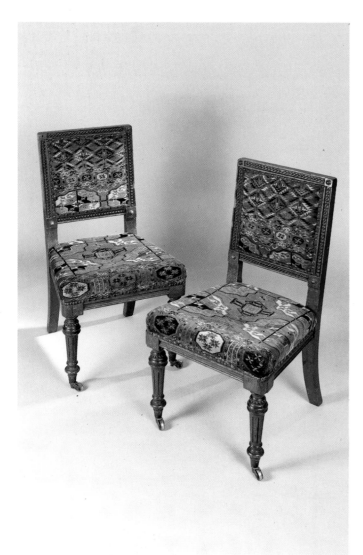

ended up in the Victorian drawing room. The saleable part of these tribal weavings was the piled area and so appendages such as ropes, tassels, hanging loops and the plain-woven backs of bags were considered a nuisance, and their shipment an unnecessary cost. They were cut off, sometimes very crudely, and simply discarded. Objects were often further mutilated to make them more acceptable: cradle-shaped bedding bags were cut up into six pieces and sold separately as little mats to cover furniture; pairs of bags were sewn together to make a small rug after a border was cut from each; 40-feet long piled bands, used to stabilise the trellis tent, were cut into 3-feet lengths, and so on.

In the 1870s and 1880s many of these small tribal weavings were cut up and used as upholstery fabric, pillows and bolster covers. Ironically this basically destructive practice has caused a number of lovely old pieces to survive which otherwise might have been lost if used on the floor. An amusing aside to this fashion is that its popularity prompted the German firm of Koch and te Kock to produce machine-made imitations of Turkmen and Qashgai weavings for sale as upholstery material.

The objects reaching the west were faced with another menace, a process known as 'chemical washing', which involves treatment of carpets with alkali followed by an acid to neutralise the alkali. Sometimes a bleaching agent is used as well. This process partially degrades the wool, softening and increasing the lustre of the pile. The colours are also altered, toned down and even bleached out if desired. The aim is to make a more attractive product. The majority of new carpets sold today have been 'washed' under controlled conditions, but in former times the finer points were not always observed and many tribal artefacts, especially those bleached, have been completely ruined by the process. Objects surviving the twin hazards of mutilation and bleaching were then subjected to shod feet and the caresses of the older type of 'beat-as-they-bash-as-they-chew' vacuum cleaners. As a result few tribal weavings made prior to the impact of European influences survive in original or complete condition.

RIGHT: *Many carpets have come to the west without any documentary information about their source. This wonderful carpet, variously classified as Caucasian, Armenian, and north-west Persian, is such a piece. The technique is that of a Persian carpet, the colouring rustic, the design distantly derived from the prayer rugs of sixteenth-century Ottoman Turkey. It was probably made before 1800 and could well be a tribal version of a more sophisticated pattern. 270 × 155 cm/ 106½ × 61 in.*

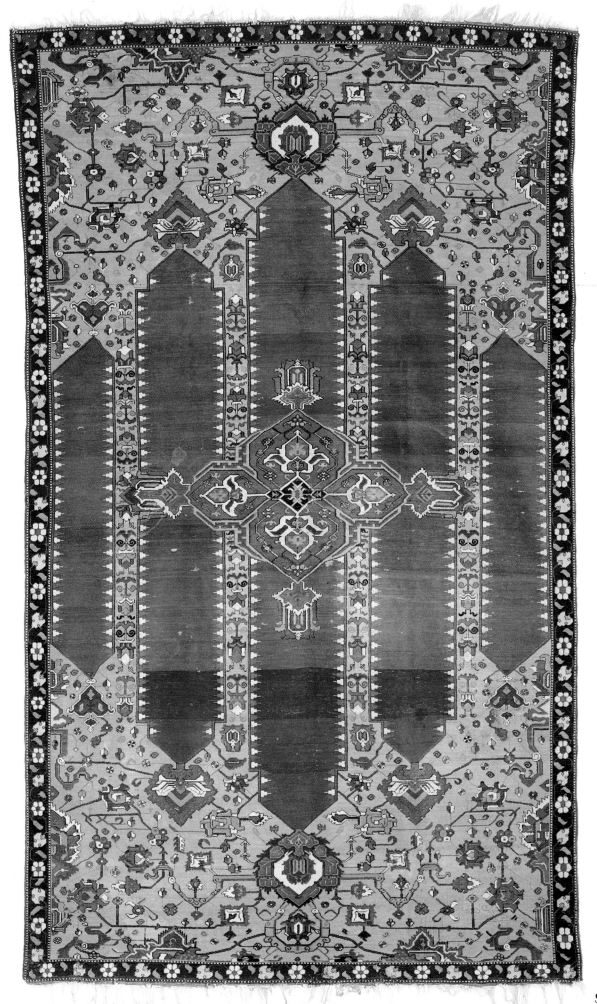

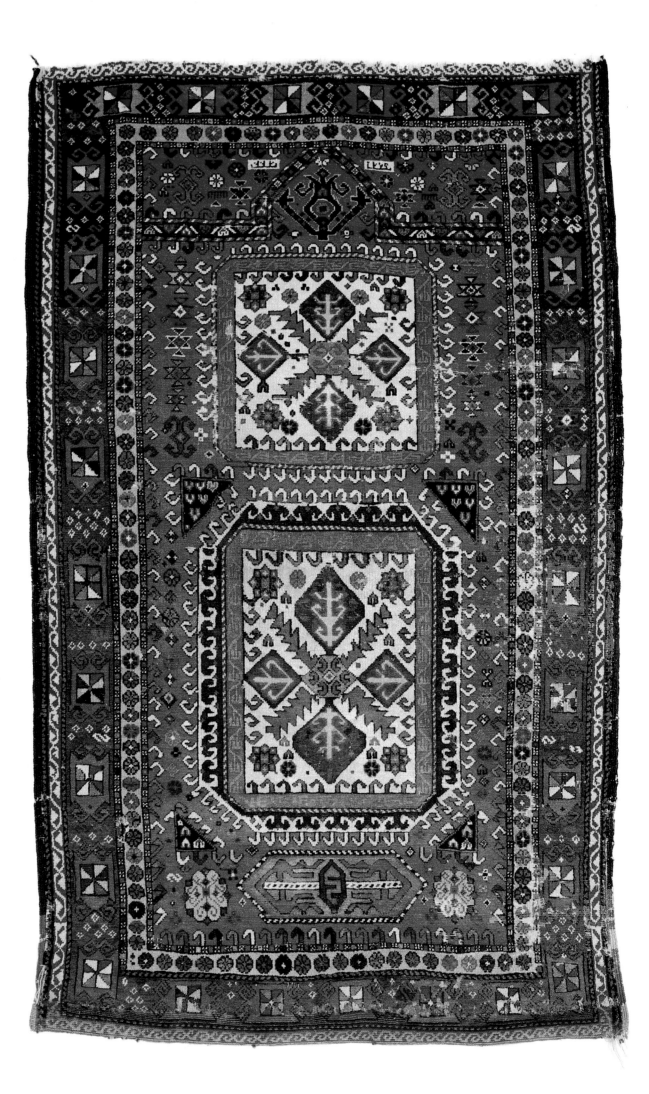

LEFT: *This prayer rug is one of a rare group of weavings from the early nineteenth century for which no one so far has discovered a source. They are thought to be Caucasian but even this is in dispute. They have top quality wool in the pile and silk in the foundation, usually a sign that a product of the highest quality was intended. 162 × 97 cm/64 × 38 in.*

BELOW: *The inscription in this north-west Persian carpet has given rise to much discussion. The style and colouring is that of*

a piece made around 1900; the inscription refers to an order made by Mizra Medhikhan in the time of Nader, dated 1124 (AD 1712). There are obviously two possibilities: that the date is wrong, or that our understanding of dating on the basis of colour and style is wrong. An inscription cannot always be relied on as it is a common practice in Persia for a craftsman to re-use the inscription on some respected object in his own work, thereby conferring dignity upon it. 335 × 238 cm/132 × 94 in.

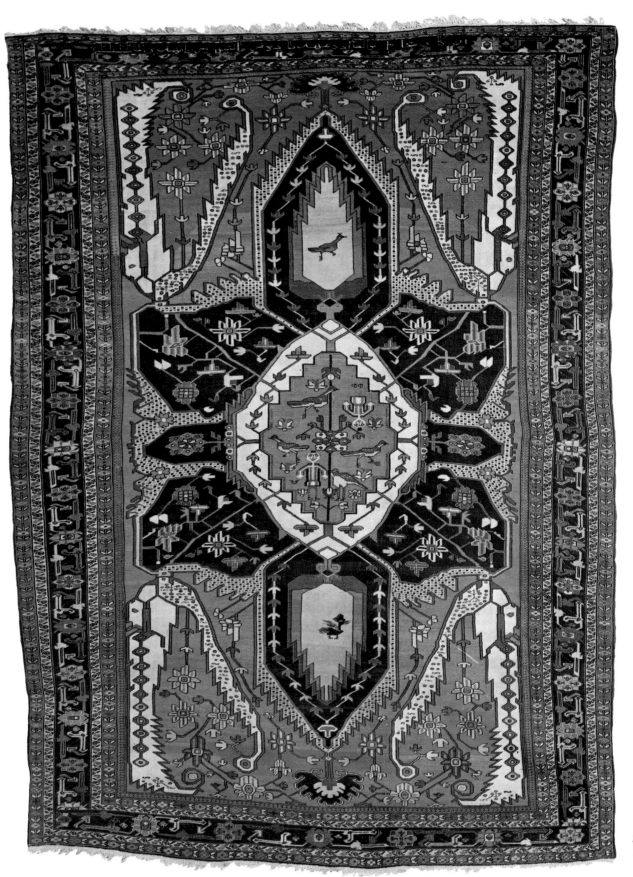

Obscure sources, unsuspected treasures

Throughout this period no effort was made to keep records of the sources of the carpets. The traders who made first contact with the weavers certainly had every commercial reason to conceal their sources so it is very unlikely that in their turn the exporters in Constantinople had any more than a general idea of the district where the goods came from. Thus a mass of material of diverse ethnic and tribal origins, from villages and encampments all over Turkey, the Caucasus, Afghanistan and Persia,

RIGHT: *Bedding bags (see below) – often mistaken for cradles – are used by several nomadic tribes in Persia. This is the base and both long sides of such a bag; it is unusual in that the sides, worked in knotted pile, show the influence of urban design, whereas the flatwoven base is decorated in the tribal style. Kashkuli division of the Qashqai tribe, nineteenth century.* 180 × 131 cm/71 × 51½ in.

BELOW: *Women of the Shahsavan tribe on migration from their summer quarters on Mount Savalan to the Moghan plain. They are expert weavers and will have made most of the woollen textiles they are using, including the woven bands, storage sacks, kilims and, on the right hand camel, the bedding bag. In the bazaar, bedding bags are often cut up and the panels sold separately. North-west Persia, 1980s.*

poured onto the market without any form of documentation, was shipped to Europe and America and sold to the public as home furnishings. And the further the carpets travelled from their origin the less people knew about them. It will ever be regretted that there were no ethnographers at this time making notes, recording dates, places and types of loom used; no Captain Cooks to bring to the west objects of known date and origin. Now only the carpets remain.

So how was the nineteenth-century householder to know what he was buying? The seller's knowledge was patchy, the buyer's ignorance total. The dealer would no doubt have done his best to tell the totally ignorant buyer all he knew about the pieces. In the case of tribal work little information of a specific nature was available but for commercially produced rugs there was more and it was generally accurate. Some valuable information has been transmitted by word of mouth within the families of dealers in the west, traditionally Armenians and Sephardic Jews, in the form of a lore of carpets, consisting of a sort of working jargon used in the everyday affairs of business. It includes an elaborate nomenclature, almost a set of nicknames, for carpets according to size, colour, pattern, place of shipment, district of origin, tribal origin, village of origin, function, shape and so on. Many terms are words from one of the local languages. As they have probably passed through at least one other language on their way to English the words have often changed into something else and their original meaning lost, giving endless opportunity for

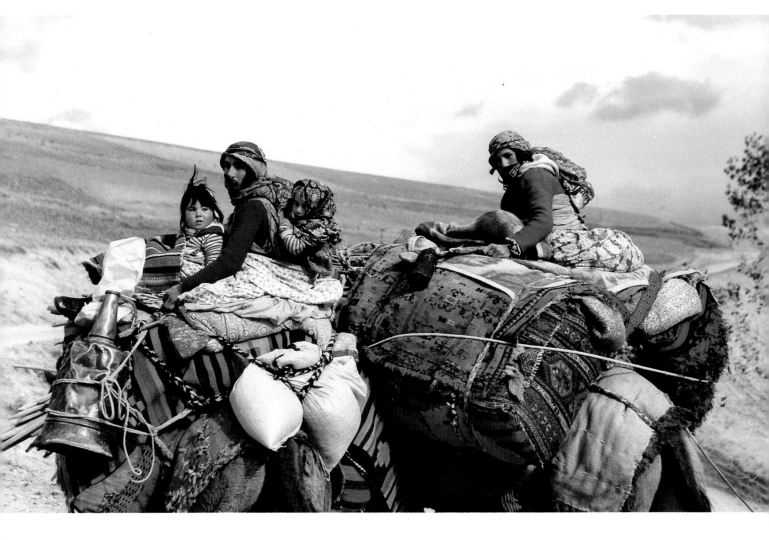

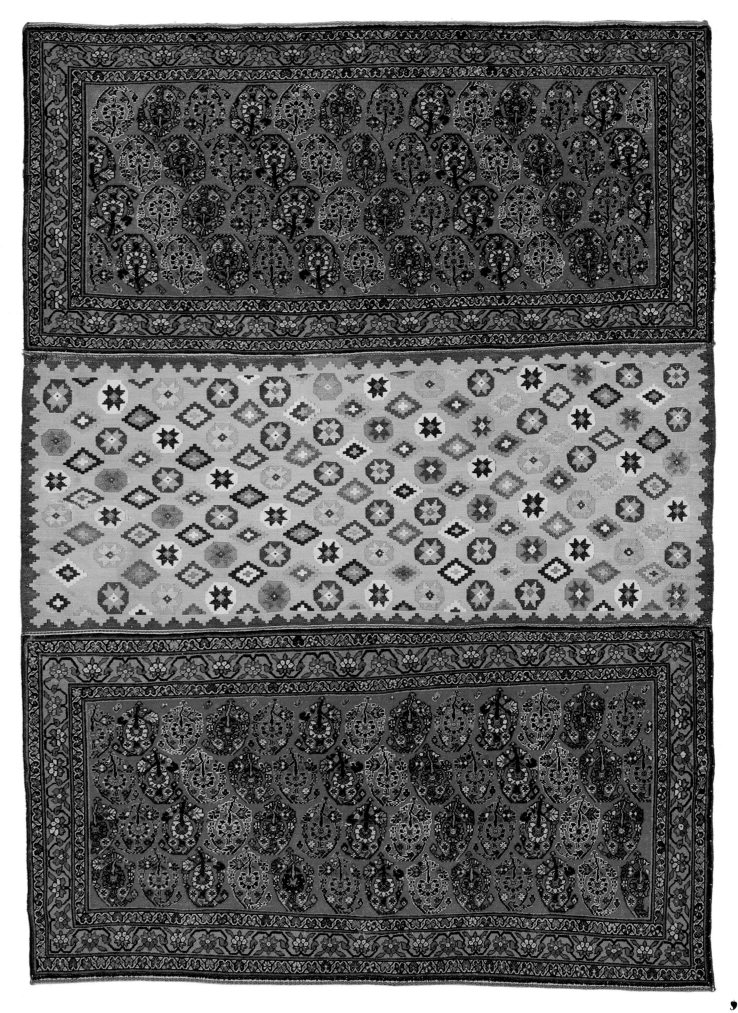

RIGHT: *Settled villagers of Bakhtiyari origin in the Char Mahal district of Persia were organised into a cottage industry at least as far back as the early nineteenth century. Their carpets are notable for their excellent wool and clear colours. The inscription indicates that it was made on the order of the Ilkhan of the Bakhtiyari, a royal appointee, in 1323, which corresponds to AD 1905. The Bakhtiyari villagers must have continued to employ traditional technology into the twentieth century, as no synthetic dyes have been used in this piece. 186 × 132 cm/73 × 52 in.*

BELOW: *In spite of its worn condition there is a life and freshness in this old village carpet from Kordestan. Small birds, animals and a host of little ornaments decorate the flower-filled field. In rural Kordestan the craft of dyeing was maintained at a high level. The colours in this carpet are strong, bright, and show the typical palette of the village dyer. In particular there is a good unfaded yellow (therefore a good green, too). The dyer also knew how to obtain the full range of colours from madder, which include apricot, scarlet and purple. Nineteenth century. 274 × 168 cm/108 × 66 in.*

misunderstanding.[2] Much of the traditional information about carpets is valuable and amounts to the only source we have, but the accumulated inaccuracies will take a generation of scholarship to untangle. More than fifty years of study have already gone into laying the academic foundations for an understanding of the earlier Islamic carpets, but the classification and documentation of tribal carpets is still a long way behind.

The student of this material is faced with immense problems. In Europe the first tribal carpets came to museums as late as the 1870s. The haphazard gathering of tribal and village weavings has made it very difficult to understand the pattern of production at this time and as a result there are large gaps in the knowledge of where and when a piece was made. Occasionally the gap can be filled by the discovery of old inventories describing a particular carpet still in a house, or by an inscription and date woven into a carpet, but more often only an informed guess is possible. To complicate matters dates can be falsified and inscriptions are sometimes copied from earlier carpets. Perhaps somewhere there are documented examples of earlier date yet to be discovered, surviving under unusual circumstances, but although in the last ten years increased interest in tribal

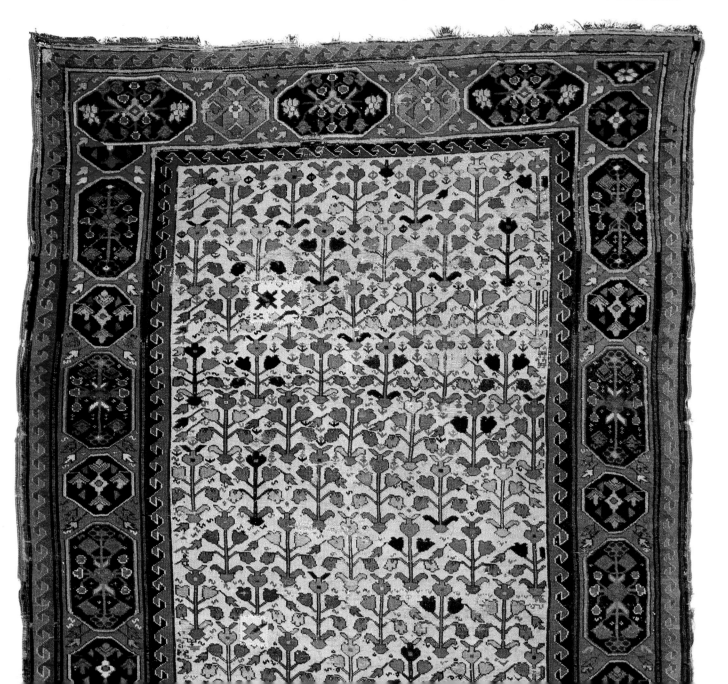

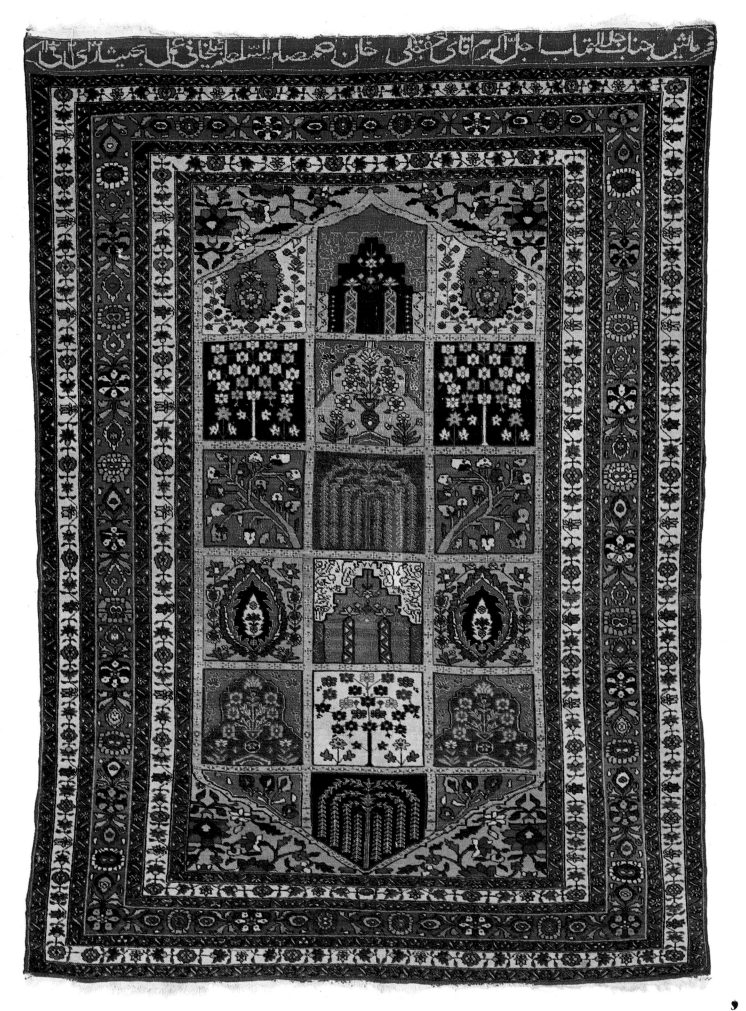

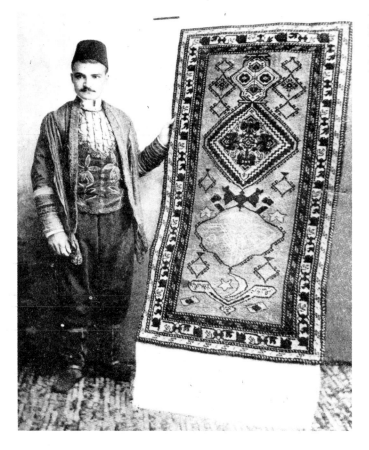

Promoting the exotic. Mr Garabed T. Pushman, a native of Turkey, displays his handiwork, 'the first rug woven in Chicago', 1905.

RIGHT: *Nomadic Baluchis in Baluchistan, the arid regions of south-east Persia and south Pakistan, produce pileless weavings. Today the distinctive dark and handsome Baluchi piled carpets are the product of settled villagers in Khorasan, north-east Persia. There are indications that in former times the Baluchis of Khorasan had a more nomadic life-style than they do today. They may therefore be latecomers to the cottage industry. This carpet is probably one of the oldest and by common consent one of the most beautiful examples known. It was brought to auction by someone who had no idea of its quality and rarity. Nineteenth century. 240 × 162 cm/ 95 × 64 in.*

weavings has brought to light numerous examples hidden away in museum storages and country houses, unfortunately none has had with it this much hoped for paperwork.

This is how in the scramble to export goods during the last century a few objects, now understood to rank among the outstanding achievements of tribal and folk art, came to be used as scatter rugs, cushions, covers for piano stools, upholstery, and simply floor covering. Age is no guarantee of quality and in case the impression has been given that every old carpet is a masterpiece of ethnic art, it is good to remember that most carpets were the consumer goods of the tribal people, made for everyday use. They were discarded when worn and new ones woven to replace the old. Weavers with great skill and artistic sensibility were few, and only rarely did a weaving pass beyond the threshold of the ordinary. Such a variety and profusion of objects came onto the market in so short a time that it was impossible for traders and public to make detailed judgements on their character. Everything was mixed up and only now, with the benefit of hindsight, is it possible to discriminate between the exceptional and the commonplace.

If a buyer had a good eye he might pick out a particularly charming piece. But mostly purchases were on the basis of price, size and colour. Price was determined by size, fineness of weave and quality of workmanship, with a premium for rarity and special appeal. As a result of this haphazard process many a treasure has been pounded into oblivion by passing feet, although almost miraculously some outstanding objects have been lovingly cherished in quite modest homes to be passed on to the next generation.

A more common story is that the owner of an old carpet, unaware that the rug the dog likes to chew is a work of art, is surprised at the interest generated by an old mat. The incomprehension of some owners is marvellous. A collector related to me how he found a fragment of an ancient Turkmen tent door rug, the oldest he had ever seen, in a dog basket. This was pointed out to the owner who not only refused to part with it under any circumstances but also declined to remove her dog's bedding from its normal place. She did, however, consent to allow it to be documented and photographed. A neighbour keeps a valuable and beautiful Caucasian rug in the hallway to prevent the wall-to-wall carpeting from being soiled by dirty feet and children's bicycles. The cost of carpeting the whole house twice over would not match the value of the rug.

In time the carpets bought long ago by grandparents or great aunts return to the market. The recycling of rugs from households back onto the market is a slow process. It may take as little as a decade or as much as three generations. Today we search among these old pieces innocently acquired so many years ago for treasures of a vanishing art which was already in decline a hundred years ago.

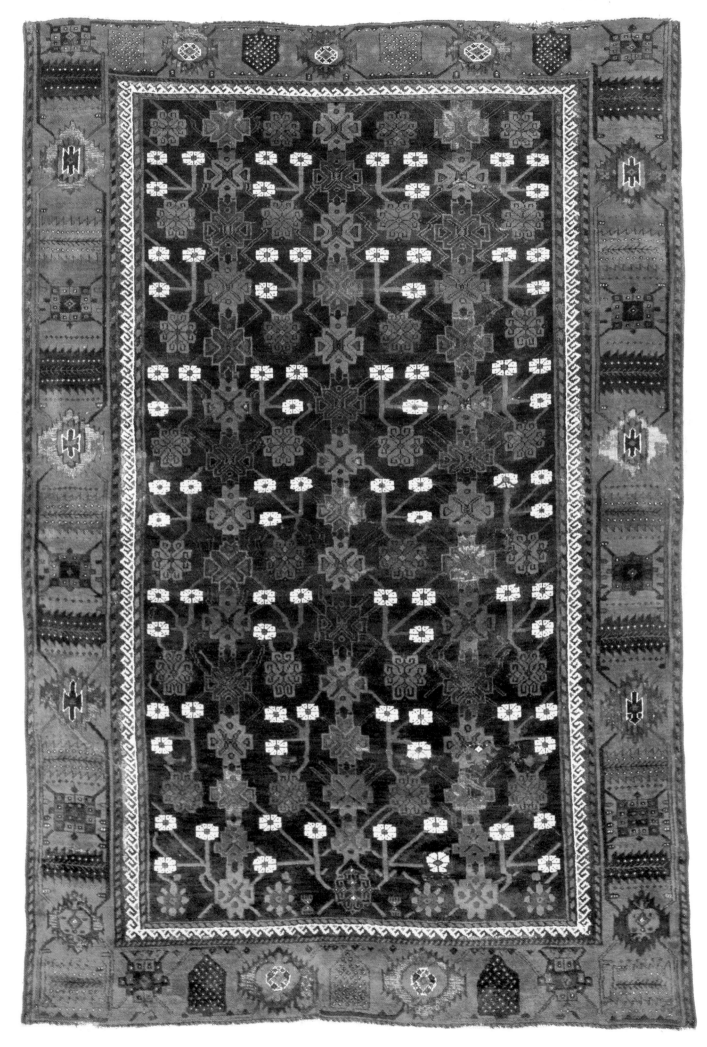

*A Turkmen child at play, learning to weave on her toy loom.
North Afghanistan, mid 1970s.*

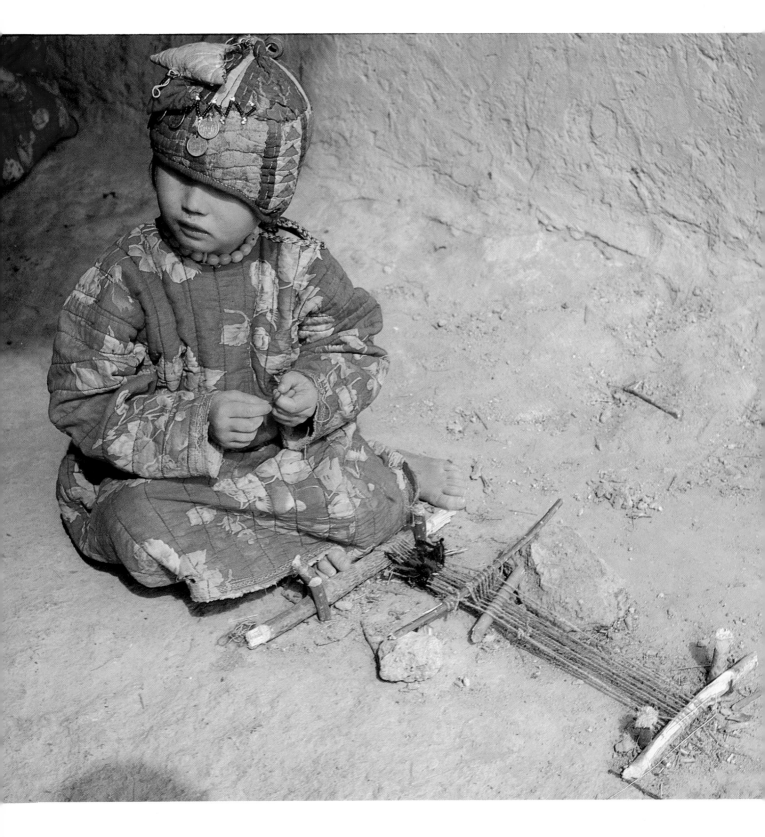

Chapter two

Making a carpet

BELOW: *Kirghiz shearing their sheep, 1975. Wool quality varies in different parts of the fleece. If wool of a particular quality is needed the fleece is pulled apart and sorted into different grades, a task requiring skill and practice. Where the pasture is good, the sheep are usually shorn once a year. If the climate is dry, sheep may not be able to find sufficient grass in the summer to grow a good fleece, in which case the sheep are shorn twice a year. The inferior summer wool and the lesser grades of winter wool are used for felt.*

Learning the craft

For as long as anyone can remember women in various parts of Asia have been weaving carpets at home. Girls learn to weave as soon as they are old enough to have the manual dexterity. Their first efforts are often made on a miniature toy loom. When they are skilled enough to make a real contribution they work alongside their mother or grandmother and other members of the family on the household carpet learning the patterns, and by the time they reach their teens they are proficient weavers, but this is only one phase in the making of a carpet. There are the other skills to be learned: wool sorting, combing, spinning, plying, stringing the warps onto the loom prior to weaving and cutting the pile of the finished carpet. Mastery of these skills means that a usable carpet can be produced without leaving the family and home. In this respect and in terms of basic skills, tribal and cottage weavers are in the same position, so the description of the carpet making process that follows applies equally to both. The main difference between them is in the type of loom used. Cottage weavers use an upright loom instead of the horizontal loom favoured by the nomads.

The materials

A carpet maker must know how to choose suitable wool for the various yarns used in a carpet. Basic wool quality is determined by the breed of sheep and not their diet or the climate, but in different parts of the same fleece there are quite large variations in quality. The best wool comes from a sheep's first clip and thereafter from the area around the neck and shoulders. When a sheep is sheared the fleece is pulled apart by hand and the clumps put into heaps of graded quality. The inferior wool is processed into felt and the better grades reserved for weaving. A different type of yarn is used for the warp, weft and pile, and the top quality wool is reserved for the pile. In making a selection an experienced wool sorter can distinguish differences in fibre diameter of three thousandths of a millimetre. Sorting wool by appearance and hand is still preferred to mechanical methods even in the west.

The wool is then prepared for spinning by making it into loose, porous coils using a special wool comb (illus. p.54). The wool is pulled, using both hands, through long metal spikes set vertically in a triangular wooden frame, usually held between the knees. The purpose of this is to arrange the wool fibres so that they all lie parallel to each other. When spun, the resulting yarn is hard, smooth and lustrous, characteristics essential for the pile yarn. Alternatively the wool can be prepared for spinning by carding. Handfuls of wool are worked into a loose fluffy ball by pulling it repeatedly in different directions between two sets of teeth embedded in hand–held wooden carding implements (illus. p.54). The aim of

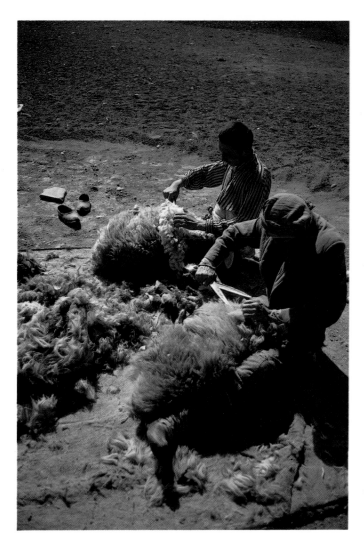

BELOW: *Drying freshly washed wool. Malatya province, Turkey.*

BELOW RIGHT: *Kirghiz women prepare wool for making felt by teasing it apart with a light wand, raising a cloud of dust in the process.*

carding, the exact opposite of combing, is to randomise the fibres so that they lie in different directions. Yarn spun from carded wool is soft, fuzzy, reflects little light and, compared to yarn spun from combed wool, has a greater strength for the same diameter. This kind of yarn is used for clothing and blankets where softness and insulation are important. As a rule combed wool is used for all carpets, kilims and flatwoven items

The coils of prepared wool are then twisted into a thread by spinning. The basic spinning implement is the hand-held spindle. A strand is drawn out from the coil of combed wool and attached to the spindle which is rolled on the thigh or twisted between the thumb and fingers to set it in motion. The spindle is allowed to hang from the thread being formed and its rotation imparts twist to the thread which gradually lengthens as more wool is teased out of the coil. The loose coils of wool are kept under the arm, up the sleeve, wound lightly round the wrist or on a distaff. When the spindle reaches the ground it is taken up and in a neat motion the thread is wound onto the spindle and the process repeated. Women can be seen spinning with practised ease while watching the animals and children out in the fields or walking along the road. The hand-powered spinning wheel is also in common use (illus. p.54). Yarns for the weft are thin and loosely spun for flexibility, warp yarns are thicker and more tightly spun for strength, and the pile yarn is thick and loosely spun.

Warp and pile yarns invariably have two or more strands twisted together. Making a thicker yarn by

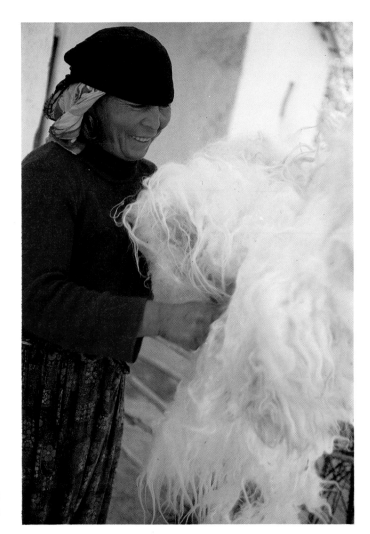

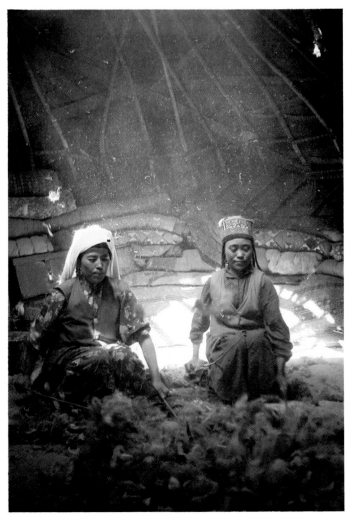

combining single threads is the process of plying and requires a special winding apparatus. Alternatively paired threads can be twisted (in the opposite direction to spinning) using a spindle (illus. p.55). After plying, the yarns are wound into hanks for dyeing.

In former times women took their hanks of wool to the dyer; some still do but the single-stage new direct dyes are easier to use and much dyeing is now done at home. The results are not always happy. The dyed wool is wound into balls in readiness for weaving.

Weaving

Next the loom, which in essence is a rectangular frame, is prepared. The loom is set up in the protection of the main dwelling, inside or just outside. Warps are stretched between the two cross-beams and held under tension by the two sides of the frame. The preparation of the foundation is time-consuming, but must be meticulously accurate to avoid distortions when the carpet is finished.

Knots are 'tied' or wrapped round a pair of warps so that the two ends face the weaver. The two ends are cut with a hand-held knife leaving a double tuft sticking out. When a horizontal line of knots is complete a weft is passed across and back, over and under alternate warps. The wefts are packed or beaten down with a beating comb onto the row of knots to hold them in place. As weaving proceeds the pile is only roughly sheared with scissors since the final clipping is part of the finishing process. Thus the carpet is built up in alternating lines of knots and wefts. Tying knots is not difficult by itself. The main physical skills are getting the tension of the knots

Felt, a woollen cloth made without weaving, is an important material for nomads living in a harsh climate. It is used to cover the outside of the tent and on the floor inside. The felts of this tent are in poor shape and this Kirghiz family is making a new one. Felt is made by placing fluffed-up wool in an even layer, pouring soap and water on it and then compressing it repeatedly. Compression is being applied here by making the felt into a tight roll and rolling it backwards and forwards with the forearms. Afghan Pamir, 1975.

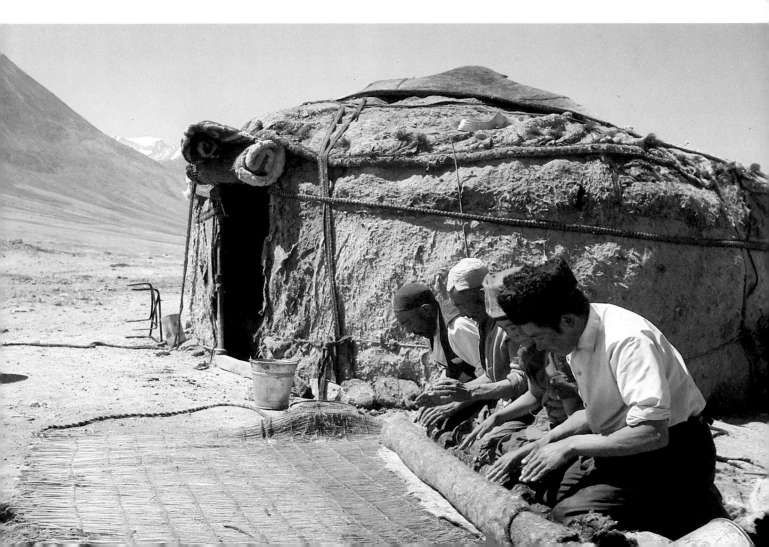

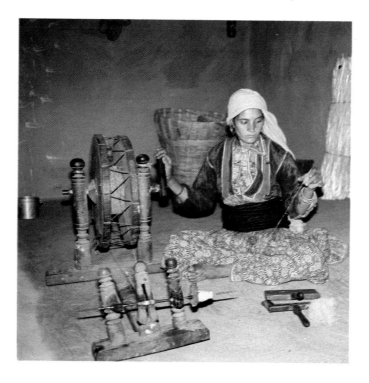

LEFT: *The hand-powered spinning wheel is in use all over Asia. This Indian woman is using a well-made model to spin carded wool for blanket making. The carding implements and the loose ball of carded wool are on the floor in front of her.*

RIGHT: *This woman is plying together two strands of yarn using a spindle. To do this she turns the spindle in the opposite direction to that used in spinning, setting it in motion by rolling it on her thigh. Plying is more commonly done with a spinning wheel. Sinanli village in the Malatya province of central Turkey.*

A Turkmen woman of the Yomut tribe combing wool by the traditional method.

Spinning wool with a spindle in Turkey. Loose porous coils of combed wool are wrapped round one wrist and, while the spindle is spinning round, an even strand is gently drawn out from the coil with the other hand.

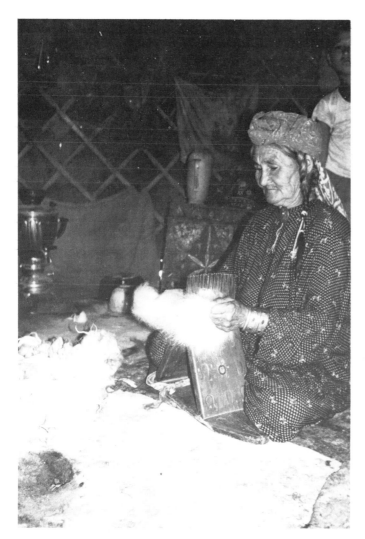

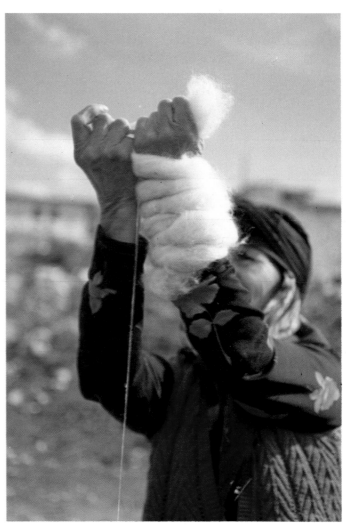

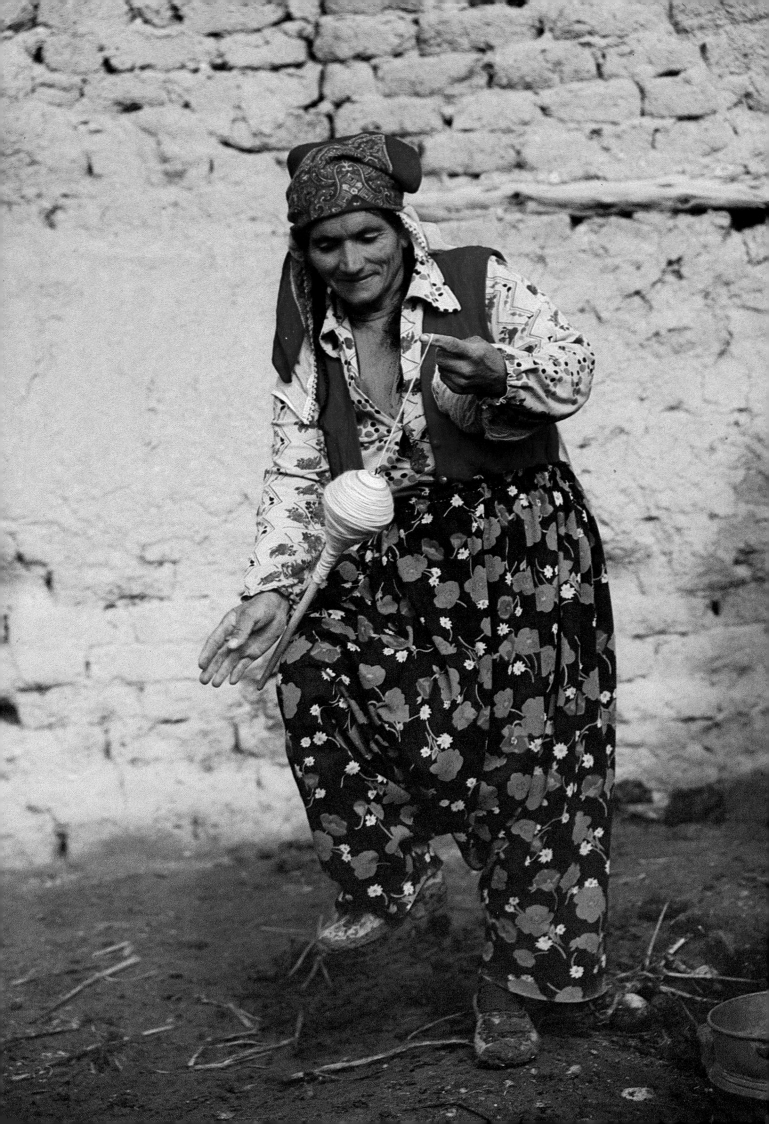

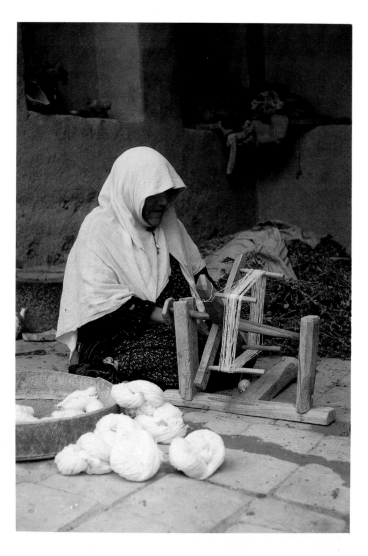

RIGHT: *Turkmen girls weaving a traditional tribal carpet on a horizontal loom. After making the knot they cut the tufts of the pile with a curved knife. Similar knives have been found in Russian Turkestan, together with spindles and needles, in women's graves dating from around 1400 BC. Ali Eli tribe, north Afghanistan, 1978.*

LEFT: *A simple winder is used to make skeins from the spun wool prior to dyeing, Turkey, 1970s.*

BELOW: *This elderly lady of the Karakoyunlu tribe is using an alternative method of preparing wool with a bow which is held in the left hand and plucked with a wooden implement in the right. The vibrating string placed against the raw wool causes it to fly apart. The fluffed wool is then loosely wound into a bundle ready for spinning or felt-making. The storage sacks along the back wall of the tent are her work (compare p.88). Beyshehir region, 1985.*

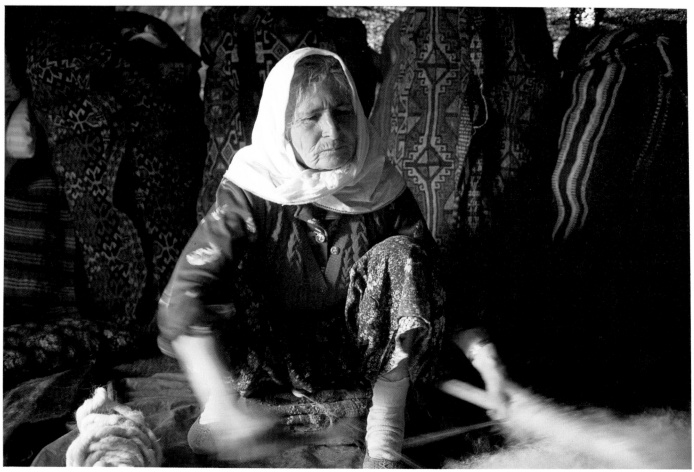

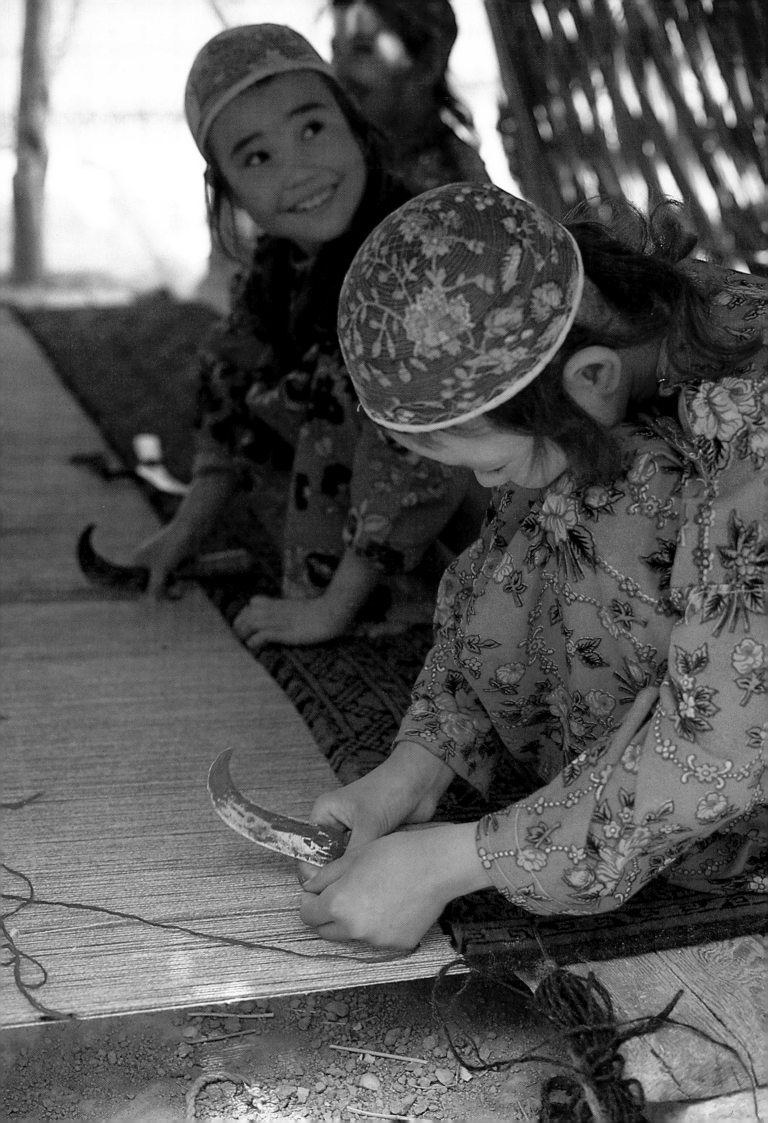

and wefts even and compacting the knots evenly so as to get straight lines. The most impressive skill is a mental one, best appreciated by drawing a carpet pattern on paper, then trying to draw it from memory. The first will turn out to be difficult, the second out of the question. The exercise shows the precision required in converting a pattern from memory or from a cartoon into rows of coloured knots which, when viewed together, make up the pattern of the carpet. It is impossible to go back and correct mistakes, so weaving a successful pattern depends on the ability to plan the exact arrangements of the knots from the beginning. There are other little things to be learned, such as how to finish the sides and the ends. The sides are strengthened with extra wrapping material as each line of knots is added, and the warp ends tied or braided in a variety of ways to prevent the ends from unravelling. The women of the house weave together or separately whenever they have time between their various household duties. The activity can be surprisingly lively. The women may sing together and their work is punctuated by the rhythmical pounding of the beating combs and the tinkling of the little horseshoe-shaped pieces of metal that decorate them. Depending on the size several months' work may be needed to complete a carpet.

When it is finished the carpet is cut from the loom and the pile is sheared to its final length. In workshops a razor-sharp curved knife held in both hands is placed on the surface of the carpet and drawn towards the user, shaving the pile a little with each stroke. The more common method is to use scissors, sometimes with a projection at the tip of both blades so that extra pressure and control can be applied with the other hand. The best result is achieved by using fairly heavy pressure on the pile and shearing it by minute degrees dozens of times. This laborious work has the effect of polishing the wool and unravelling the twist in the pile wool so that the fibres in each tuft lie parallel. Both actions increase the lustre of the pile.

Before sale many carpets are washed with soap in a local stream or river, to remove accumulated dust. It is said that some streams are especially good for bringing out the colours. For instance the shade of red in wool dyed with madder can be altered by the acidity or alkalinity of the water and this may be the reason for the claim, but the softness of the water could also be a factor.

Dyeing
In former times dyeing was a hereditary craft practised by a few respected specialists. In the last hundred years, since the introduction of synthetic dyes, much traditional knowledge relating to the old methods has been lost. In many areas people have forgotten how to use common dye plants and do not even know their names. Some of this lost knowledge has been recovered by the chemical analysis of small samples of coloured yarn taken from old carpets. A dye chemist can tell us the mordant (a metallic salt used to attach the dye to the fibre), the nature of the dyestuff, and often the actual species from which it was derived, but knowing the ingredients is not the same as knowing the recipe. There is still much to be learned about the old technology.

Turning first to tribal carpets, none of the main nomadic communities still uses natural dyes so it is difficult to be sure how they organised their dyeing. They could have taken their wool to the local dyer and paid him to dye it for them, or they could have gathered the dye plants, bought or bartered the other ingredients, and dyed the wool themselves. They probably did both because, with the exception of blue and green, the colours found in the typical tribal palette are fairly easy to produce. Blue dyeing with indigo has become a simple procedure, but years ago getting the insoluble dark blue cakes into solution was a process too lengthy and difficult to have been possible for nomads or the average villager.

For the cottage industry we have more information because natural dyeing still survives in Persia. The community dyer has a key role. He is not called on to do all the dyeing, because the women prefer to cut costs by doing as much for themselves as they can. He does the indigo dyeing and has the knowledge and materials for all the common colours. He has the advantage that he can cope with large batches of wool if a sizeable carpet is to be made. To dye the wool in small batches at home is to run the risk that they will not come out the same shade. The effect of using two different batches of wool is seen in the blue background of the carpets illustrated on pages 41 and 128. Changes in colour of this kind are acceptable in a tribal or village rug but would be regarded as a fault in a workshop carpet.

For workshop carpets a typical system is for a merchant–entrepreneur to have a number of looms under contract to him, either gathered in one place or dispersed in individual houses. He decides what sort of carpets he is going to produce and orders the shades and quantities of wool that he needs from the dye house which is under his direct control. Dyeing is done in large batches to a high standard. Numerous shades are produced with reproducible accuracy – over twenty in the better pieces. Skilled urban dyers are often familiar with both traditional and synthetic dyestuffs.

Dyestuffs and colours
For blue, nothing surpasses indigo. The name comes from the ancient Greek word for Indian. For thousands of years the indigo plant, *Indigofera tinctoria*, which requires a sub-tropical climate, has been cultivated in India. The dyestuff extracted from it was exported in the form of dark blue cakes which found their way through trade into every corner of the ancient world. Another source of blue dye was dyer's woad, *Isatis tinctoria*, native to eastern Europe, which was known in pre-Roman Britain. The dyestuff obtained from both plants is identical, though *Indigofera tinctoria* contains thirty times as much indigo as woad. The availability of synthetic indigo, which is identical to the plant extract, has virtually put an end to the cultivation of the indigo plant in India.

Indigo exists in two forms: a blue form which is insoluble, and a yellow form which is soluble. For dyeing, indigo must first be dissolved in water. The process is one of chemical reduction in the absence of air. The traditional method was to ferment it for several weeks in a vat alkalinised with urine. Wool was dipped into the heated vat and exposed to the air. The yellow soluble form oxidises spontaneously to the blue insoluble form which is deposited on the surface of the fibres in the form of a protective coating. Wool dyed with indigo is more resistant to wear than undyed wool. In theory it can be rubbed off, but in practice indigo-dyed woollen textiles do not develop the well-used look of cotton clothing dyed with indigo. The saturation or depth of colour depends on the amount of indigo deposited on the fibres, so a dark blue is expensive. The lavish use of midnight blue is a popular extravagance in Persia (illus. p.61).

For reds the most important source is the madder plant, *Rubia tinctorum*, which is easy to cultivate. The dyestuff is in the roots. These are dug out, dried, and then ground into a powder. Madder contains not one but at least six dyestuffs, three major and three minor, which between them produce a remarkable range of colours. The hue is mainly determined by the three major components, purpurin, pseudopurpurin and alizarin. The amount of each present on the wool fibre depends on four variables: the mordant used, the quantity of madder present in the dye bath, its acidity–alkalinity, and its temperature. All dyeing with madder requires the wool to be pre-treated with a mordant. The commonest mordants are potassium aluminium sulphate (alum) and iron sulphate. The full spectrum of madder colours includes pink, rose, apricot, a brilliant scarlet (of the type used for flags and old military uniforms), rust red, numerous brown-reds, purple and brown-purple.

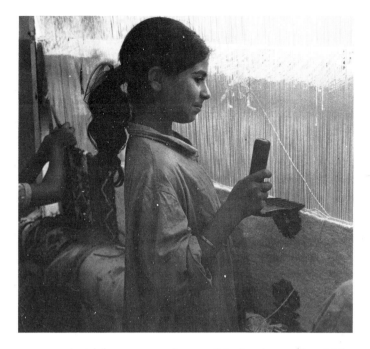

ABOVE: *A girl demonstrates the use of the beating comb, which is used to compact the line of knots after the insertion of the wefts. Tunisia, 1970s.*

BELOW: *Washing carpets in a stream to remove dust prior to sale. Dowlatabad, south Persia.*

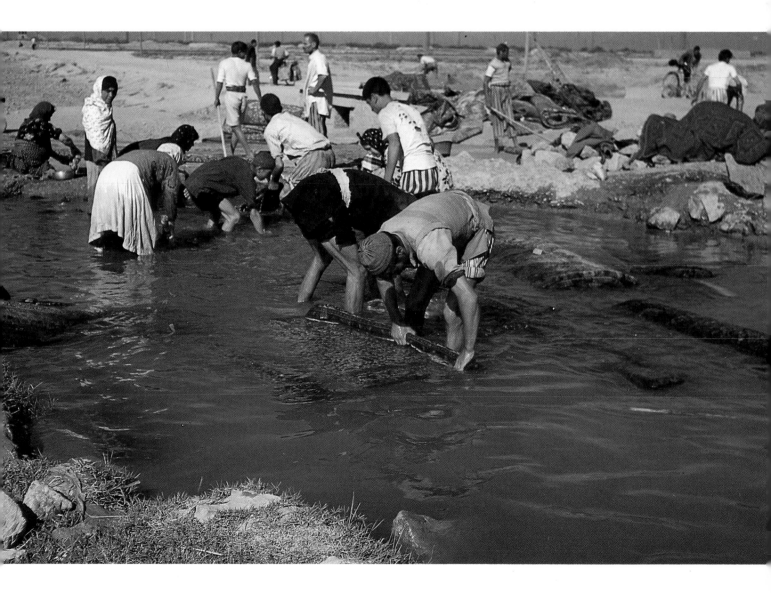

RIGHT: *In the sixteenth century and throughout the seventeenth, many fine carpets were woven in Khorasan, north-east Persia. In the eighteenth and nineteenth centuries, while carpet production was in decline throughout the whole of Persia, the workshops in Khorasan remained active (p.139). The scale of this carpet, together with its perfectly balanced composition, deep blue field and crimson background, give it a classical look, although irregularities in the pattern at the corners indicate that a complete cartoon was not used. The crimson-red has the characteristic hue of a dye derived from an insect, either lac from India or cochineal. Possibly Dorokhsh village, nineteenth century. 589 × 269 cm/232 × 106 in.*

BELOW: *Indigo dyeing has always been a specialised craft. Here cloth is being dyed after it has been woven. The dark colour is obtained by repeated dipping and consumes an enormous amount of the dyestuff. The broad expanses of midnight blue so popular with Persians are therefore an expensive luxury (opposite). India, 1970s.*

Yellow dyestuffs are found in a great variety of plants. Most fade quickly on exposure to light. Of the few plants known to have been used by dyers in former times, weld (*Reseda luteola*) is one of the best. With alum mordant it gives an extremely light-fast yellow.

To obtain black, wool is mordanted with iron and dyed with oak galls or acorn cups which contain tannins. With these six materials – oak galls, a yellow dye plant, alum, iron sulphate, madder root and indigo – the rural dyer is equipped to produce the typical village and tribal palette of between six and thirteen colours which are: two blues (sometimes three), red (sometimes two), apricot (weak madder), purple, orange (sometimes), yellow, green, black and undyed white. For green the wool is dyed with indigo plus yellow, and for orange with madder plus yellow.

One more category of dyestuffs must be mentioned here – the insect dyes. On wool and silk they produce a set of bluish reds varying from pink-lilac through bright crimson to deep red-brown-purple (see illus. p.153) – the last, the colour of congealed blood, is sometimes called oxblood. These colours are common in court carpets and textiles. They were obtained by using Indian lac, a dye derived from the insect *Coccus lacca*. In the mid-nineteenth century cochineal took the place of lac when Europeans discovered how to cultivate the Mexican cochineal insect and its use extended to village and even tribal carpets (see pp.61, 145, 151).

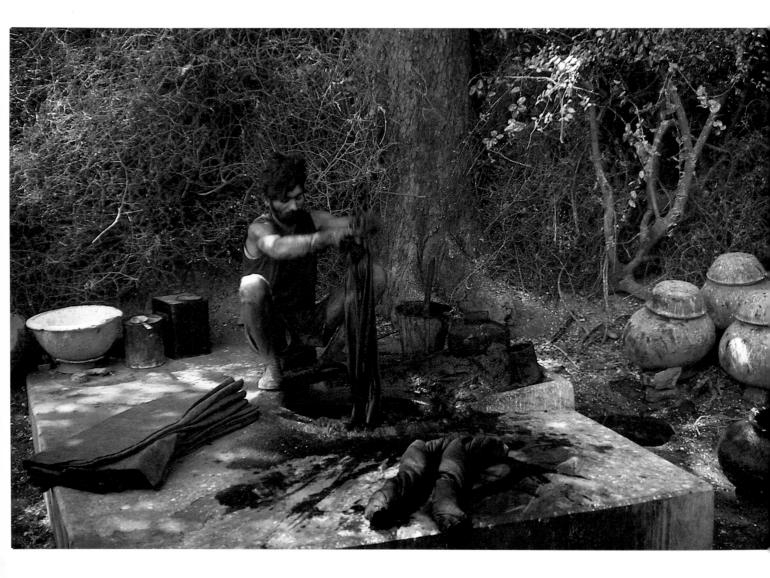

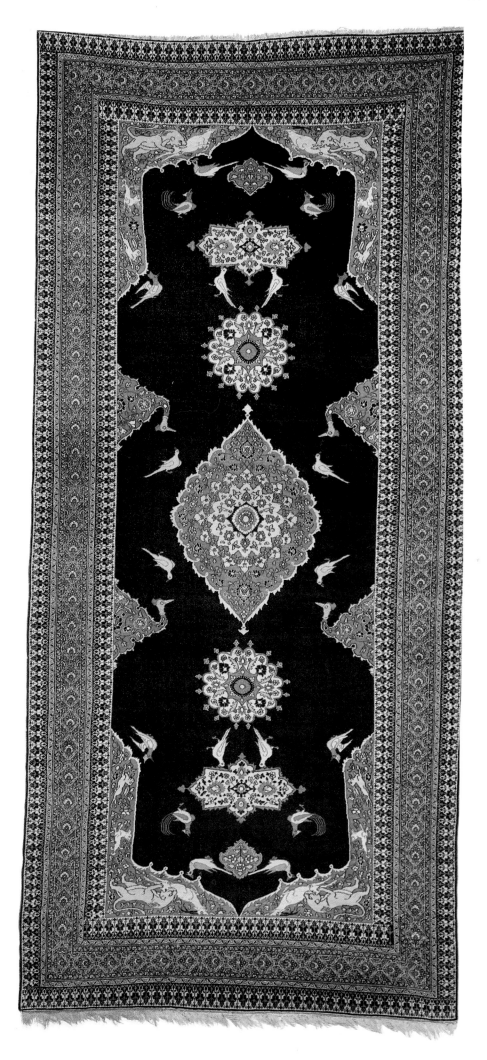

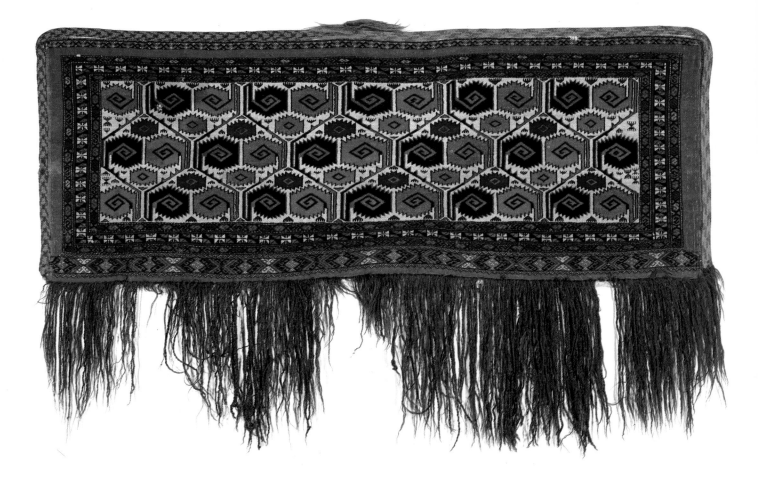

ABOVE: *An important event in the life of any woman is her wedding. Among the Turkmen it was and is customary for young women to weave special hangings, often with a white ground, to decorate the bridal tent and the animals taking part in her wedding procession. This example was woven by the Salor tribe of Turkestan in the mid nineteenth century before synthetic dyes came into use. The brilliant effect is enlivened by the use of silk dyed with cochineal. Nineteenth century. 48 × 140 cm/19 × 55 in.*

RIGHT: *A professional dyer. North Afghanistan, 1971.*

An important feature of rural carpets is the non-uniformity of their colours (see illus. pp.4, 13, 21, 37, 41, 75, 128). Where at first glance we see an area of plain colour, a second look reveals that the eye has been deceived. In reality the colour consists of innumerable variations of the same shade. This vibrato in colour, known as abrash (meaning dappled, mottled or speckled), is an attractive feature of natural dyes. It gives them a vitality and interest which makes uniform colours appear flat and lifeless by comparison. This non-uniformity results from the action of variations inherent in the dyeing process on hand-prepared yarns. Hand spinning produces a yarn of non-uniform diameter and variable twist. In the dyeing process the dye and mordant penetrate unevenly. Abrash is most pronounced with hand spinning, vegetable dyes and village technology, and may be absent with machine-spun yarns and synthetic dyes.

Effectively, synthetic dyes began in the 1860s[3] but did not come into general use until the 1870s, reaching many of the nomadic tribes in the 1880s. Even so they were not adopted everywhere (illus. p.157). As is well known, the early results were often disastrous: the colours were brilliant but they tended to fade or run, which gave them a bad name (see p.86).

Recent work on synthetic dyes has added greatly to our knowledge of the age and source of carpets woven within the last hundred years. For example, a rug dyed with a particular synthetic dye cannot have been made before that dye was marketed. A particular red dye used by the Turkmen was patented in Russia. Pieces with this dye all appear to have been woven in Turkestan within the Russian sphere of influence, whereas in Afghanistan a synthetic yellow of British manufacture was used.

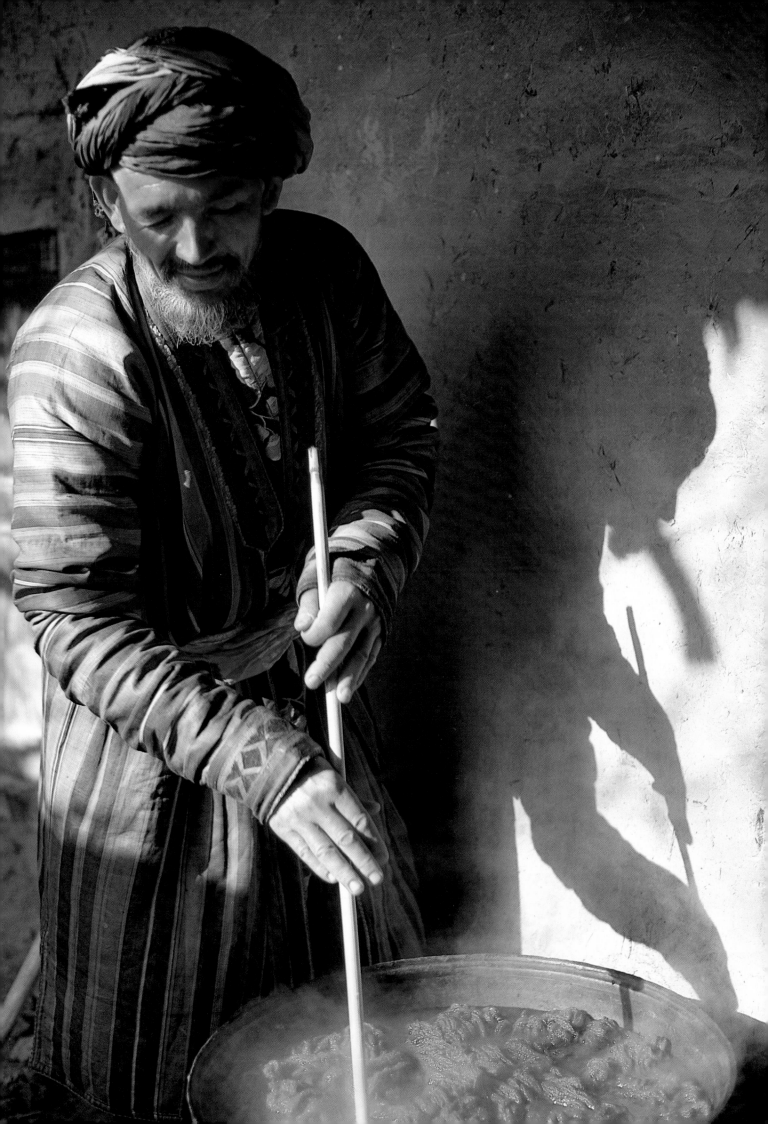

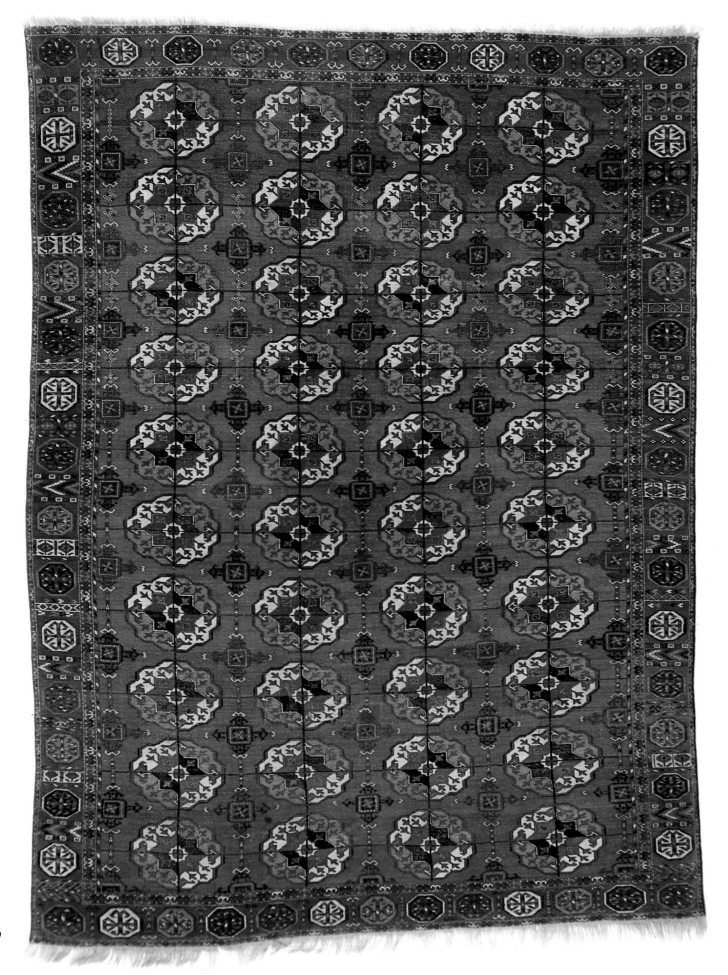

Chapter three

Tribal and domestic weavings

The origin and history of carpet weaving

I believe that the art and craft of the knotted pile carpet began where it has always flourished, among the pastoral nomads. Wool and leather are absolutely basic to their way of life. They are as much masters of wool as the ancient Egyptians were of stone. They process it into the covering for the roof and the walls of the tent, ropes, girths, bags and containers of all sorts, felt rugs for the floor, clothing for man and animals, and a variety of household items from oven gloves to blankets. It also serves them as a medium for artistic expression, for that deeply felt desire to make things pleasing to the eye, and the humblest item is decorated with a variety of colours and patterns. However only the more western tribes

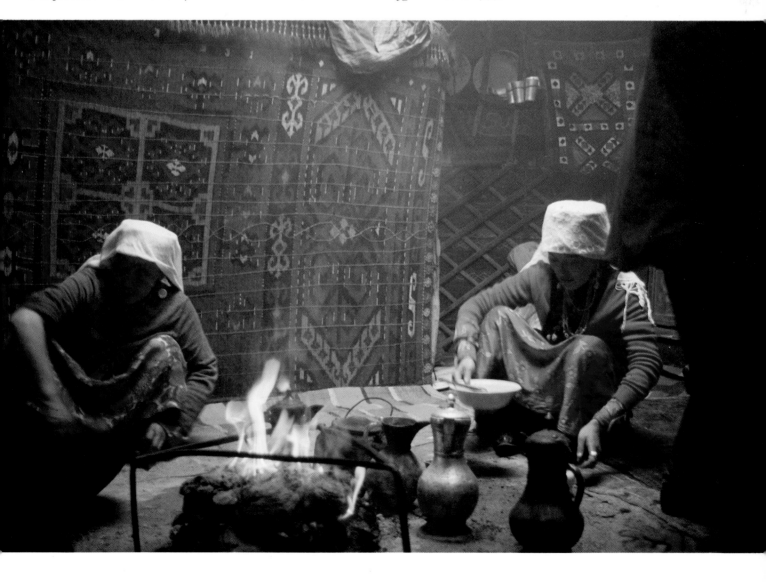

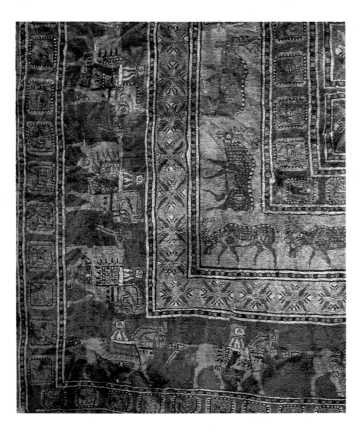

LEFT: *A section of the famous carpet excavated from the frozen tomb of a nomadic chieftain at Pazyryk in the Altai mountains of southern Siberia, now in the Hermitage Museum, Leningrad. It dates from the fifth century BC and its decorative style derives from the art of Achaemenid Persia. Whether or not it is a nomadic carpet with a Persian design or a Persian carpet acquired by the nomads is still in dispute.*

BELOW: *Throughout Turkey mosques are carpeted with rugs and kilims given by local weavers. From the layers accumulated over the centuries, it is possible to reconstruct a fairly complete history of Turkish carpets. The carpets covering the floor of this mosque in Karapinar are a good cross-section of local production. Central Turkey, 1970s.*

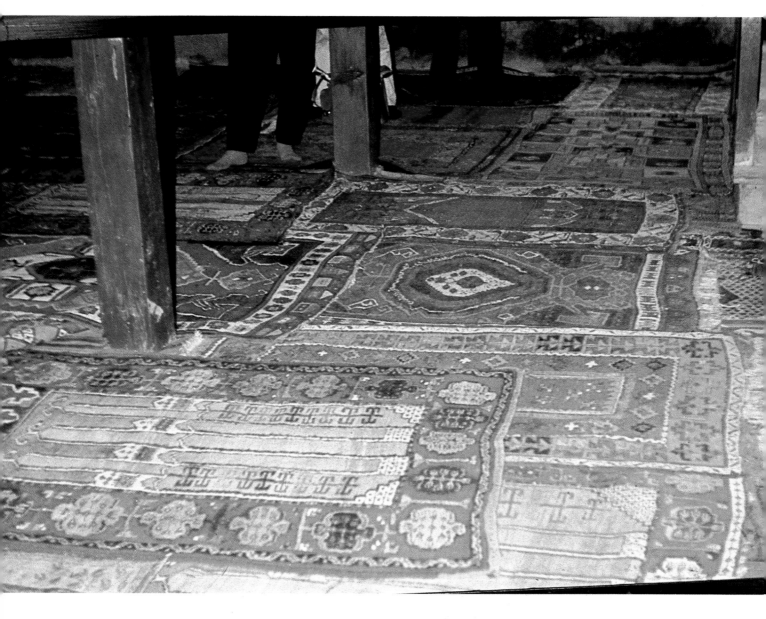

developed the knotted pile technique to a high technical
and artistic level; the Mongols, who have a very similar
life-style to the Kazakh, Kirghiz and Turkmen, have no
knotted pile carpet tradition.

The first piled carpets may have imitated the texture
and insulating properties of animal pelts. Some carpets
made by nomads for everyday use have just this quality
(illus. pp.11, 29). The oldest complete carpet was found
in the frozen tomb of a nomadic chieftain at Pazyryk in
southern Siberia, close to the border with Mongolia. In
it, preserved in permanent ice since the fifth century BC,
were perishable articles including felt, leatherwork,
wood carvings, woollen textiles and Chinese silks – great
rarities in the world of archaeology. The carpet is on
view in the Hermitage Museum, Leningrad. It is two
metres square, quite finely knotted and of velvety texture
– nothing like an animal pelt. There is disagreement as to
who made it. Its design suggests an origin in Achaemenid
Persia, an idea rejected by those who believe it was made
by the nomads themselves.[4] Nearby at Bashadar another
piece of piled carpet was found. It is only a fragment but
finer than the Pazyryk carpet and older by a century.

Apart from some poorly documented archaeological
scraps from the sand-buried cities of east Turkestan
(Sinkiang), and from the rubbish heaps of old Cairo,
nothing more is known about the history of the carpet
until the thirteenth or fourteenth century, the date of the
earliest material from Turkish mosques. (As a result of
the long-standing custom of giving carpets to the local
mosque, Turkey has a richer inheritance of old carpets
and a more complete record of its carpet weaving history
than any other country.) Practically every rug book calls
a well-known group of early carpets found in a mosque
in Konya Seljuk court carpets (i.e. twelfth or thirteenth
century), but they have the character of cottage-made
carpets and must have been made during the early
Ottoman period some time after the year 1300.[5]
However there are carpets in Turkey which could indeed
be court products of the Seljuk period. They are of a
much higher technical order than the Konya group, but
they are little known.[6]

From the fifteenth century onwards Turkish carpets
survive in sufficient quantity to give a good idea of their
history. For Persia the record is fragmentary. A few court
carpets have been preserved from the sixteenth century –
works of astonishing technical virtuosity and artistic
refinement. Carpet weaving was evidently an important
branch of courtly art in Persia. The record of Persian
tribal and village carpets made prior to the eighteenth
century is very scanty.

Modern carpet history really began in the nineteenth
century but to understand the pattern of production in
each of the carpet producing countries it is necessary to
know something of the history and composition of their
peoples. Turkish carpets can be better understood if we
remember that this formerly Greek-speaking country
became, in the course of four and a half centuries
beginning around AD 1000, increasingly dominated by
the westward movement of Turkish-speaking people
who were originally steppe nomads of Turkmen origin.
Pockets of Greek speakers continued to live in western
Turkey until the first quarter of this century when, as a
result of war, there was a mass migration of them to

BELOW: *In 1905 three early carpets and several fragments were
noticed in a mosque in Konya. The design of this example,
now in the Museum of Turkish and Islamic Art, Istanbul, is
based on a Chinese textile pattern. It probably dates from the
fourteenth century though an earlier date is often given.*

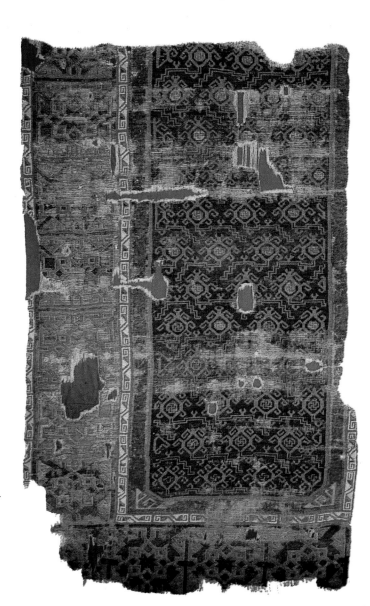

RIGHT: *Some interesting carpets woven in Turkey – usually called simply 'Yuruk' or nomad – are made by Kurdish-speaking nomads and villagers in the eastern part of the country. They have a distinctive colouring and use a variety of designs, some borrowed from their urban neighbours. The design of this rug is derived from motifs originating in court art of the fourteenth century. Nineteenth century. 162 × 96 cm/ 64 × 38 in.*

BELOW: *Over a period of 450 years, Turkish-speaking people moved westwards and settled in Greek-speaking Asia Minor. Until the early decades of this century there were many Greek villages in Turkey, some producing carpets as this example reveals. The central medallion has an inscription in Greek characters which reads 'the peacock', and a date which can be read as 1280 (AD 1868). The peacock is sacred to Hera, goddess of marriage and maternity. It is clearly a wedding carpet, and is woven in the style of Kula, a village in western Turkey noted for its active cottage industry in the last century. 355 × 380 cm/140 × 149½ in.*

Crete. Some may still remain in eastern Turkey. (The Greek community also wove carpets (illus. p.68 below), as the occasional inscription in Greek reveals, but the details of their output is unknown.) The nomad Turks migrated all over the country to find suitable pasture. Some settled down, but others have continued their nomadic life to the present day. Similar movements of people, in more than one wave, went into Persia, Azerbaijan, parts of the Caucasus, Turkestan, and parts of Afghanistan. In all these places there has been a trend towards settlement of these originally nomadic, Turkish-speaking people.

Wherever these nomads went there is a strong residue, more or less expressed, of Turkic design, but the longer the community has been settled the more diluted with other influences the designs have become. A typical example is the Ersari tribe, a large Turkmen group with many subdivisions, some of whom settled in the Oxus river valley during the seventeenth century. Their nineteenth-century weaving has a strongly tribal

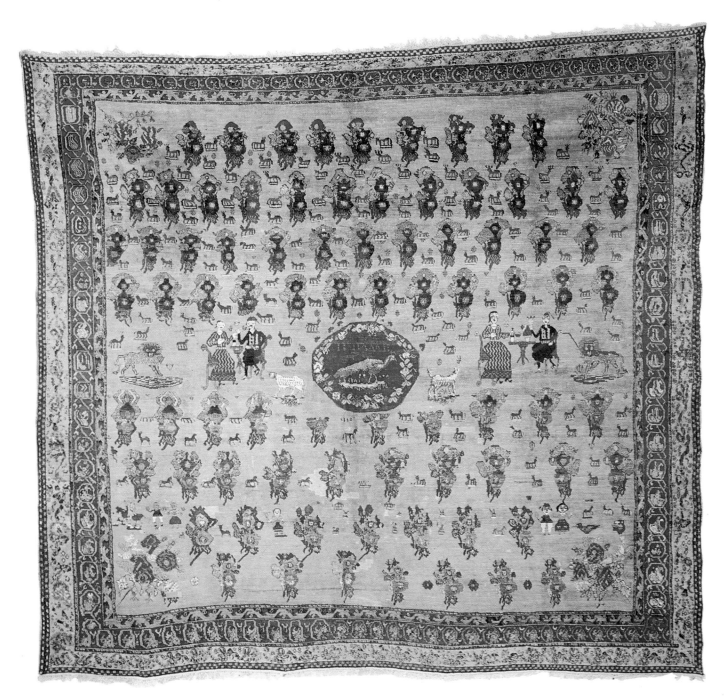

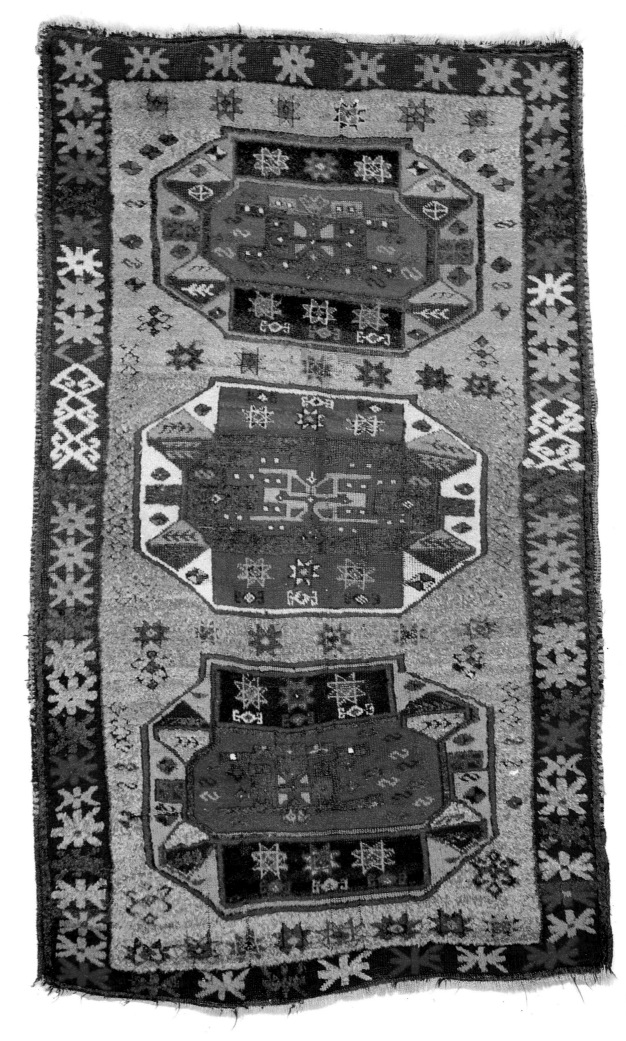

RIGHT: *The colouring and decorative style of this carpet are immediately recognisable as the work of Turkmen weavers of the Ersari tribe settled in the Amu Darya (Oxus) river valley in the Emirate of Bukhara. But by no stretch of the imagination can this be thought of as a tribal carpet. In fact the formerly nomadic Ersari had been settled since the seventeenth century and by the nineteenth century much of their output had taken on the character of a cottage industry. This huge carpet must have been made as a special commission for a palace or public building on a loom built for the purpose. Nineteenth century. 589 × 427 cm/232 × 168 in.*

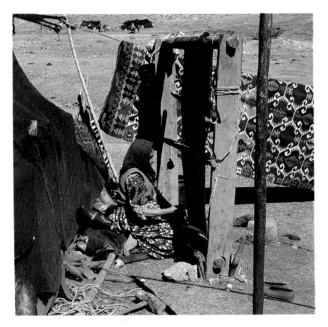

ABOVE: *The next day her family will start migration to their winter pasture, so she is hurrying to finish a simple sack needed for the journey. A kilim she made hangs over the guy rope. Karakoyunlu tribe, Beyshehir region, 1985.*

BELOW: *Functional objects such as the pannier bags made by these nomads rarely find their way to the market place. Old examples are extremely rare since when too shabby to use they are discarded like old clothes and new ones are made. Near Pamukkale, central Turkey, 1970s.*

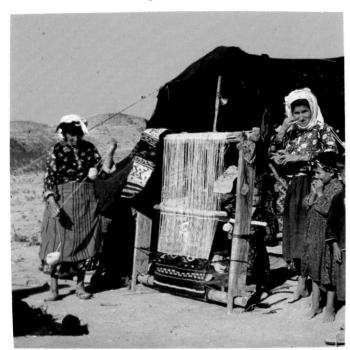

character but, compared to their nomadic cousins' work, includes many assimilated elements from the patterns of Persian carpets and locally made silks. Carpet sizes are often more suitable for houses rather than tents (illus. p.71 opposite), and in many instances their work has taken on the character of a cottage industry.

Tribal communities

The term tribal is used here rather loosely as a practical description of carpets and the circumstances of their production and not as a definition of the social structure of a weaving community. It refers to weavings made primarily for personal use within a community. The tribal category includes the weavings of a few groups that are unlikely to be accepted within the technical anthropological definition of the term. A better term might be tribal-style. The truly tribal groups, such as the Turkmen of Turkestan and the Qashqai of Iran, who are organised into clans or lineage groups and maintain some degree of large-scale tribal coherence, are typical producers of tribal-style carpets. But many weavings of similar character are also produced by peasant women in small village communities with no tribal allegiances, who are unaware of their larger relationships and often ignorant of their origins. These communities are often of particular interest because in their relative cultural isolation they may retain long-standing customs, an unusual life-style or even their own language. The term tribal is intended to exclude the products of communities where weaving is carried out solely as a means of livelihood, but does not exclude groups of weavings just because their makers sell a portion of them. Selling or bartering surplus weavings has always been a source of revenue for skilled tribal weavers.

Tribal and domestic weavings have a strong local, traditional, even cultic character and their traditional designs have often been in use with little change for many centuries. The point of excluding weavers working primarily for money is that market demand soon becomes an influence of such importance that it overrides any considerations of tribal convention or communal tradition. Weavers are then at the mercy of market pressures and soon they and their work are transformed into a cottage industry

The output of such weavings is considerable and in addition to articles sold and exported there are innumerable domestic weavings made all over Asia which never reach the market place. There are communities in eastern and central Turkey, for example, whose weaving tradition might have gone unrecorded but for the discovery by ethnographers of old carpets in local mosques. Turkey in particular has a strong tradition of kilim, or pileless weaving, which has attracted serious attention only recently. It is not known if kilim weaving in Asia Minor or Turkey was brought by the carpet-weaving Turkic nomads in the eleventh century or if it is a truly ancient and indigenous art form.

The numerous weaving communities, scattered in small, more or less independent groups throughout the carpet producing areas, have life-styles ranging from the pastoral nomadic to the settled agricultural. The most self-sufficient and independent of these live wholly in tents and move their flocks seasonally between summer and winter grazing. Others have both tents and houses,

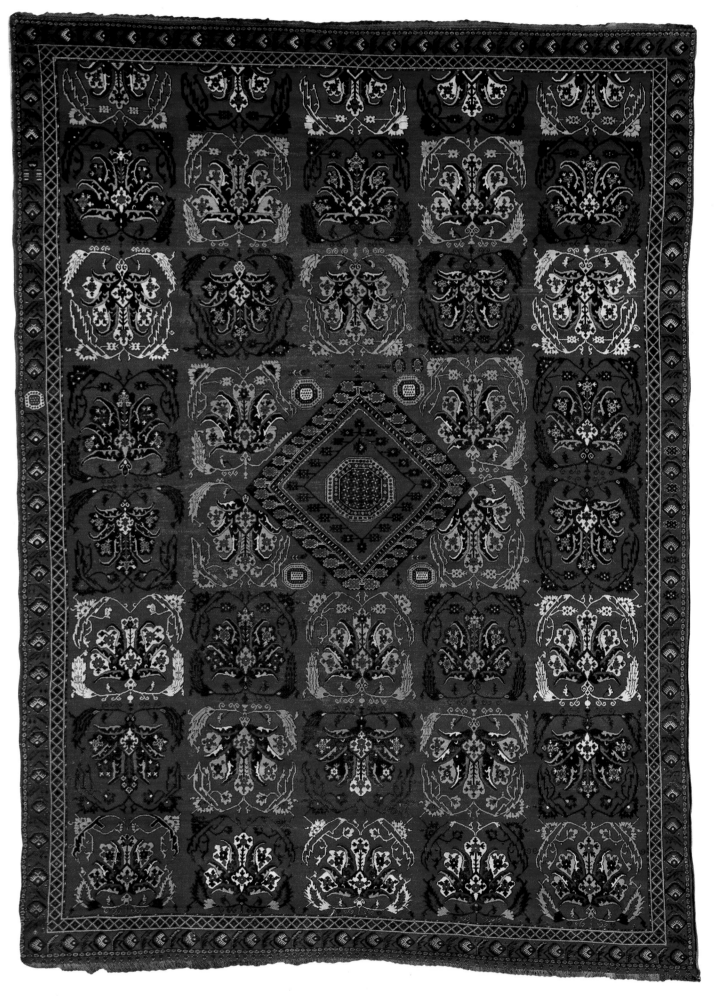

BELOW: *In parts of Turkey piled carpets are used as a bed (Yatak). They are squarish and rather coarsely knotted. As they are purely domestic products their patterns tend to be conservative, which makes them difficult to date with any accuracy. This example has an archaic repeating pattern in many colour combinations with deliberate ambiguity between the motifs and the ground colour – both typical devices of the tribal weaver. Although probably made in the nineteenth century it could well be much earlier. 198 × 167 cm/ 78 × 65½ in.*

RIGHT: *Although the design of kilims tends to be conservative, no tradition is impervious to change. This kilim has a design of stylised carnations which can be traced back to the Ottoman court style, in fashion some two centuries before it was made. In the interval the carnation has been transformed into a typical tribal-style design consisting of a bold repeating pattern in different colour combinations. It was woven on a narrow loom in two halves. Nigde region, central Turkey, nineteenth century. 307 × 182 cm/121 × 71½ in.*

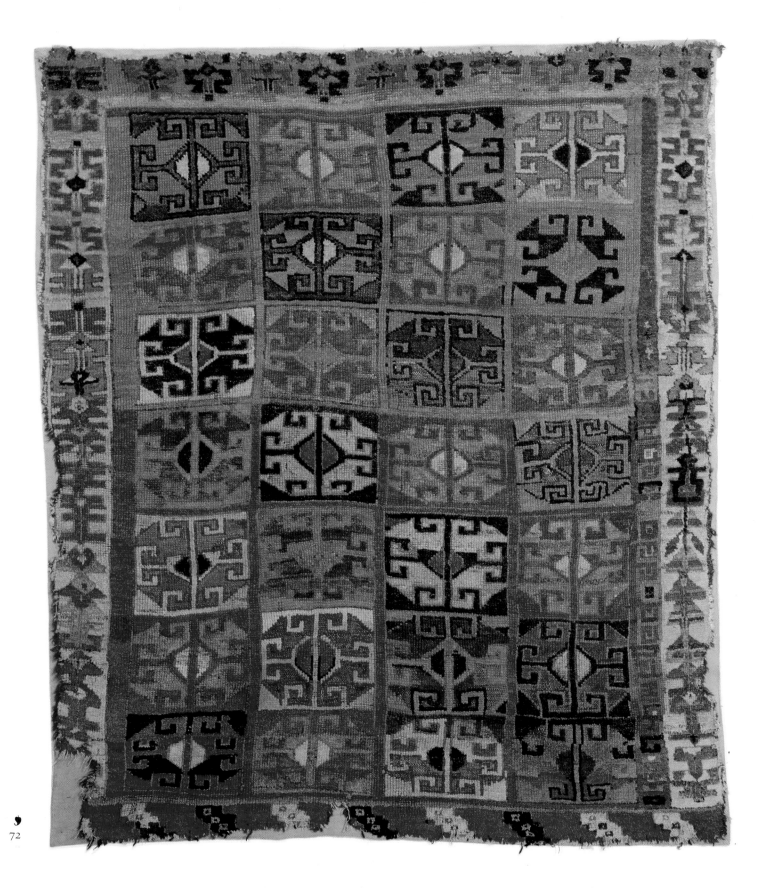

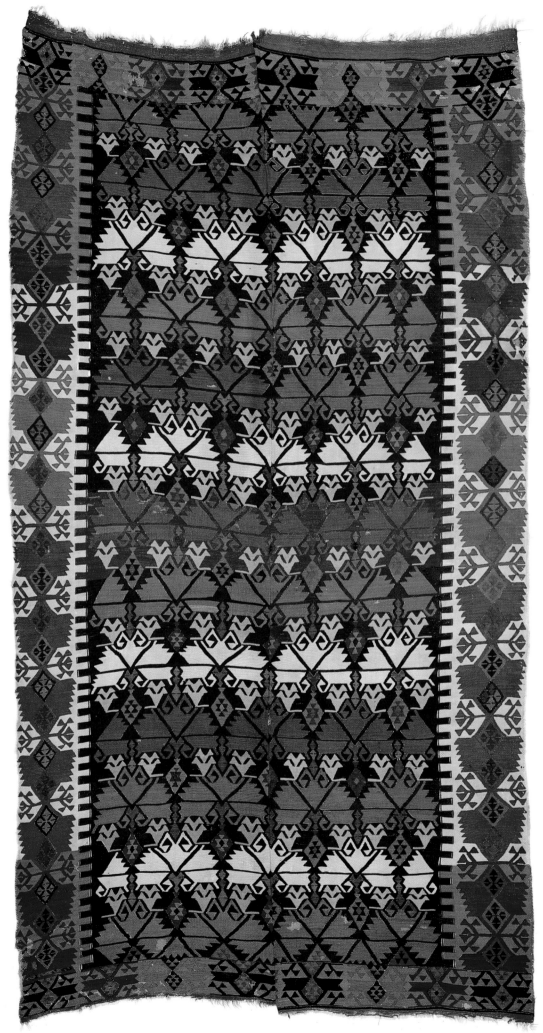

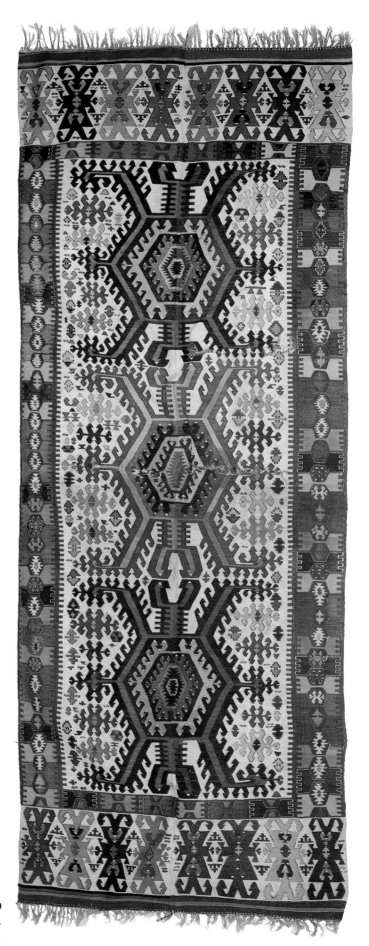

plant annual crops but migrate with their flocks. Yet others live in houses in the winter and tents in the summer within the same village compound. Lastly many are purely settled, with a self-contained life-style of tribal character.

From the carpet point of view these nomadic or village-based groups were, if not now, primary producers of wool and the source of many of the tribal carpets found in the market place today.

The nomadic life

When discussing tribal carpets, the nomadic tribes invariably come to mind first. It is easy to be romantic about the wide open spaces, the wonderful scenery and the self-sufficient life-style enjoyed by many of the pastoral nomads, while overlooking the extremes of climate, the ceaseless work and the ever present possibility of sudden poverty if livestock are lost in a hard winter or an epidemic.

The nomadic life-style has a long history. The technical advances in animal husbandry and the development of suitable light-weight, portable housing seem to have occurred in the third millennium BC. Once the breakthrough had been made the great Asian steppe was populated by a variety of unrelated groups of diverse ethnic origins sharing a common life-style and, at times, common religious and artistic conventions. Historical and archaeological evidence indicates that the life-style of the early steppe nomads 2400 years ago is very similar to that of the present-day steppe-dwellers such as the Mongols, Kazakh, Kirghiz, Uzbegs and Turkmen. There is an uncanny resemblance between the artefacts found in the famous frozen tomb of a nomadic chieftain at Pazyryk in the Altai mountains of Siberia, dating from around 400 BC, and those of the Kazakh people of today.[7] Apart from the adaptation of tent design to the local climate and conditions these nomadic groups maintain a way of life which is basically extremely conservative.

The nomadic life may have romantic appeal for western city-dwellers but it clearly also has a very real attraction for its long-standing adherents who continue to cling to it with extraordinary tenacity in the face of ceaseless suppression. Historically the more independent

LEFT: *A lively debate is in progress over the origin of Anatolian kilim designs. On the basis of resemblances to the patterns of archaeological wall paintings dating from the sixth millennium BC, one side claims that they have their origin in the neolithic period, and have been woven locally ever since. The other claims that the kilim is essentially an object made for the tent and that the craft was brought by nomadic Turks from central Asia. Aydinli tribe, Balikesir region, nineteenth century. 416 × 160 cm/160 × 63 in.*

RIGHT: *Until recently this type of kilim was unknown in the west. Their makers, the Yuncu tribe from Balikesir in western Turkey, consider them to have sacred and magical significance and are reluctant to part with them. When this is the case the appearance of such weavings on the market usually follows a weakening of tribal traditions. With the Yuncu it is probably no more than an erosion of old ways of thought brought about by prolonged contact with western influence. Nineteenth century. 277 × 133 cm/109 × 52 in.*

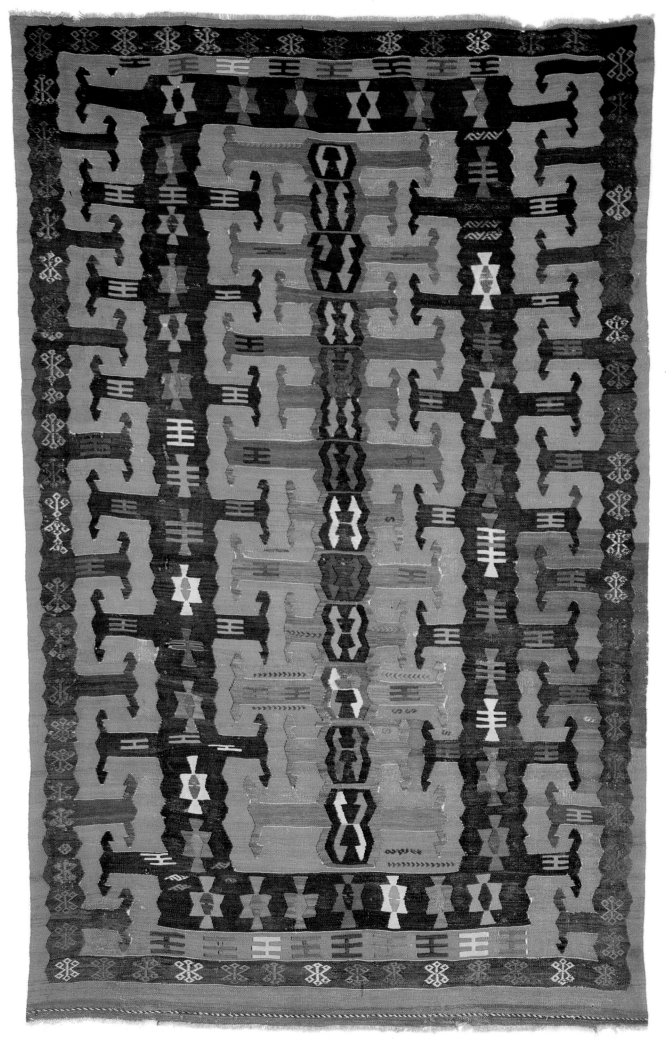

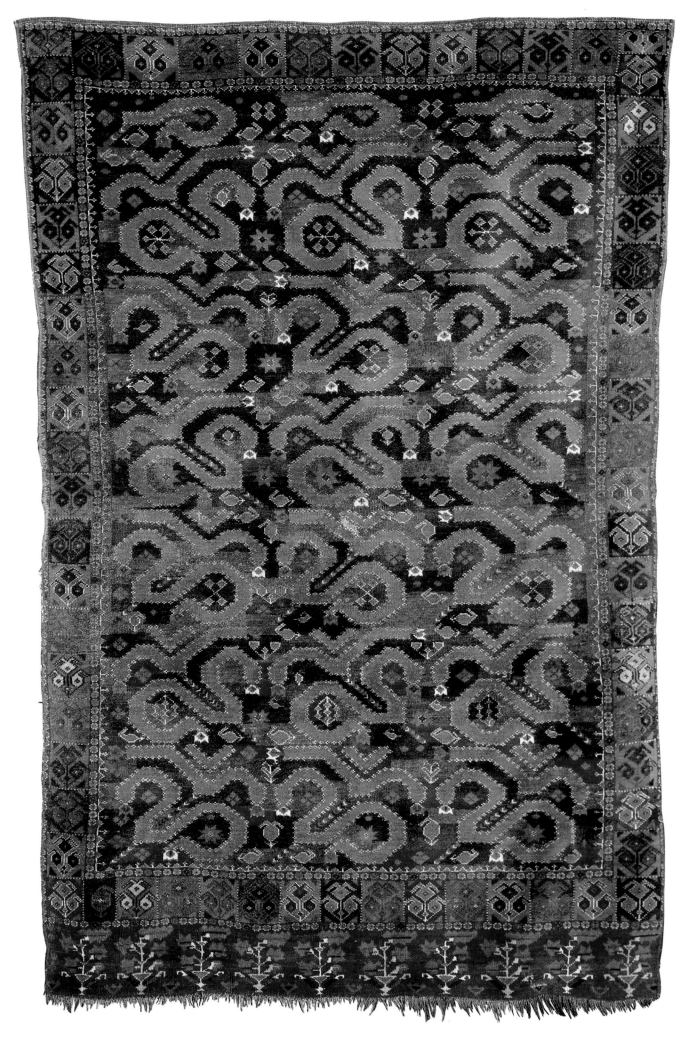

tribes have always been seen by central government as a potential threat and have tended to suffer as a consequence. In Persia in the first half of the eighteenth century Nadir Shah forcibly relocated several tribes on the periphery of his territory to act as buffers against potential invaders, though forcible suppression has been a commoner fate. The last hundred years have been a difficult time for the nomadic tribes. Some survive intact, others cling precariously to their old way of life, but within this period many have succumbed to superior forces and vanished.

For three decades the Russian authorities tried to convert the Kazakh nomads to the orthodoxy of fixed housing and agriculture. In spite of the liquidation and expulsion of 'reactionary' leaders, collectivisation, 'land reform' and 'livestock reform' – in effect a programme of confiscation and redistribution – and a fall in the number of sheep and goats to 10 per cent and horses to 5 per cent of their former numbers, the Kazakh way of life survives. The huge losses of livestock, capricious rainfall and the marginal nature of much of the steppe grazing land has forced those in authority to adopt a more flexible attitude to nomadism. Camel breeding programmes have now been launched and the nomadic family has been restyled as a 'brigade'. As an acknowledgement of the validity of the nomadic life, the 'red tents', housing adult educational activities, have joined the nomadic encampments.

LEFT: This Turkmen rug has the typical shape, size and lower panel of tent door rugs, but not the characteristic design (see p.91). The apparently complex field pattern consists of a fairly simple unit of design in horizontal rows. In succeeding rows the design inclines to the left and to the right alternately. This departure from the traditional door rug form is a reflection of the settled state and greater receptivity to outside influences of its makers, the Ersari tribe. Russian Turkestan, nineteenth century. 187 × 120 cm/73½ × 47 in.

A Kirghiz family cleaning the tent. They are shaking out a floor rug which is curved to fit the shape of the tent. It is made out of coloured pieces of felt which are cut out and sewn together in bold patterns. A white cord outlining the patterns conceals the seams and gives contrast to the design. The technique is often called appliqué but is more like a mosaic. Rolled up above the entrance is a door rug of similar construction. The Turkmen in former times used a piled rug for this purpose (see opposite and pp.31, 91). Afghan Pamir, 1975.

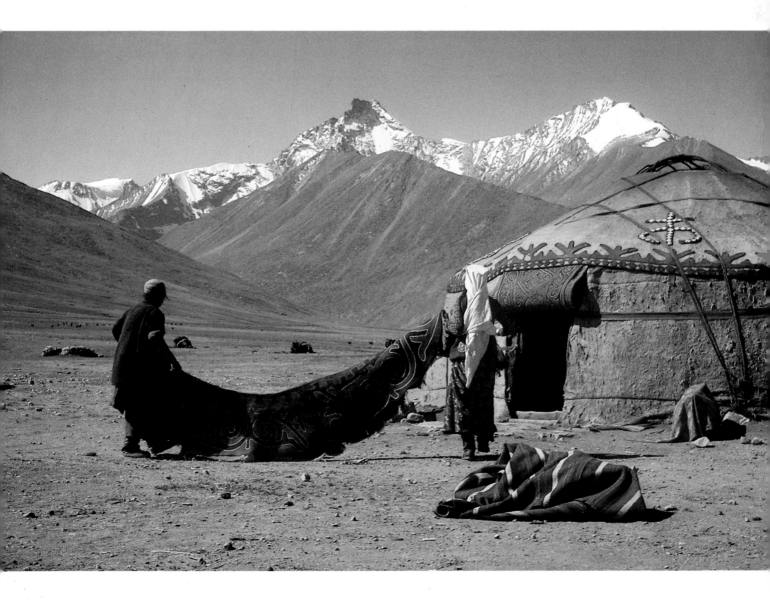

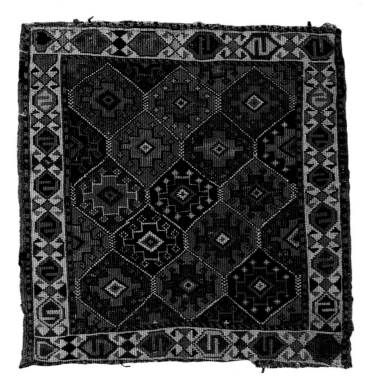

LEFT: *The Shahsavan, a confederation of Turkic tribes in north-west Persia, are known in the west for their attractive pileless weavings, especially small bags, which have usually lost their backs on their way to the west. The square faces of these bags are delicately brocaded in the weft wrapping (Soumak) technique which gives great clarity to their varied and interesting designs. Their flat surface makes them well suited to display on a wall and as a result they have become popular as an inexpensive alternative to abstract paintings. 46 × 46 cm/18 × 18 in.*

BELOW: *A distant view of an encampment of the nomadic Shahsavan tribe on Mount Savalan, north-west Persia. The woollen felts covering the tents are white when new and darken with age. They are replaced every five or six years.*

RIGHT: *It is not known for certain what sort of piled carpets the Shahsavan wove, but this piece, probably made before 1880, could be one of them. It has, in common with their known weavings, stylistic features which relate it to Turkey, Persia and the Caucasus, and in appearance is almost certainly of tribal origin. 427 × 142 cm/168 × 56 in.*

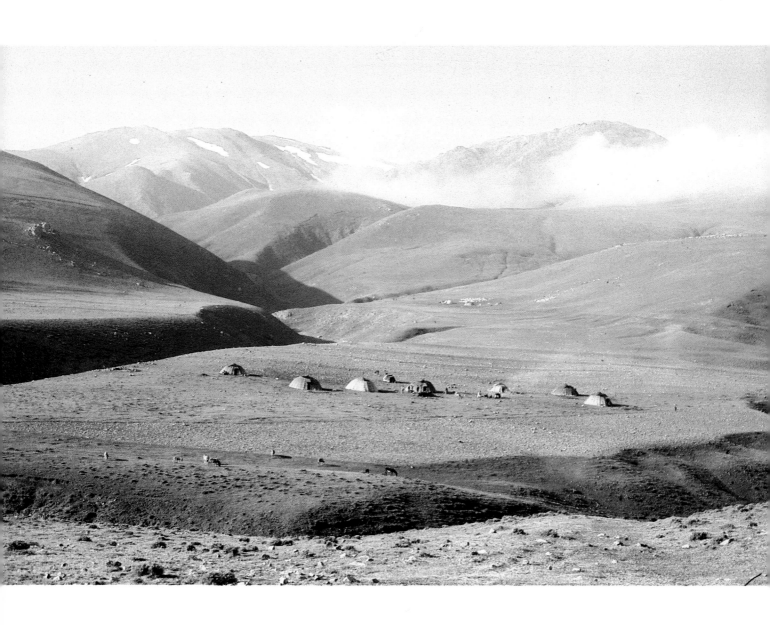

A similar educational programme in Iran during the last twenty years, intended as a peaceable means of reforming the thinking and life-style of the nomads, has had the curious result that the Qashqai, a resourceful people, now provide the universities of Iran with more than their fair share of scientists and university professors, while members of their families still retain their pastoral way of life. The Turkmen of what is now Turkmenistan have not done so well. The defeat of the czarist Russian army by the Tekke tribe brought a crushing reprisal at the battle of Gok Tepe in 1881, the culmination of several decades of action against the Turkmen, from which the Tekke never recovered as an independent nomadic group. Large numbers fled to Afghanistan and Persia and many of those that remained changed from pastoralists into cotton farmers.

Many people have the idea that nomads wander about because they are unable to do any better for themselves and think of them as scruffy, impoverished loafers camping by the roadside with a few goats and chickens. The exact opposite is the case. Nomads, in order to pursue their way of life successfully, require a fairly high level of material wealth. They must have the apparatus for living – tents, felts, ropes, bedding, cooking utensils and so on – which is costly by itself and requires horses and camels for its transportation, and they must have livestock which provide meat, milk, leather and wool. The real wealth of the pastoralists lies in the size of their flocks and their holdings of livestock. When a community reaches a certain level of poverty, the nomadic life-style is no longer possible.

As a general rule nomadic groups prosper when central government is weak. In times of strong central government, they tend to suffer, and those on the poverty line are obliged to settle. Their seasonal migration between two sets of pasture is the most efficient use of marginal land yet devised, and settlement means that livestock can only be supported for part of the year; extinction is a matter of time. When the power of central government declines some groups may be able to revert to nomadism, as has happened in Persia recently with the Shahsavan tribe.

Tribal breakdown

It might be imagined that the energetic activity of local buyers in the nineteenth century, described earlier, would have sought out and perhaps cleared out every single carpet from the remotest tribal sources. This was far from the case. Some tribal groups have hardly been influenced by the changes of the twentieth century and have continued to produce work of full tribal significance, and a few, such as the Yuncu tribe of western Turkey, who considered their weavings to have sacred or magical properties, resisted the attempts of outsiders to obtain them.[8] Such people have sometimes been forced to sell under extreme economic pressure resulting from famine, war, or political manipulation. When this happens jewellery, carpets, needlework, anything that can be, is sold and so dispersed. Suddenly there is a brief flood of goods onto the market, which dries up equally quickly as the stock is exhausted. This has happened many times in the last hundred years with different groups, the last recently in Afghanistan when a mass of Turkmen tribal goods appeared in the market place.

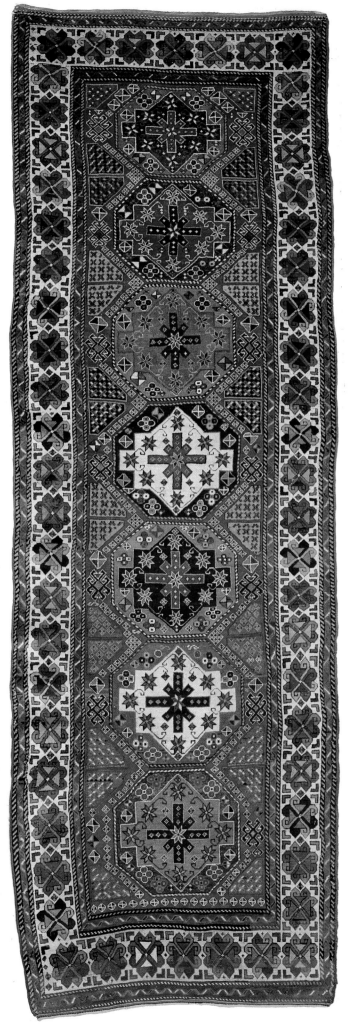

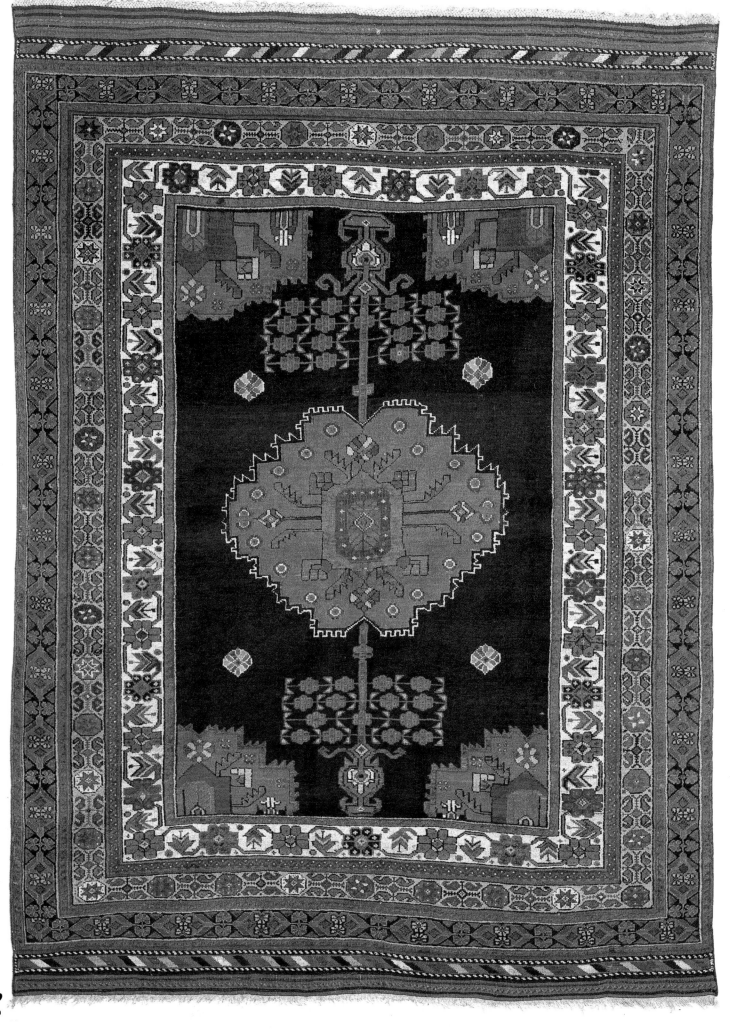

LEFT: *In the south-east Persian province of Kerman, tents of the Turkish-speaking Afshar tribe can still be found, though the major part of the tribe is now settled. In the last century some lovely Afshar weavings came onto the market, among them saddle rugs, small bags and soumak-woven covers. They are little known and deserve further study. Their rugs have a rich variety of patterns. Some are adapted from urban models, while others, such as the design of this rug, with its flower-filled vases and formal layout, have ancient roots (see p.154). The seven borders are a typical feature of Afshar work. Modern Afshar rugs are among the most original on the market. Nineteenth century.* 186 × 141 cm/73 × 55½ in.

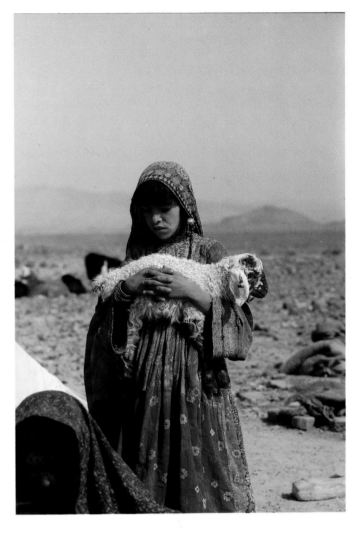

RIGHT: *Sheep are all-important in the life of the nomad. Pakistan, 1970s.*

BELOW: *Evening milking time at a Kirghiz encampment. Afghan Pamir, 1975.*

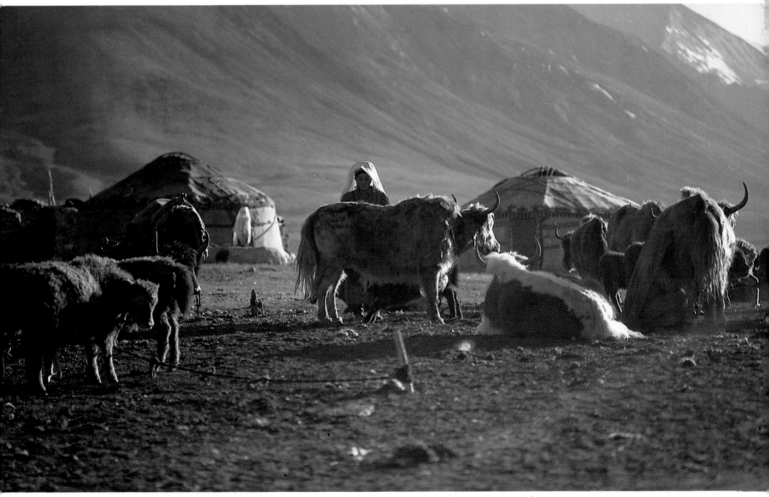

After such a catastrophe some tribes revive, but others are reduced to a level of poverty from which they never recover and are absorbed, dispersed, simply die out, or are forced to change their life-style from sheep herding to cotton farming, for example. In any event many of the tribal groups weaving in the early nineteenth century no longer exist. The recent arrival in Istanbul of a virtually unknown type of domestic weaving from the Konya area of Turkey presumably heralds the decay of such a local tradition. Uzbeg rugs of a particularly interesting type (illus. p.11) have recently come out of Afghanistan and one wonders what may be happening to their tent dwelling makers who inhabit some of the remotest parts of the world.[9]

The character of tribal weaving

The best way to appreciate tribal weaving is to understand its character. A carpet is made knot by knot, line by line, across its width, beginning from one end. It is possible to record every knot of the pattern on paper as a sequence of signs, one for each colour: two red, six blue, one black, ten white and so on. Carpet patterns written down in this way are called talims and are commonly used in workshops. The advantage of the talim is that it enables a weaver to execute a complex pattern without the higher weaving skill of being able to work in detail from an exact cartoon. A tribal weaver has to have the

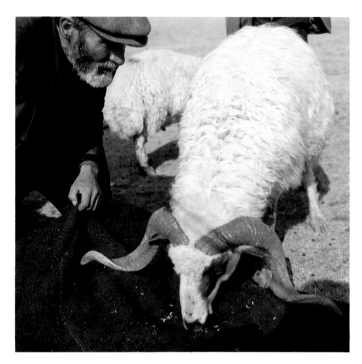

ABOVE: *Making sure the ram is well fed while on migration. Sachikara tribe, Marash province, Turkey, early 1980s.*

BELOW: *Men rest while two women weave a kilim. A loom has been set up vertically in the tent by burying the lower part of the frame in the ground, a common technique in Turkey. Karakoyunlu tribe, central Taurus, 1986.*

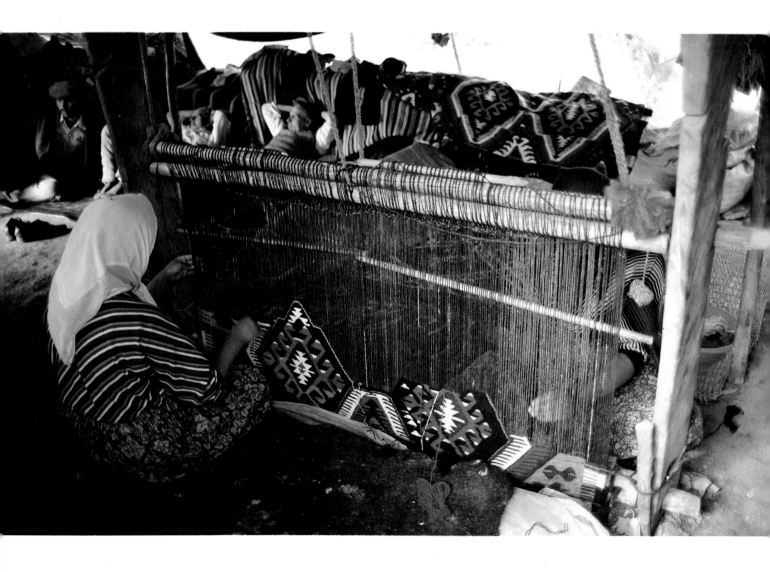

equivalent of a talim in her mind. Remembering a large complex pattern is comparable to knowing by heart a complete orchestral score. Remarkable feats of memorisation are on record but the average weaver has an average mind and patterns cannot be too extensive. The way the tribal weaver gets round the problem is to learn a fairly large number of small patterns and use them in a variety of combinations and colours. The advantage of this is best understood in terms of telephone numbers. It is easier to remember twenty or thirty seven-figure numbers than six or seven numbers of thirty figures. Tribal weavings therefore tend to have repeating patterns of fairly small size. Without the mind-engaging quality of complex designs, expressive power in tribal carpets is achieved through the use of space, proportion, colour, and the tactile allure of good wool.

It is a common belief that repeating patterns lack depth and subtlety and are only woven by people of limited originality who know no better. Long acquaintance with tribal carpets has convinced me otherwise. The ornaments in a classical repeat pattern look natural and relaxed as if they just fell into place by themselves. Yet their placement was no accident, for the difference between the effortless calm of a well-planned tribal design and one in which the subtleties of spatial organisation are not understood can be spotted immediately. It is a mistake to think that a simple design is necessarily simple-minded.

BELOW LEFT: *A boy is weaving a carpet in a Turkmen design, known also as the Bukhara pattern (see pp.64, 65), in a Pakistani workshop. He has not yet learned the pattern by heart so he is consulting his piece of paper, written in special notation like a knitting pattern, called a talim. The talim records the sequence of colours in each row of knots.*

BELOW: *A striking effect is achieved by the use of blocks of colour on a white ground in this kilim woven by one of the nomadic groups from around Karapinar in central Turkey. Nineteenth century. 395 × 163 cm/155½ × 64 in.*

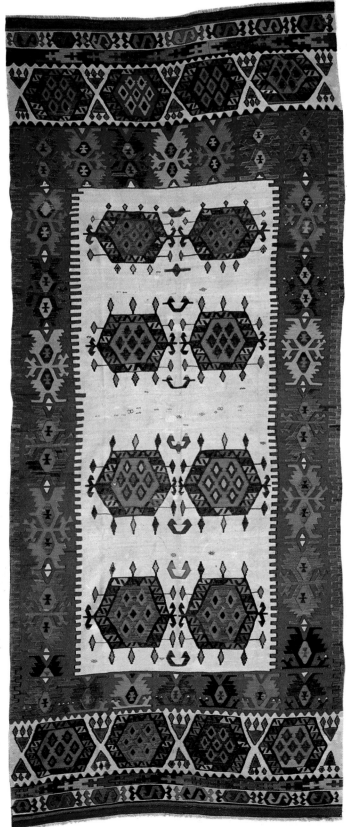

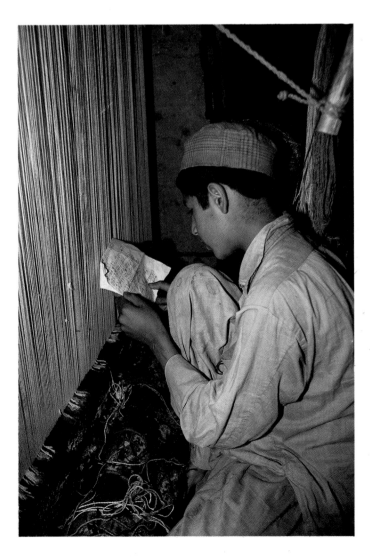

The decline of tribal weaving

The best of the tribal carpets which came to the west in the nineteenth century, in the first flush of public enthusiasm, have a vigour and clarity in their design, a quality of colour and workmanship lacking in later tribal work. The time when carpets were first sought out for

RIGHT: *The tribal weaver can make interesting patterns out of quite simple elements. Here the camel motif is repeated in different colour combinations to create a charming effect. The use of a single main motif means the pattern can be memorised quite easily. The little animals in between are improvised as weaving proceeds. Azerbayjan, around 1900. 300 × 200 cm/ 118 × 78½ in.*

BELOW: *The art of tapestry woven kilims was a speciality of the Turkish nomads who developed among themselves a corpus of tribal designs analogous to that of the Turkmen in their piled weavings. In common with the Turkmen, the Turkish nomads were subjected to an inexorable pressure to settle and the majority of their known weavings date from a period of cultural and artistic decline brought about by impoverishment and a changed way of life. Occasionally an old kilim can be found which bears witness to the artistic standards of times past, as in this example, woven by a nomadic group in the Karapinar region. Long kilims, draped horizontally, are still used to cover the pile of bedding at the back of the tent (see p.88); this one has been woven in two halves. Nineteenth century. 404 × 146 cm/159 × 57½ in.*

export coincides with the beginning of a gradual downhill slide in tribal fortunes, and artistic achievement. In terms of carpet weaving we are observers of the very end of an ancient art form. The interest taken by the west in tribal weavings during the nineteenth century played a part in the lamentable decline which followed. Fortunately enough examples survive from the period prior to significant contact with Europe for us to have an idea of the vigour and quality of tribal weaving at its best (illus. p.5), and were it not for those early examples we might have an altogether different view of tribal carpet art. So consistent is the downward drift in standards that it can be used as a method of sequential dating. It did not, of course, happen overnight in every household. The rate varied considerably in different geographical areas; in some districts the decline occurred within as little as two decades while in some remote areas traditional standards have been maintained into the middle of the twentieth century.[10]

Asking why these changes occurred raises questions beyond the scope of this enquiry. Instead we will look at the circumstances of the decline to see what actually happened. Of course the problem of rapid decline is by no means peculiar to carpets. Similar changes have taken place and are still occurring in any number of traditional art forms throughout the world.

There were many influences in the second half of the nineteenth century bringing about change in the world

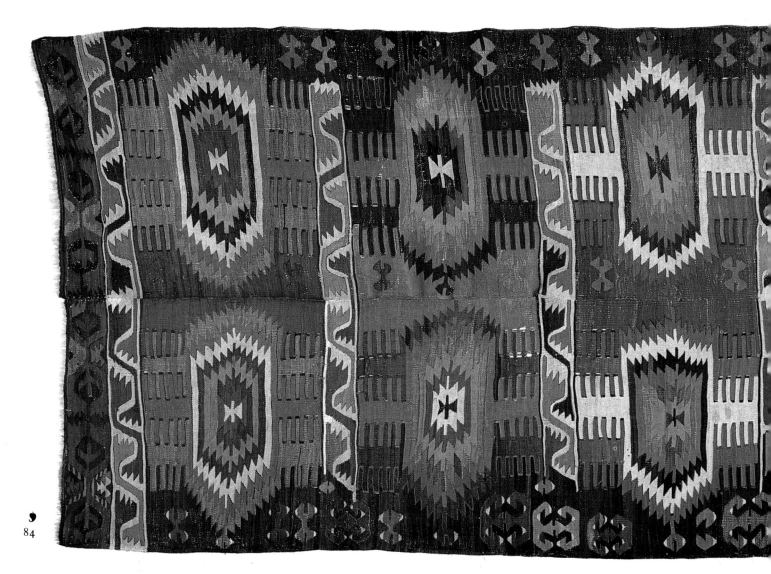

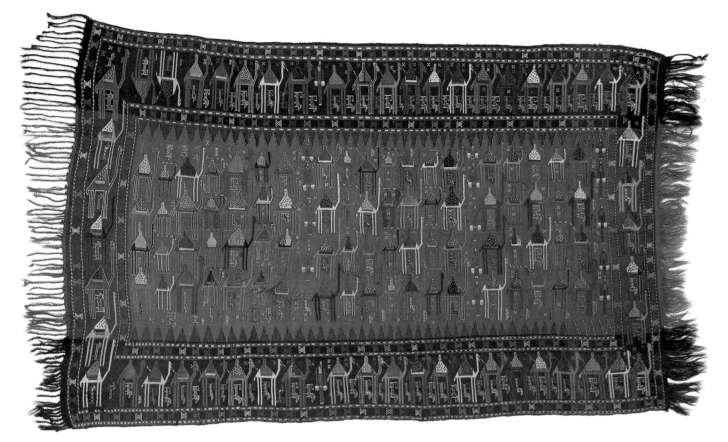

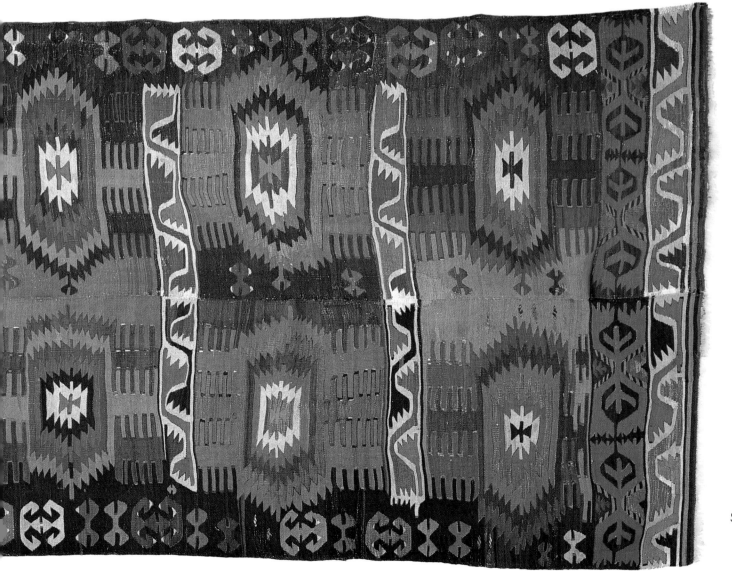

RIGHT: *Though many of the nomadic (Yuruk) tribes of southern and eastern Turkey speak Kurdish, an Indo-European language, their carpets are often patterned with Turkic designs. The large indented ornaments in the field of this Kurdish rug resemble the Turkmen 'gul' patterns, here interpreted with a vigour of expression typical of Turkish carpets in general. Nineteenth century. 264 × 132 cm/ 104 × 52 in.*

BELOW: *A Kurdish woman at an overnight encampment near Maku in the extreme north-west of Persia. Her tent has been taken down and family belongings are stacked ready for loading. Camels are still used by this tribe, although tractors are slowly replacing them. On migration, the large goat-hair tents are kept packed and light canvas ones used instead; storage bags are turned inside out to preserve the patterned surface. An interesting feature of the tribe's dress is the beadwork collar.*

of carpets, most of them arising from the increasing economic and cultural domination of Europe, America and Russia. Technology, industrialisation and new farming methods had a general erosive effect on the rural communities. Tribal and village life in Asia has been no exception to the rule that, wherever western cultural influences are felt, the traditional and indigenous culture tends to fade away. The influence of western culture was gradual, introducing new methods of transport, improved communications and different habits of living. Changes also occurred in people's expectations. Drift of the population from the land to the cities began but did not become a torrent until the middle of the twentieth century. There was also a general move against certain sections of the population which accelerated the decline. Nomadism in particular, as we have seen, was considered undesirable and to be discouraged by every means possible.

The introduction of synthetic dyes in the 1860s was a particular misfortune for the carpet makers.[11] While the dyers of today can achieve excellent colours, fast to light and washing, with a variety of fabrics, the results with the early synthetic dyes were far from happy. Rapid fading, running colours and a harsh discordant tone were the more obvious problems. In retrospect it is difficult to understand the sequence of causes and effects which led to what appears to have been a loss of colour sense among so many rural weavers in the late nineteenth century. Many people have assumed that the corruption of traditional taste was caused by the dyes themselves, but this seems to be an over-simplified explanation. In the beginning only small quantities of synthetic dye were used, as highlights,

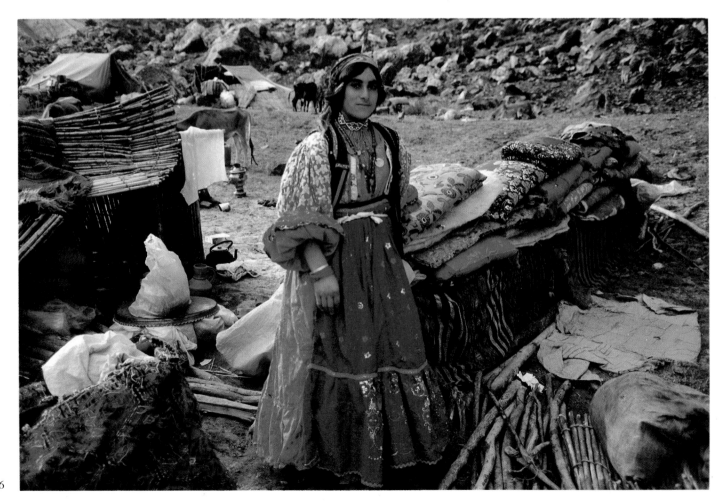

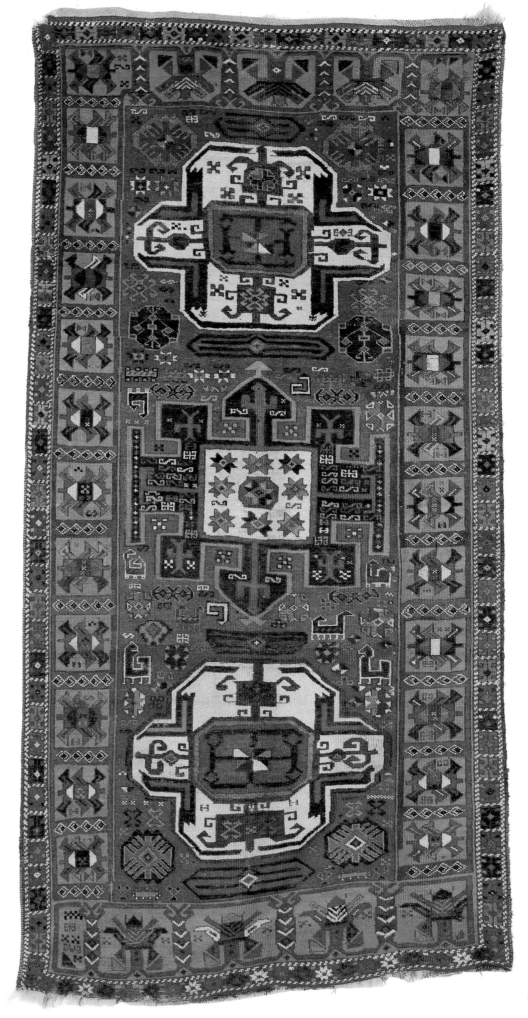

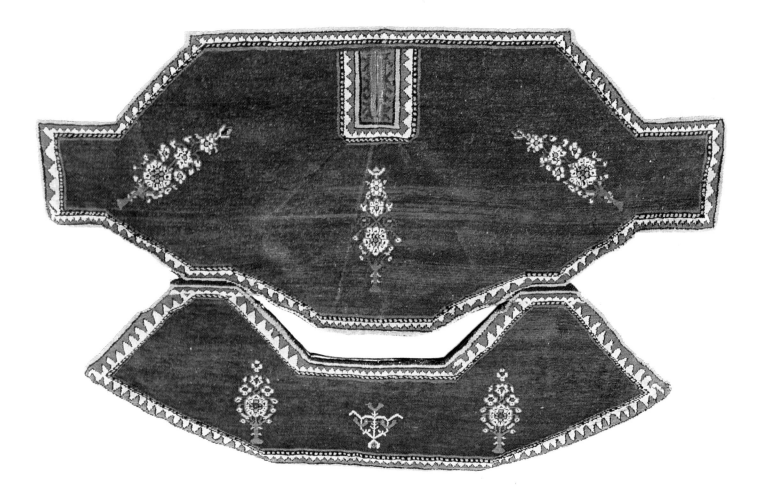

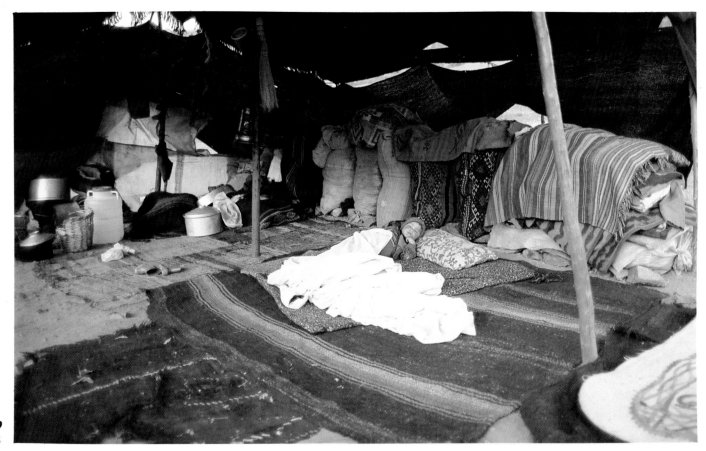

adding touches of colour to little details in the design. One has the impression that the new colours were used not because they were cheap but because they were a novelty. Cost may not have favoured the adoption of the new colours in the beginning, but the introduction of dyes that were easier to use probably facilitated the acceptance of new colours once the new dyes had acquired a price advantage over traditional ones. I should point out here that because nomads have been observed dyeing their own wool it cannot be assumed that they have always done so. This is in fact unlikely. Indigo dyeing, a comparatively high technology, was usually practised and maintained as a craft in towns and villages, trade secrets being passed from one generation to the next within families. The high standards of dye technology in former times, and incidentally the existence of local colour styles, were probably the result of nomads and villagers taking their prepared wool to these professional dyers.

To say that standards declined raises the difficult question of the validity of making aesthetic judgements from our twentieth-century viewpoint on the weavers of a hundred years ago. It is almost a function of getting older to complain of falling standards in the younger generation, so many claims can be discounted on the grounds that the elderly simply dislike change and regard

LEFT: *In the last century animal transport was so important that life was not possible without it. In Persia saddle rugs were popular with all levels of society. Nomads made their own while urban workshops catered for a more expensive taste. This unusual example is probably Bakhtiyari work. Around 1900.*

BELOW LEFT: *A child having his afternoon sleep. The typical black goat hair tent has a row of decorated storage bags arranged along the back wall. They rest on a low platform of stones to keep them off the ground and the bedding is piled on top. Each tribe uses different designs for the decoration of their storage bags (see also p.56). Honamli tribe, Beyshehir region, Turkey, 1986.*

BELOW: *Nomads have been settling in Turkey for centuries and are still doing so. This house is not only shaped like a tent, but also furnished in the same way, with its row of decorated storage bags piled high with bedding. The family settled two generations before the photograph was taken. Some of the weavings are part of the dowry of this woman's daughter. Even in villages occupied by former nomads, known to have settled more than a hundred years ago, the tent-like arrangement of their stone houses can still be seen. Gaziantep province, Turkey, 1981.*

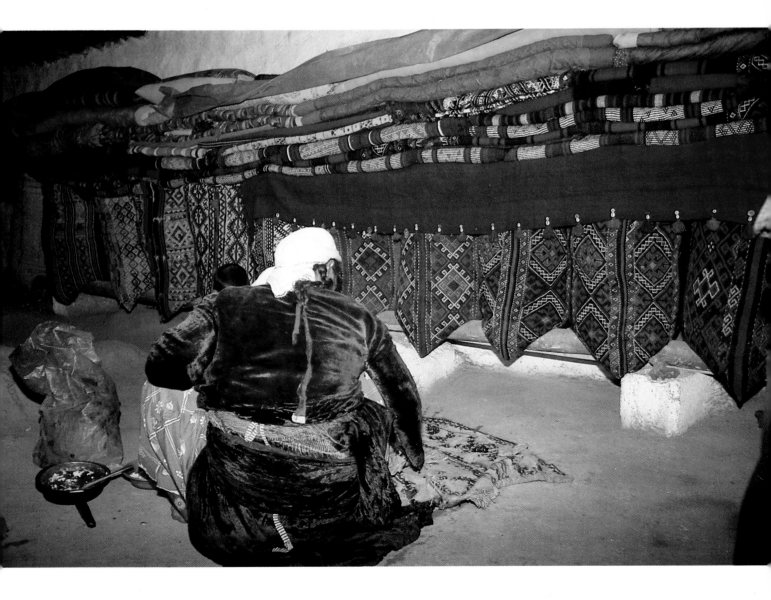

BELOW: *Strong colours and vigorous designs contribute to the appeal of the weavings of the Ersari tribe, a group of settled and semi-nomadic Turkmen in Russian Turkestan and Afghanistan. This is the face of a large bag. Nineteenth century. 97 × 133 cm/38 × 52½ in.*

BOTTOM: *A good example of a tribal weaving which could easily be overlooked by someone unfamiliar with carpets is this incomplete strip, originally a shallow Turkmen bag. When this piece surfaced it was recognised by a collector as a hitherto unknown design, the work of the Salor tribe, which barely survived a military defeat in the 1850s. Nineteenth century. 35 × 97 cm/14 × 38 in.*

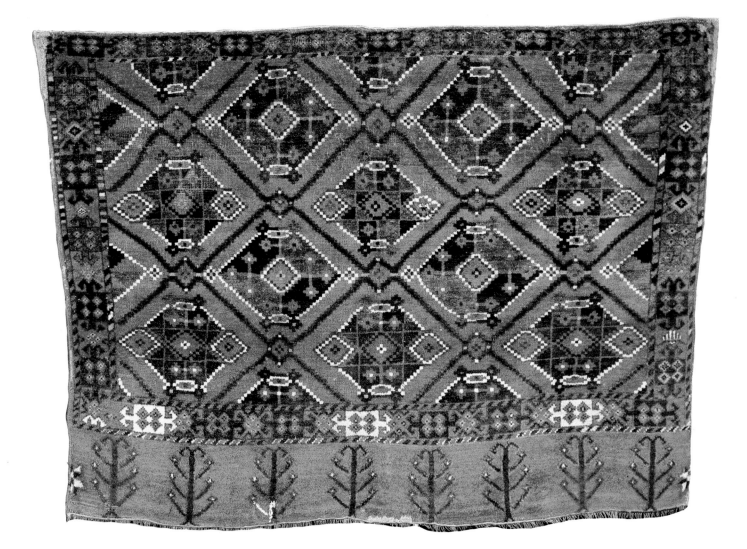

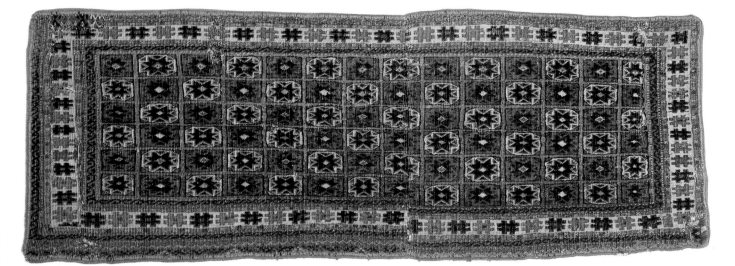

BELOW: *In the past the Turkmen used a piled carpet for the door of the tent (see p.77) but the custom lapsed around a hundred years ago. The door rugs of all the main tribes have a similar panelled layout which seems to represent something specific. Some believe it to be a garden, others the panels of a wooden door, but so far no satisfactory explanation has been found. Ersari tribe, Amu Darya valley, nineteenth century.* 157 × 137 cm/62 × 54 in.

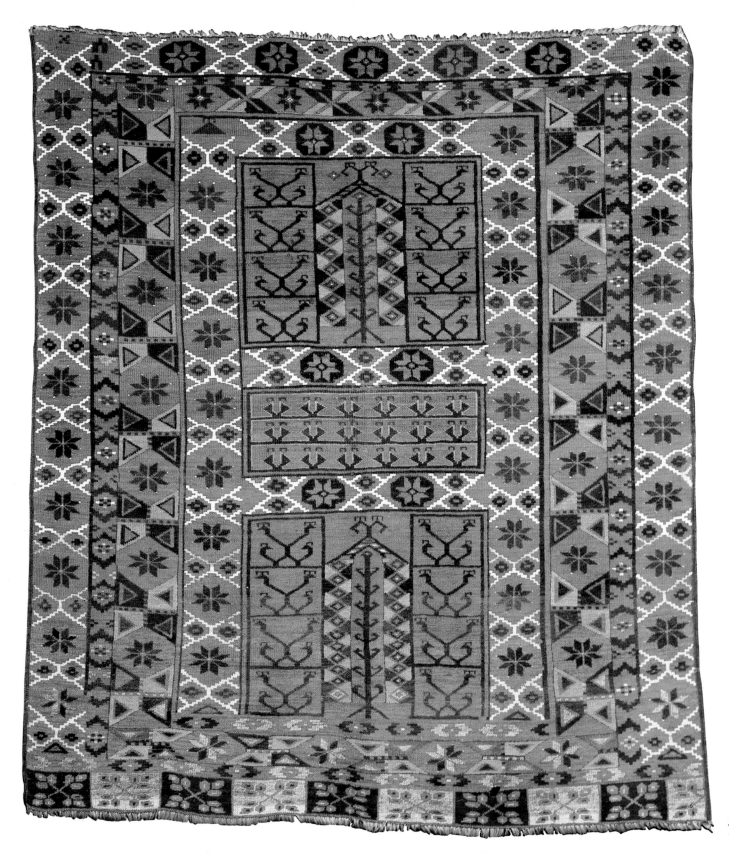

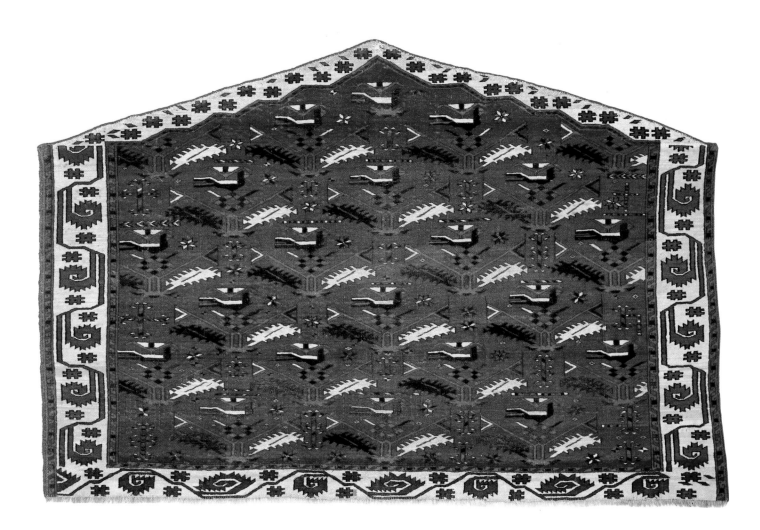

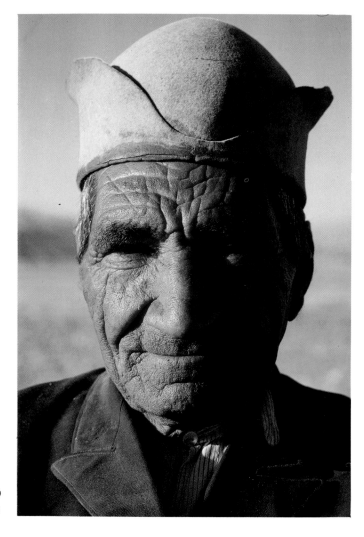

ABOVE: *The use of trappings by the Turkmen to decorate the bridal camel has already been mentioned (p.62). This example, with its design of birds within a lattice, is the work of the Tekke tribe. This rare type does not appear to have been made since the 1880s, and there are only two examples in western museums, both acquired in the 1980s. 99 × 146 cm/ 39 × 57½ in.*

RIGHT: *The Qashqai are skilled copyists. The pattern of this carpet has been copied from a Persian workshop carpet of the early nineteenth century. Such copies are themselves copied, the design becoming progressively more angular and distorted each time. This carpet is so close to the original that were it not for the unmistakable Qashqai colour style, some hesitancy in the curves, and an interruption in the rhythm of the main border design at one end, it could easily be taken for a workshop product. The presence of silk in the foundation and the excellent workmanship indicate that the weavers were aiming to produce a carpet of the highest quality. Nineteenth century. 318 × 171 cm/125 × 67½ in.*

LEFT: *Felt hats have been traditional dress among the nomadic tribes of south Persia for centuries. This type with its two flaps is worn by members of the Qashqai tribe. Its specific form was invented in the 1940s.*

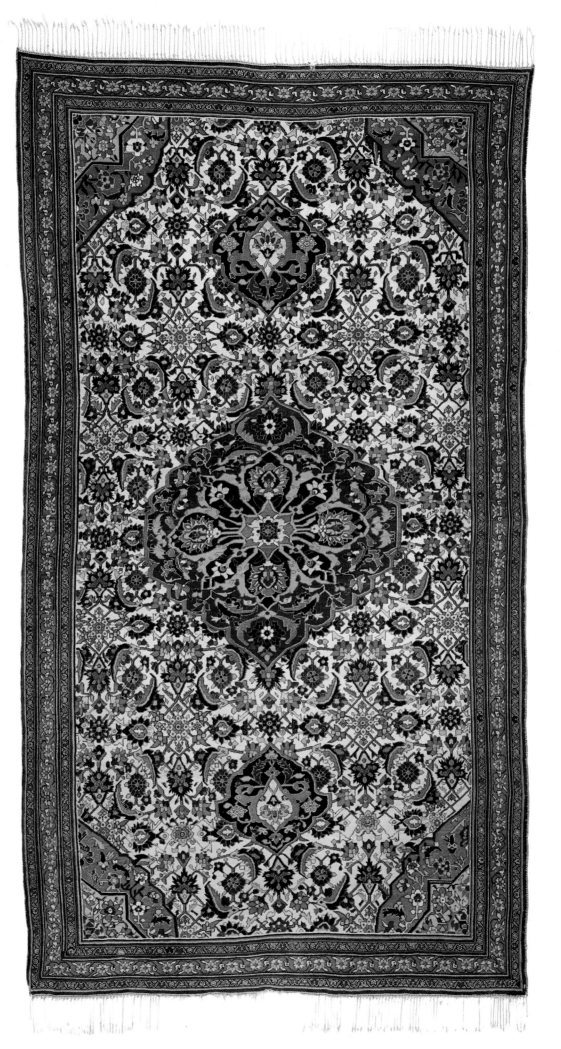

RIGHT: *No one is certain of the function of this little weaving. Such pieces are believed to have been used to decorate the entrance to the covered litter in which the Turkmen bride travelled to her wedding. It is Tekke work and dates from the mid nineteenth century.* 45 × 78 cm/17½ × 30½ in.

BELOW RIGHT: *Two women getting the pattern sorted out. Love of bright colours and brilliant effect is evident in their clothing and in their choice of yarns for their weaving. The pink is almost luminous. Bechkan village, Gaziantep province, Turkey, early 1980s.*

BELOW: *The joyous profusion of camels and other animals has been achieved by the use of a small number of individual motifs which have been skilfully arranged in a variety of colour combinations by a weaver working entirely from memory. Probably Shahsavan tribe, eastern Turkey or Azerbayjan, nineteenth century.* 210 × 200 cm/82½ × 78½ in.

it as decline. Again preference for colour is a matter of personal taste, even more so preference for colour combinations. But the changes that occurred in the wool dyes, and the resulting appearance of the carpets are more fundamental than a passing phase of taste. Indeed many later tribal and village weavings show an astonishing apparent loss of the sense of colour and form, and it would be easy to convince the sceptic that the dull, muddy, faded and running colours of some synthetically dyed rural weavings around the turn of the century are nothing short of a calamity.

The question of the harsh and clashing colours we see in later rural weaving is more difficult to judge. In rural communities today, for instance, it is common to find textiles worked in colours of the brightest, most luminous hues available, including yarns with glaring fluorescent dyes. Here one has to remember that the weavers have always preferred the clearest and brightest hues, so this is nothing new. These combinations may be

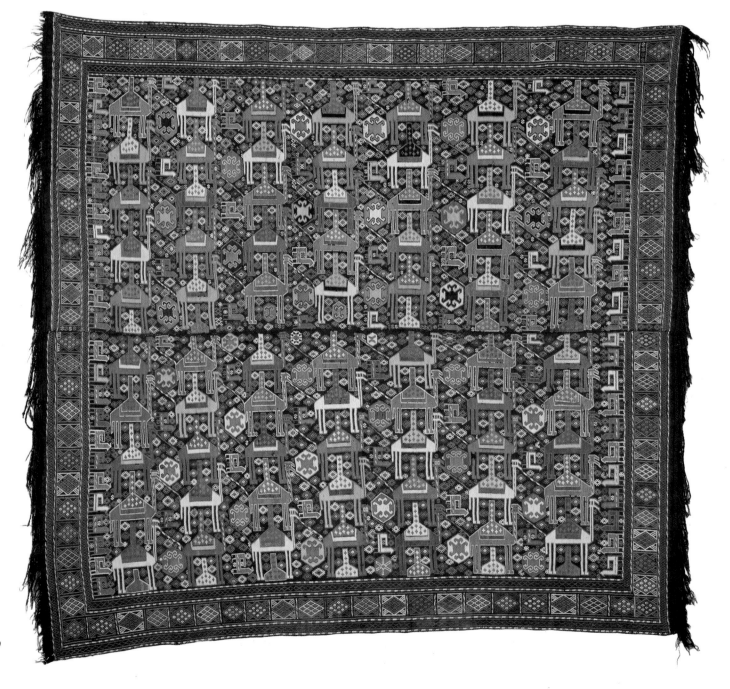

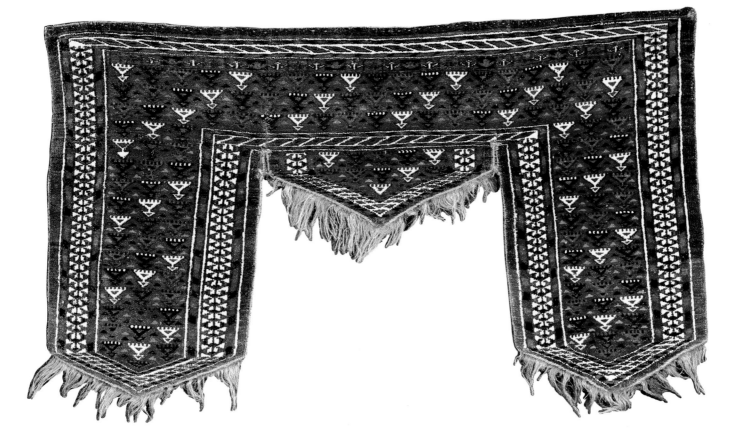

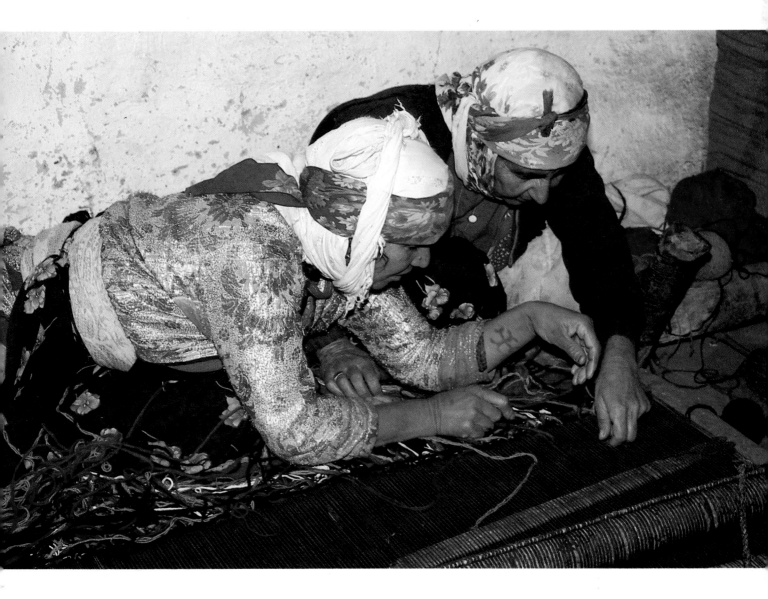

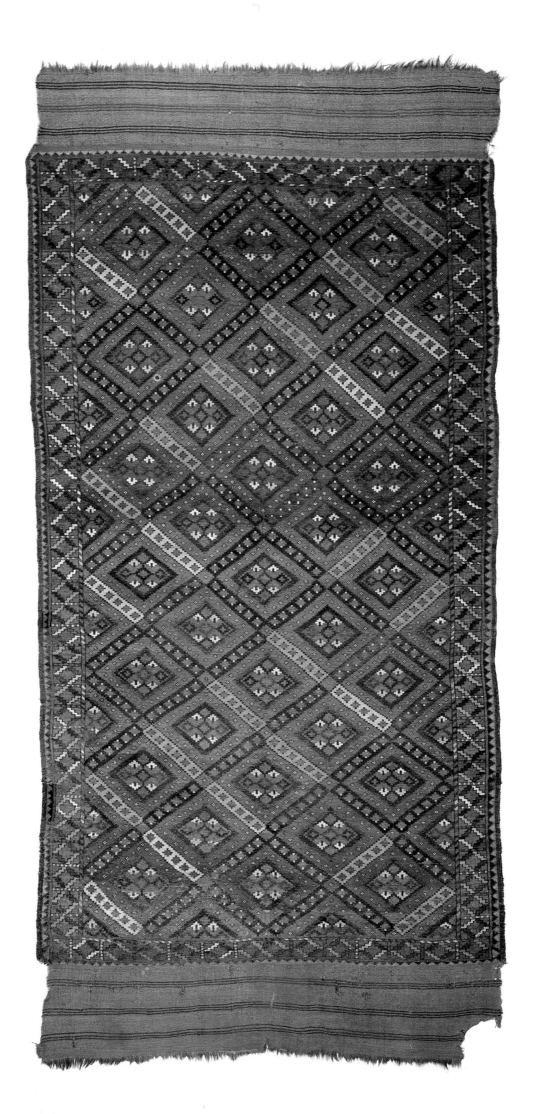

harsh and clashing to our eyes but it seems to bear out the idea that the raw preference of the weavers was for brilliance of effect. As a corollary it should be mentioned that it is practically universal that children and those with an uneducated or unprejudiced taste prefer clear bright colours to dull muddy ones.

The changes we are discussing are intimately tied up with what the weaver thought and felt about the object she was making. The main pressure on the tribal weaver was not sale and export but making things for the home and special occasions, with the chance of some surplus if time permitted. Everything had to be functional as well as decorative. Some pieces, such as those made for a wedding, were highly important for the weaver and had a significance rooted in the traditions and expectations of the whole community. As long as community life retained its old rhythms the weaver was eager to give everything to the task in hand, which was to make something precious and beautiful for the adornment of the home and the honouring of guests. Therefore the declining standards we are discussing reflect a funda-mental change in the whole fabric of community life.

Major changes in a tribal weaving tradition over a short period of time generally mean that the women are no longer weaving for themselves but for the market. They have become part of a cottage industry. This is not to say there is anything wrong in selling one's handicraft, rather the period of changeover is one of difficulty and confusion. For example, the carpets produced by the generation immediately following the defeat and forcible settlement of the Tekke tribe in Turkestan are finely worked but show increasing decorative elaboration and confusion of the traditional patterns. It is as if some restraining hand had been removed leaving the weavers free to add more and more to the pattern in an attempt to make it attractive. It was no longer their peers who were scrutinising their work but some imagined public. The tribal society no longer nurtured and gave meaning to their weaving, it was the necessity to earn money. At first they wove their usual bags and pouches but they changed rapidly, departing further and further from the usual sizes, shapes and traditional patterns. The need to weave for money was a direct consequence of the dissolution of tribal society, which in turn was mirrored in the change in their weavings.

From a collector's viewpoint the dominance of commercial pressures leads to the production of articles which as tribal artefacts are meaningless and insignificant. To be significant today a tribal rug must have been charged with significance by its maker and her society at the time it was made.

LEFT: *The shape and size of this Turkmen carpet is close to the traditional long, narrow shapes made in the cottage industries of Persia. Its dramatic character and vibrant colours are typical of Ersari work so it may well have been made by a group long settled on the banks of the Oxus who had abandoned their tents and were perhaps on the way to becoming a cottage industry. Russian Turkestan, nineteenth century.* 312 × 178 cm/ 123 × 70 in.

RIGHT: *The people of the nomadic Bakhtiyari tribe, who undertake the most arduous seasonal migration of any tribe, are well known for their carpets but only recently has their rich tradition of pileless weaving become known in the west.* 508 × 137 cm/200 × 54 in.

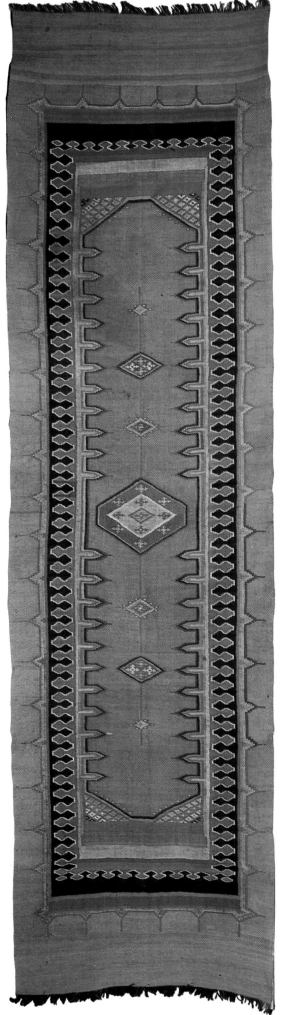

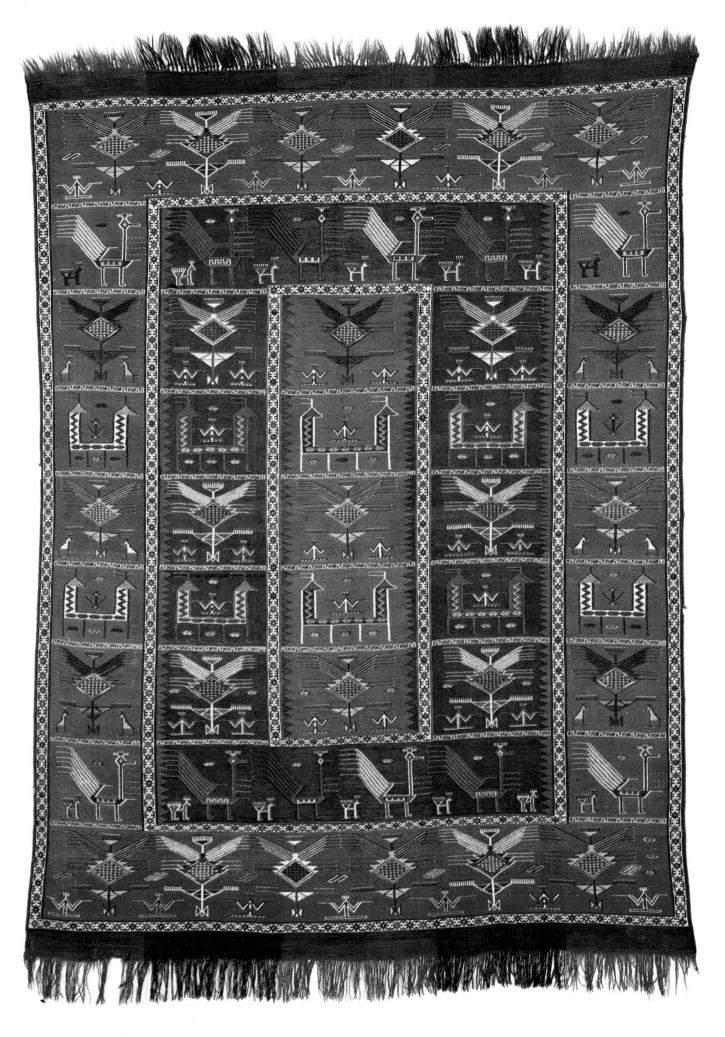

LEFT: *In many books these striking pileless weavings are called simply 'Caucasian'. It is now known that they were made by the Shahsavan (see p.78) who used to migrate across the border between Persian and Russian Azerbayjan before it was closed in 1884 (around the time that synthetic dyes were introduced). They are also called 'Verneh', a term of uncertain meaning. Nineteenth century. 200 × 150 cm/78½ × 59 in.*

RIGHT: *The inscription at the top conveys a message of blessing and good fortune for someone getting married and was probably made as a wedding present. Fars district of south Persia, possibly Afshari work. Nineteenth century. Approx. 75 × 35 cm/29½ × 14 in.*

BELOW: *This typical tribal weaving was originally the decorated face of a storage bag, one of a number hung on the wall of a Turkmen tent and used to contain personal effects such as clothing. The pattern is ancient and has a powerful simplicity. Part of its visual effect is the result of a peculiar Asiatic design concept in which the border acts as a window onto a portion of an endlessly repeating design. The disappearance of the design beneath the border, which at first sight looks strange to the western eye, is the means whereby this idea is conveyed. The sober calm and highly developed sense of colour evident in this piece relate to the artistic traditions of an earlier period which slowly vanished in the course of the last century. Salor tribe. Nineteenth century. 79 × 127 cm/ 31 × 50 in.*

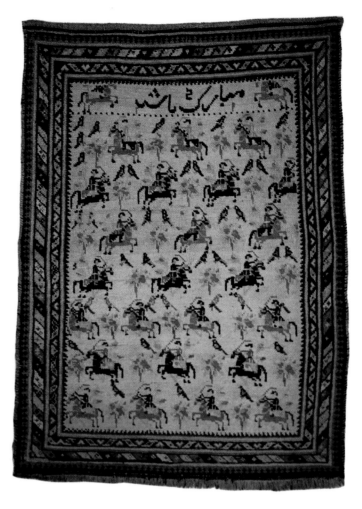

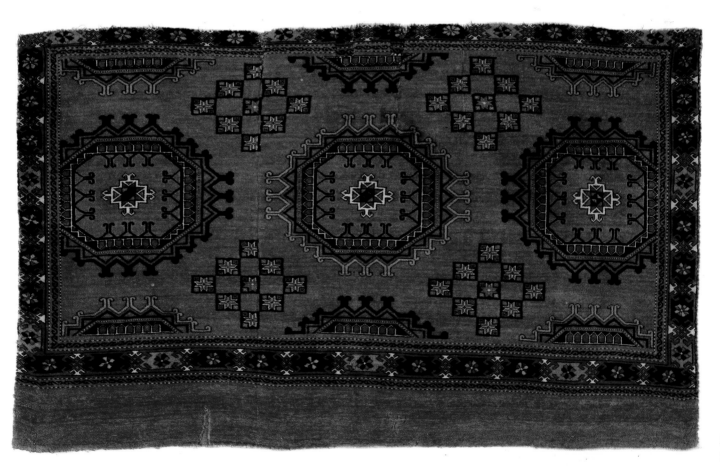

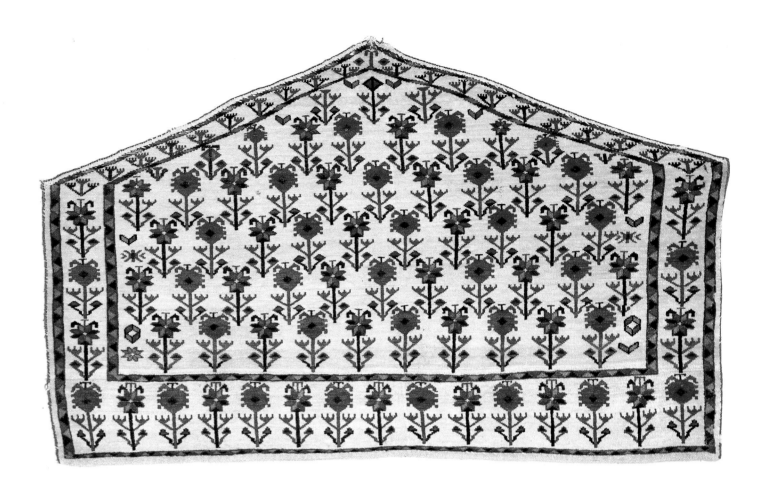

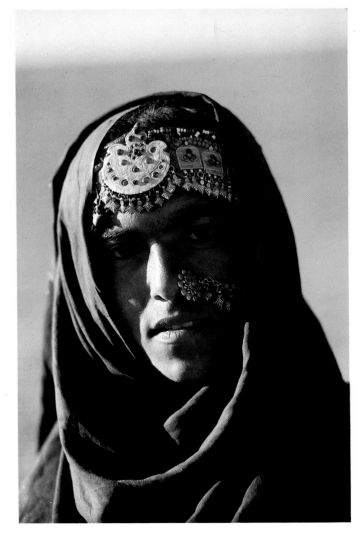

ABOVE: *Among the Turkmen it is the custom for the bride to ride to her wedding in a covered litter on a camel decorated with trappings she has made specially for the occasion. Naturally she devotes great care to making things for such an important event and the best Turkmen work is to be found in items made for the wedding tent and procession. Five-sided trappings are used in pairs to decorate the flanks of the camel. White is the colour for weddings among the Turkmen and the white ground blotched with red is associated in many cultures with the idea of fecundity in marriage. Nineteenth century. 84 × 135 cm/ 33 × 53 in.*

LEFT: *A woman of the Suleyman Khail clan, a Persian-speaking nomadic group from north Afghanistan. 1981.*

RIGHT: *Such pieces, often loosely called Baluch, are made by women of the nomadic Timuri tribe in the Herat region of western Afghanistan and in Persian Khorasan. The dark colours are a speciality of the tribe and it should be pointed out that it is more costly and difficult to produce dark blue than light blue. The colouring has therefore been chosen intentionally. As a work of art this example has a wonderful grandeur and dignity and to be appreciated must be seen in daylight. Twentieth century. 279 × 165 cm/110 × 65 in.*

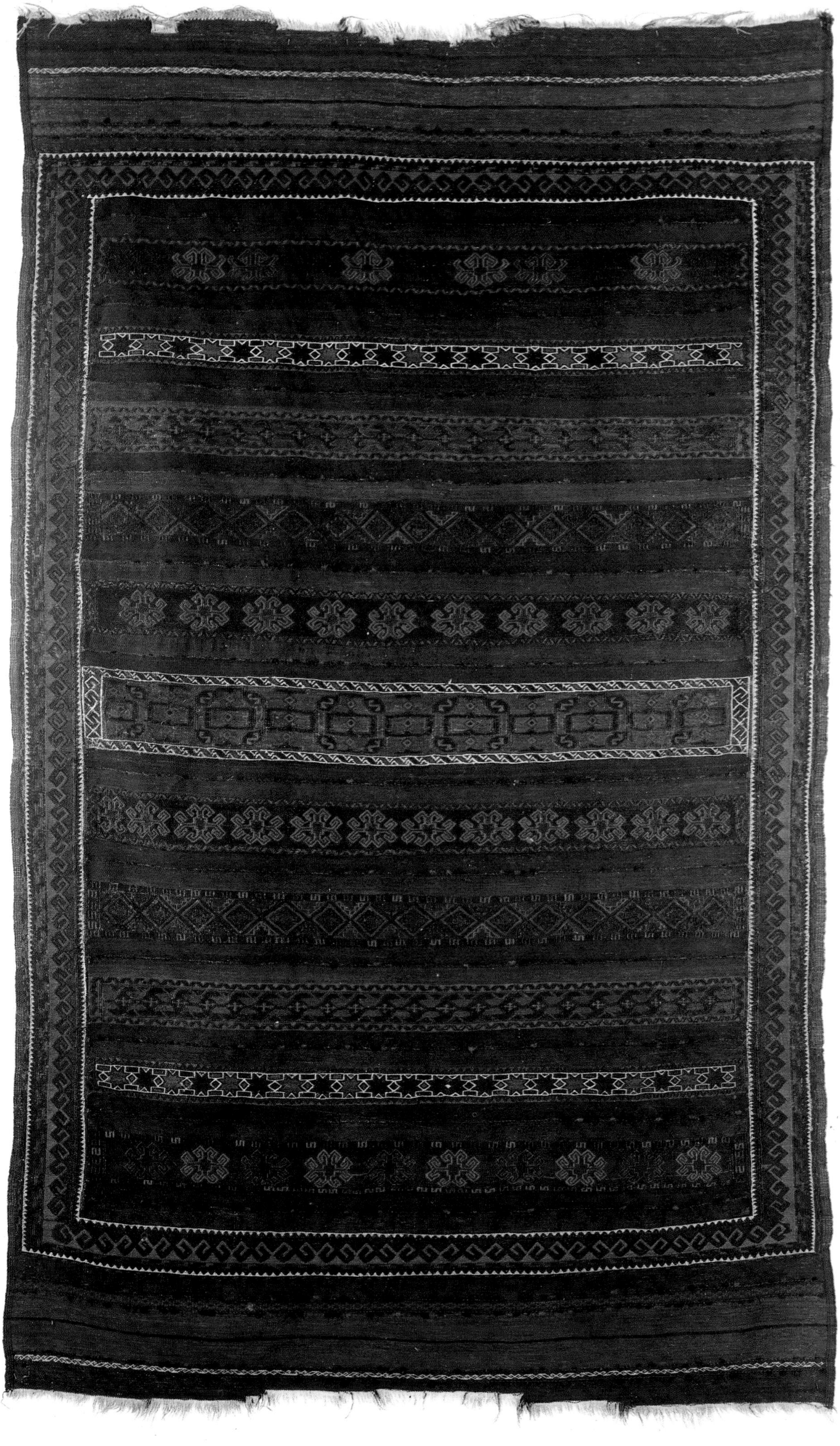

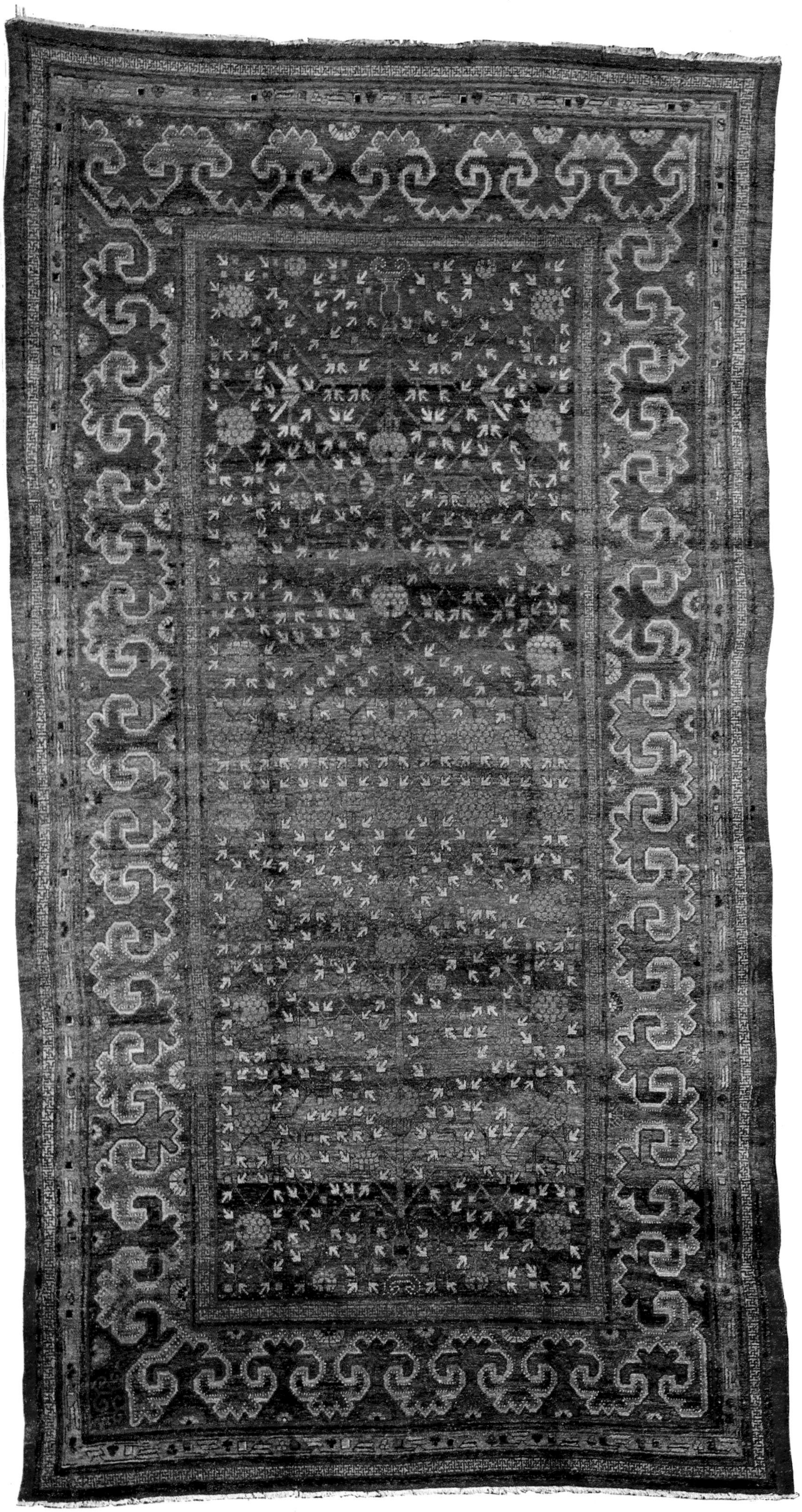

Chapter four

The cottage industry

Organisation

In the cottage industry the weavings are by definition for sale. The advantages of having a loom at home are obvious: weaving can be fitted in at any convenient moment, and an eye can still be kept on the children. The women are in effect taking on part-time self-employment to increase the family income. Raw materials can be obtained in a variety of ways. The family may have its own sheep; alternatively village women may buy woollen yarn direct from neighbouring producers, often local tribal people, or from the bazaar. Wool bought in the bazaar is likely to be of inferior quality and is often 'skin wool', that scraped from hides before tanning. The wool and the cost of having it dyed may represent a capital outlay which a poor villager can barely afford, especially as it may take three months or more to complete the carpet, sell it to a merchant and get the money. Instead of buying the materials herself the cottage weaver may obtain ready dyed yarn from a contractor who pays the weaver on delivery of the completed carpet. This system appears to have been introduced into Persia in the second half of the nineteenth century but has a longer history in Turkey. The arrangement allows the contractor to exercise a direct influence on the type and quality of work by specifying the size, colour, fineness and pattern. The main drawback is that no agent or buyer can possibly supervise the work of hundreds of separate looms so there is no effective quality control. In this respect the cottage industry differs markedly from workshop production where quality control is a critical factor in successful marketing.

The cottage industry system is fairly responsive to the demands of the market place. When the market is flourishing more looms are set up and more hours devoted to weaving. The cottage weaver is always on the look-out for new ideas. Successful patterns are copied and learned and new ones tried out. Sometimes sample carpets were made to show a selection of field and border patterns, or a new design such as bunches of flowers (illus. p.104), which, at the time it was made, must have been adapted from a European textile pattern and considered suitable for the European market. With the help of such a sample an order could be placed, the client specifying the size and which field and border patterns he wanted.

Cottage weaving is long established. In the seventeenth and eighteenth centuries many rugs were exported to Europe from western Turkey from this source. Large numbers of these survive in churches in the Transylvanian district of Rumania (illus. p.105). They are small and woven in a typical cottage industry style much as the rugs of the Milas district were in the nineteenth century and are still today (illus. p.126). One feature of this style is that many of the designs are rustic

It was in the sand-buried ruins of east Turkestan (Sinkiang) that Sir Aurel Stein found scraps of piled carpet dating from the sixth to the ninth centuries. Carpet making continues in the region today. This example from the oasis of Khotan has a design of a pomegranate growing out of a vase at each end of the field, an ancient motif conveying the idea of life and plenty. The older carpets, of which this is a good example, have soft lustrous wool and harmonious colours derived from natural dyes. Synthetic dyes were adopted rather early in this region, during the 1860s and 1870s. Mid nineteenth century. 374 × 200 cm/147 × 78½ in.

BELOW: *A carpet pattern can be transmitted and reproduced in three ways: first, by committing it to memory while working with someone who knows it (typical for tribal weaving); second, by copying another carpet knot for knot (common in the cottage industry); and third, by using a cartoon (the norm in workshops). A weaver in the cottage industry wishing to use a new design might make a small pattern-carpet (vagireh), such as this example, including in it at least one repeat of each motif. She would then copy the designs from her sample-rug. Bijar, north-west Persia, nineteenth century.* 152 × 152 cm/ 60 × 60 in.

RIGHT: *During the seventeenth century a cottage industry in western Turkey successfully supplied the export market with small, attractively coloured rugs with patterns based on the Ottoman court style. They appear in American and European painting and survive in fairly large numbers in Italy, Hungary and Rumania. There was a custom at this time, in the Transylvanian district of Rumania, for merchants to give gifts of Turkish carpets to the local church, where many are still to be seen. Turkey, seventeenth century (often referred to as 'Transylvanian').* 177 × 117 cm/69½ × 46 in.

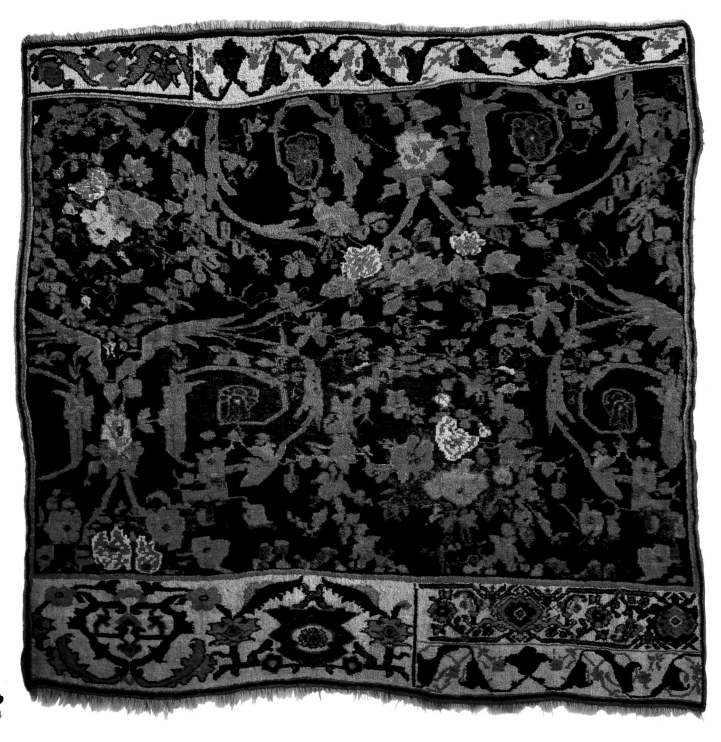

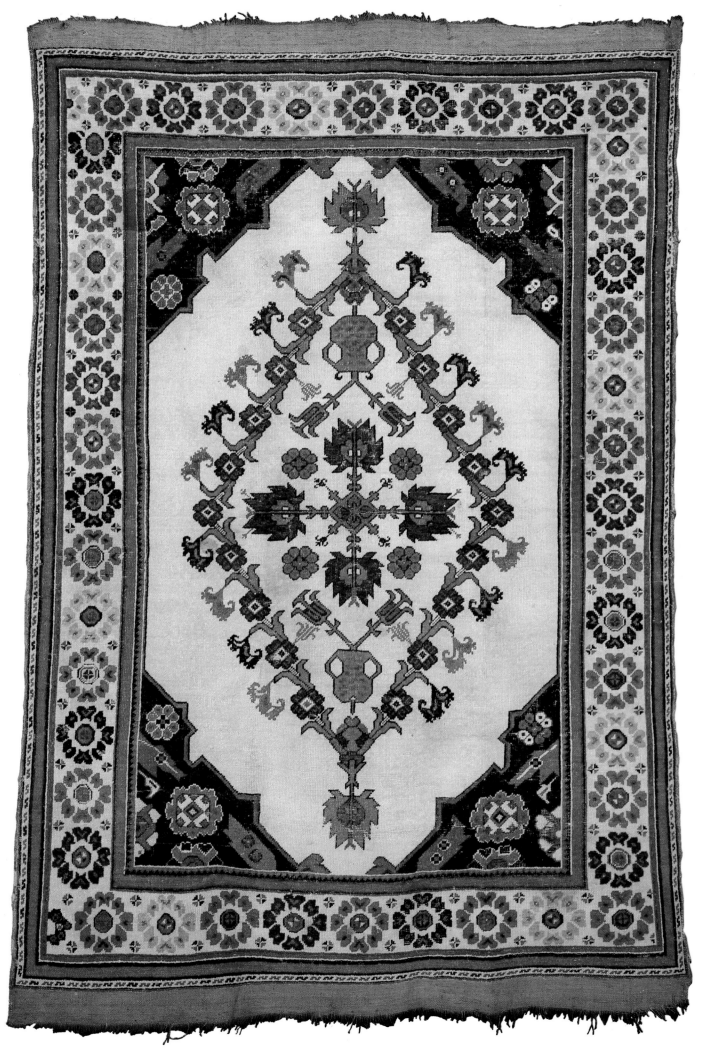

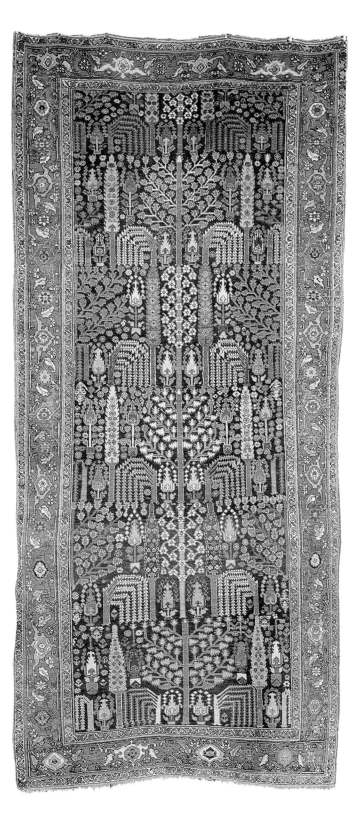

ABOVE: *The design of this carpet from Bijar, north-west Persia, is traceable to a seventeenth-century workshop original. A characteristic feature of the cottage industry is an angular stylisation of patterns derived from curvilinear models. Nineteenth century.* 358 × 158 cm/141 × 62 in.

RIGHT: *The cottage industry has a long history in the Caucasus. In the seventeenth century Caucasian weavers were making rustic versions of Persian workshop carpets. This dragon carpet, with its primary colours and angular rendering of curves, is a typical example. The term 'dragon' refers to the stylised S-shaped dragons in the design which can be identified by reference to other carpets.* 469 × 223 cm/184½ × 88 in.

versions of earlier more sophisticated patterns (illus. p.129), particularly those in vogue in the Ottoman court.

An interesting parallel occurred around the same time in the Caucasus, then under Persian rule, where circumstances never seem to have been suitable for the establishment of court-quality workshops such as existed elsewhere in Persia. Instead there was a flourishing cottage industry making adaptations of Persian designs on looms not more than two and a half metres wide (just over 8 feet), about the maximum for cottage weavers but often exceeded in the technically more advanced workshops supplying the courts. Although the patterns are clearly based on complex and sophisticated originals, in the hands of the Caucasian cottage weavers the carpets are coarsely though sturdily woven, all the graceful curves have been changed into a succession of straight lines and angles, and the colours have an unsophisticated primary character. They include the well-known dragon carpets (illus. p.107 opposite), which are believed to be based on Persian originals, although no Persian carpets in this design are known. They were evidently made in large numbers and successfully marketed abroad. Many survive in Turkish mosques and they even reached Europe, as paintings of the period reveal.

The strongly individual, local character of these Turkish and Caucasian weavings is typical of the cottage industries in general which tend to become concentrated in definite areas with a definite style in each. The local identity of a style is maintained not by policy but as the natural result of children learning from their parents and grandparents. Regional accents and dialects are maintained the same way; the style of speech acquired in childhood persists throughout life; likewise children learning to weave do so in the style of those around them. Communal weaving styles are observed to be remarkably constant over several generations and serve as the main guide in determining the source of a carpet. As already mentioned the dyeing of the wool is often handed over to specialised dyers. If everyone takes their wool to the same few dyers, this will give some uniformity to the colours used in the area and tend to reinforce the consistency of the local style.

Before contract work became common, cottage weavers would have a small repertoire of patterns peculiar to the village or locality, and every community would have its own characteristic weaving technique, colour style and patterns. The growth of the contract system has meant that what the weaver produces today is more often determined by the policy of central buyers than by local tradition. This is particularly so in Turkey where in theory some degree of official control is exercised over all commercial looms. If a cottage industry becomes highly organised, to the point that all weavers are under contract to a single agent and all are using cartoons supplied by the contractor, who incidentally may supply the loom as well, then there is little to distinguish this set-up from a commercial workshop. These are the kind of conditions found in Kayseri, Turkey, and in a large part of Pakistan's production.

Some workshops allow weavers to work at home. For example, at Hereke, where the most technically advanced carpets in Turkey are produced, a highly skilled weaver who has worked for years in the workshop may elect to work away from the hurly-burly of the shop floor in a

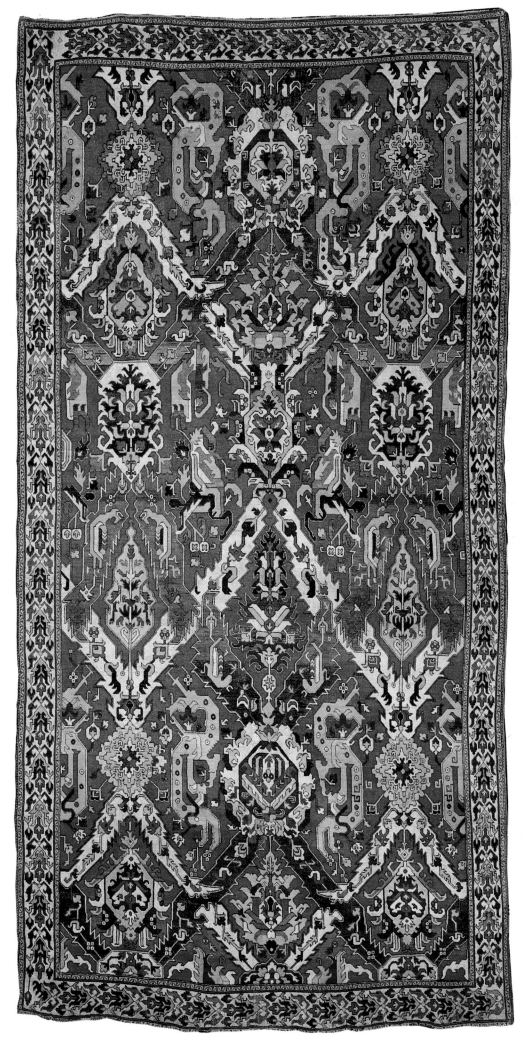

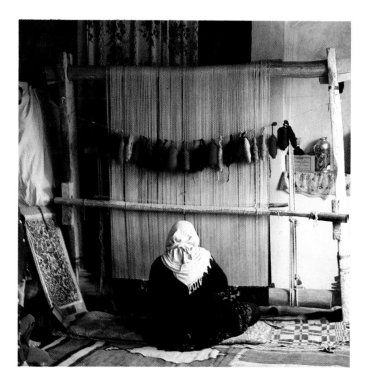

A woman weaving a carpet at home using a cartoon with a medallion design she has bought in the local market. The simple upright loom has few technical refinements. The warps are kept under tension by wedges above the lower beam. Bijar, north-west Persia.

RIGHT: *What later became the huge production of Saruk began as a cottage industry. The early examples, made in the late nineteenth century before weavers had learned to use detailed cartoons, have an attractive slightly rustic quality compared to the more refined later pieces. This prayer rug may well be one of the carpets which in the early days helped Saruk to gain its great reputation.* 193 × 132 cm/76 × 52 in.

local cottage. In this case all that has happened is that some work has been decentralised from the main workshop; the weaver has not suddenly become a worker in the cottage industry. The same applies in some Persian towns, such as Qom, where weaving is actually carried out at home but the superior technical quality of the work, the use of original cartoons from a central design studio and the quality control make the finished carpet indistinguishable from a workshop product.

The style of cottage industry carpets

Since carpets are woven for sale weavers must always be prepared to learn new patterns. One way of doing this is to copy another rug knot for knot. This is a common practice and it can be very confusing to find a pattern typical of a particular region woven in unusual colours. The give-away is always the weaving technique which is usually sufficiently distinctive to pinpoint the origin.

Another method of working is to use a cartoon, a skill developed by the more specialised workshop employees and not usually possessed by the average housewife weaver. The most she would be able to do is to follow a drawing of a design to get the general shape and spacing and fill in the details by eye. For example she might have a drawing of a section of the border or part of the field pattern and use this as a guide to her weaving without following it knot for knot. In doing so she is faced with two main problems and her solution to them gives cottage-made carpets their characteristic appearance. First is the problem of how to make graded curves. She is quite able to produce curves of a sort, but they tend to progress in fits and starts, with straight bits and angles throughout. The minutely graded elegantly swirling lines of the workshop carpets are replaced by irregular, somewhat clumsy, angular curves. Second is the problem of how to make neat corners in the border. Borders normally have a rhythmical, alternating pattern which repeats all the way round the carpet. At the corners designers prefer to make a neat transition by placing a motif in each corner, at exactly forty-five degrees, so that the border design changes direction smoothly. The cottage weaver (and this applies also to the tribal weaver) may start off by managing to place motifs neatly in each corner but she is unlikely to be able to do the same when she comes to the transition between the side borders and the end border (illus. p.46). Only a border worked from a cartoon continues uninterruptedly round all the corners. It is interesting to examine the finely worked Qashqai carpet (illus. p.93) to see if the border, which at first sight seems to have 'corner solutions' (meaning that it was worked out by a designer before weaving started), actually goes right round the carpet without a break in its rhythm.

Some cottage weavers have the unusual skill of being able to 'compose' a complete carpet from a simple sketch. Cecil Edwards, who travelled extensively throughout Persia in the 1930s, relates an amusing incident which occurred in the Heriz area. One day he noticed an interesting carpet being woven in a house and when he inquired about the pattern the weaver showed him a handkerchief printed in two colours in Manchester with a floral border and medallion with corner pieces. She had used this as the basis for weaving a full-sized carpet in twelve colours. All the curves, being too difficult to copy

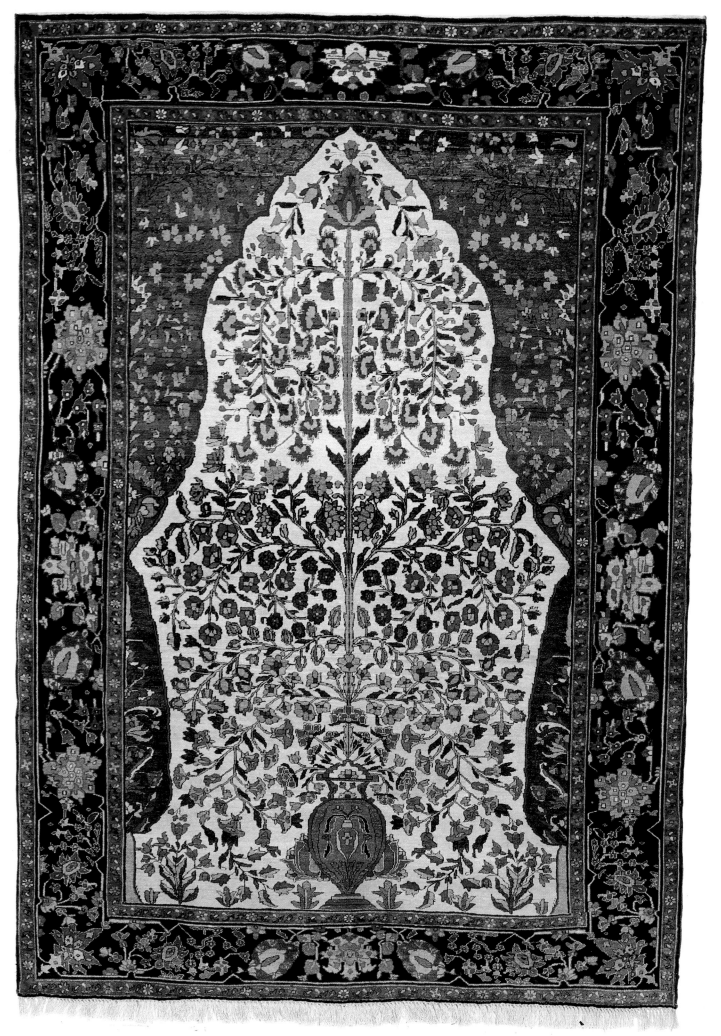

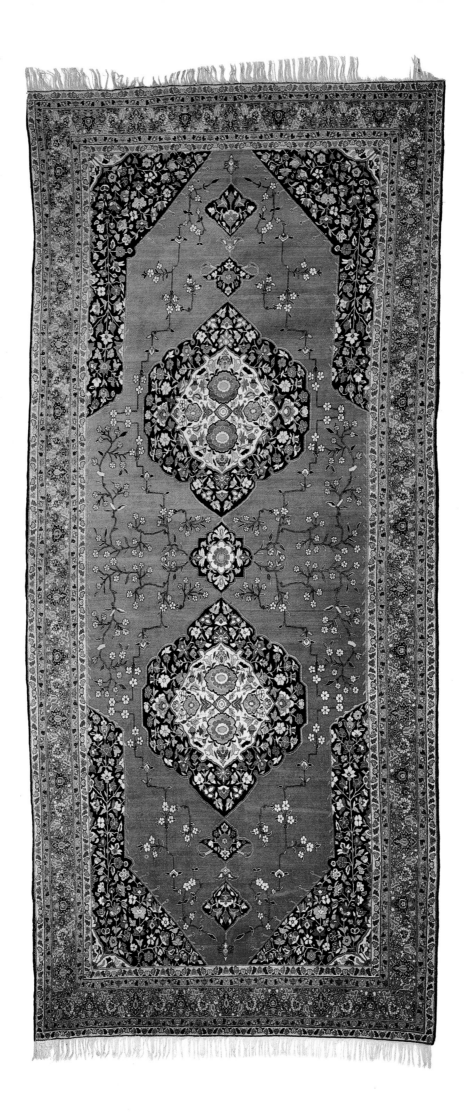

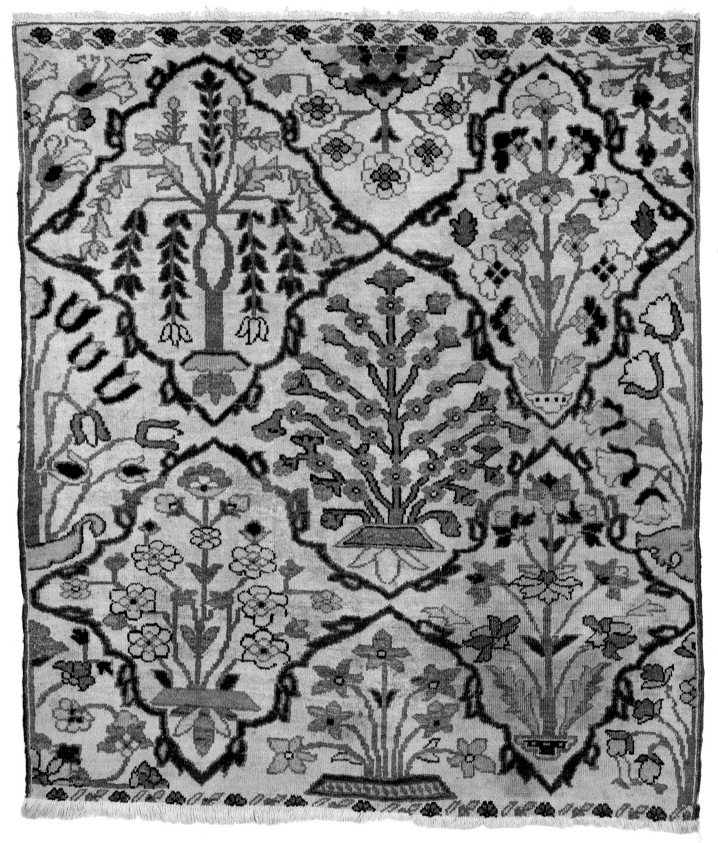

LEFT: *Tabriz, a major weaving centre in Persia, is represented by this delightful carpet, with its plain field enlivened with sprigs of flowers. It was in Tabriz that the first of the modern carpet workshops was set up in the 1870s. This carpet, made for the Persian market, was woven before the establishment of these workshops, and, like the Khorasan carpet (p.61), has something of the character of a cottage product. Nineteenth century. 570 × 270 cm/224½ × 106 in.*

ABOVE: *When the firm of Ziegler and Co. set up a merchant operation in Sultanabad (now Arak, central Persia) in 1883, they took up the idea of using small pattern-carpets (vagireh, see p.104) to introduce new designs. Having chosen a design they thought would sell well, they ordered a number of pattern-rugs to be made of the type shown here, which were distributed in the villages for weavers to copy, using as many repeats as necessary for the size of carpet required. The design comes from an eighteenth-century east Persian carpet (see p.139). 173 × 150 cm/68 × 59 in.*

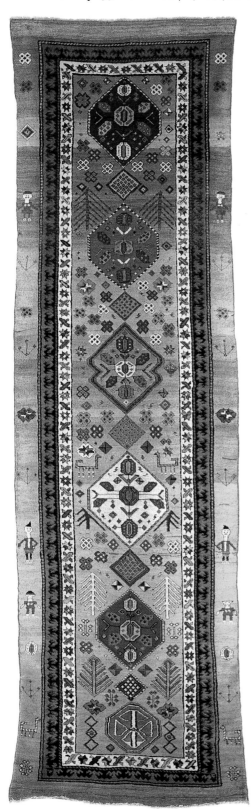

exactly, had become angular, in the typical cottage manner.

To summarise, weavings made within a cottage industry tend to have strong primary colours and bold emphatic designs; their patterns often incline towards the sophisticated but in execution always retain an element of the rustic, and in style exhibit a distinct local character.

Local traditions

Before discussing the more technically advanced workshop carpets some comment must be made on local traditions, although the output of individual villages and districts are too numerous to describe in detail.

The Caucasus is an area rich in both carpets and mysteries. Very little dependable information is available for this remarkable part of the world, a mountainous district containing a profusion of ethnic minorities, each with its own character and language, where problems of origin and history, such as that of the Basques of the Pyrenees, are repeated many times over. The Caucasus has a long history of cottage production and exportation which continues today. Most of the output from the region has the typical character of cottage work and is named according to the village, town or district of origin. Many designs can be traced in an unbroken succession of transformations back to modified Persian patterns of the seventeenth century. Some weavings have a strong tribal character (illus. p.87) and resemble the weavings of tribal groups in Turkey and Persia, and those of the Turkmen of central Asia. As no one is certain who made them they are difficult to classify. The sensitivity of the cottage industry to new ideas and influences is well illustrated by the Caucasian weavers who were among the first to introduce European design in the form of a field pattern decorated with cabbage roses in the 1840s and among the first to use synthetic dyes in the 1870s. In Turkey the cottage industry system was established long ago and is so deeply embedded in rural life that truly tribal carpets are few and far between. Anatolia is particularly rich in kilims – now the subject of a major scholarly dispute. One school claims that kilim weaving is an indigenous craft dating back to the neolithic period. The other holds that it was imported by immigrant Turks. The view taken here is that kilims are tribal artefacts, furniture for the tent rather than the house.

Not much is known of Persian cottage weaving before the nineteenth century as little reached the west, but occasional datable carpets give evidence of a vigorous and diverse industry. In the first half of the nineteenth century carpet production in Persia had fallen to a low level, but the cottage industry, charmingly described by one Persian dealer as a 'side job' never ceased. Once stimulated by foreign demand Persian village women responded energetically and output increased enormously. Demand reached such a point late in the nineteenth century that western engineers were stimulated to try and invent a machine for making knotted pile carpets. This was achieved in 1910 by the British firm of Tomkinson who obtained a patent from Renard Frères of Nonancourt, France, for a loom based on the Jacquard principle. Initially the Tomkinson carpets imitated the popular red and blue Turkey carpets but they were never very lucrative and they had difficulty in competing with the weavers of Hamadan

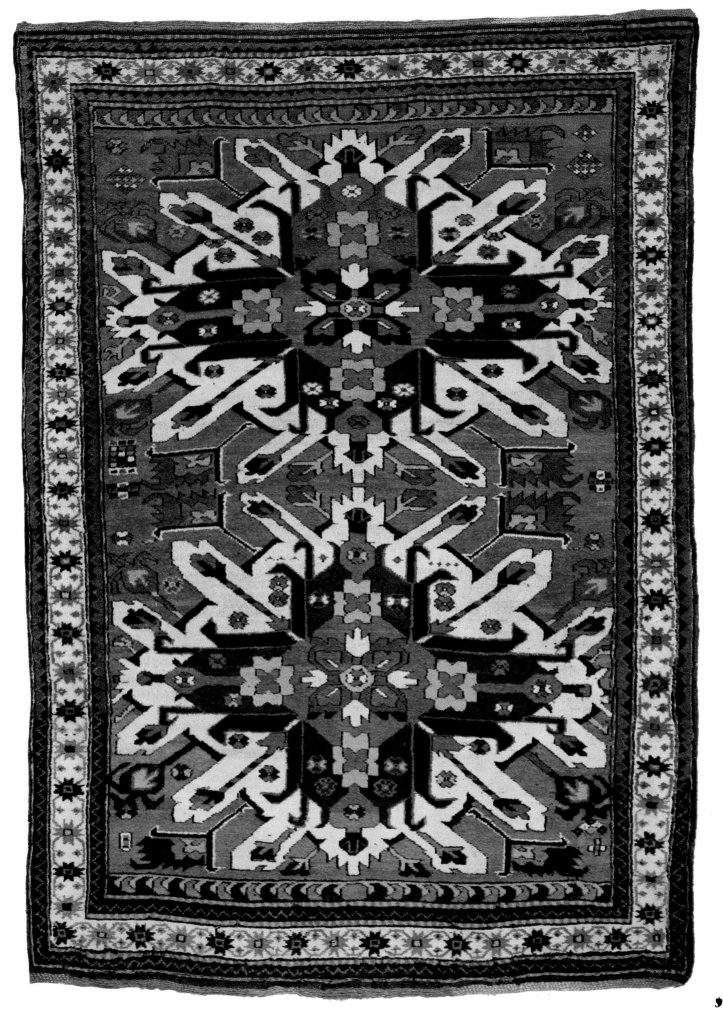

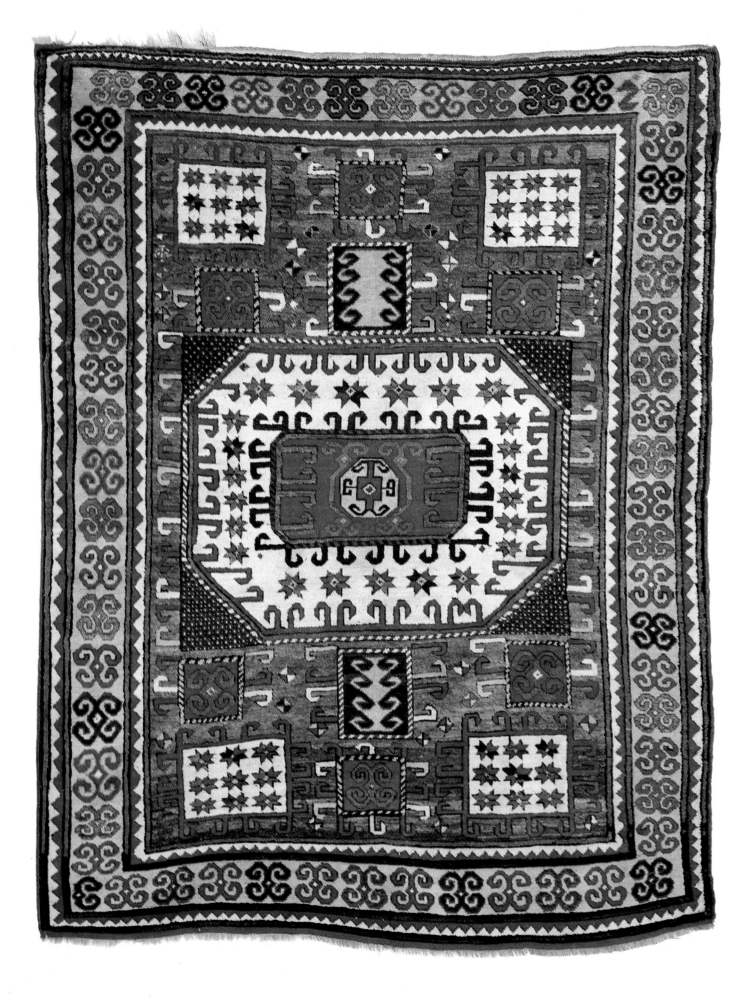

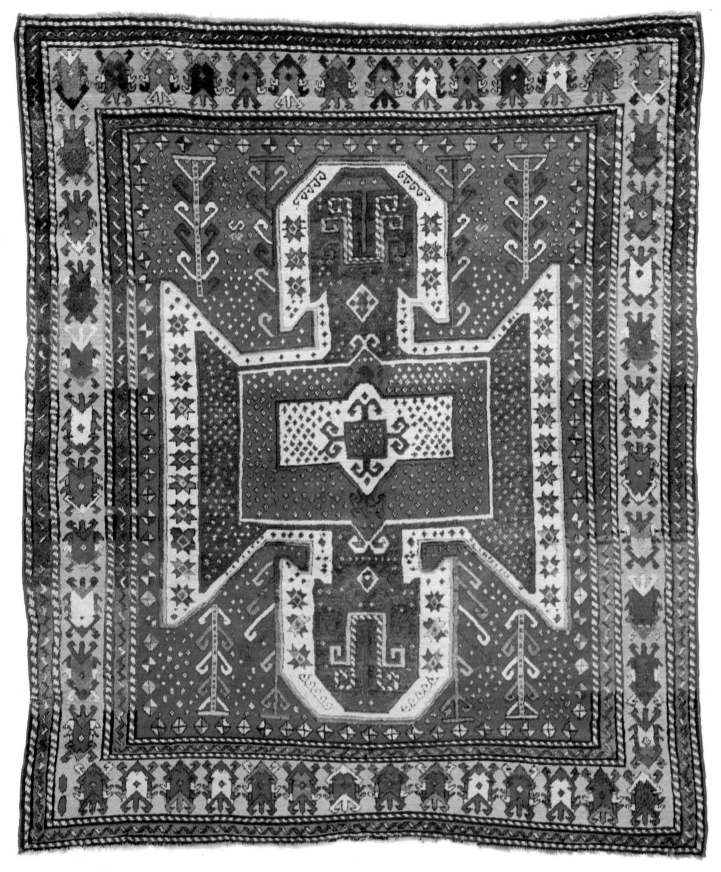

LEFT: *This Kazak carpet has what is known as the Karachop design, an ancient pattern found both in Caucasian and Turkish carpets. Its bold abstraction has made it and other Kazak carpets popular as a focus of interest in the modern home. Nineteenth century.* 225 × 170 cm/88½ × 67 in.

ABOVE: *The Sevan design, another of the range of Kazak types, is well seen in this example. It has the long shaggy pile and strong colours so typical of Kazak rugs. A related form of its field pattern is also found in Turkish carpets. Nineteenth century.* 220 × 183 cm/86½ × 72 in.

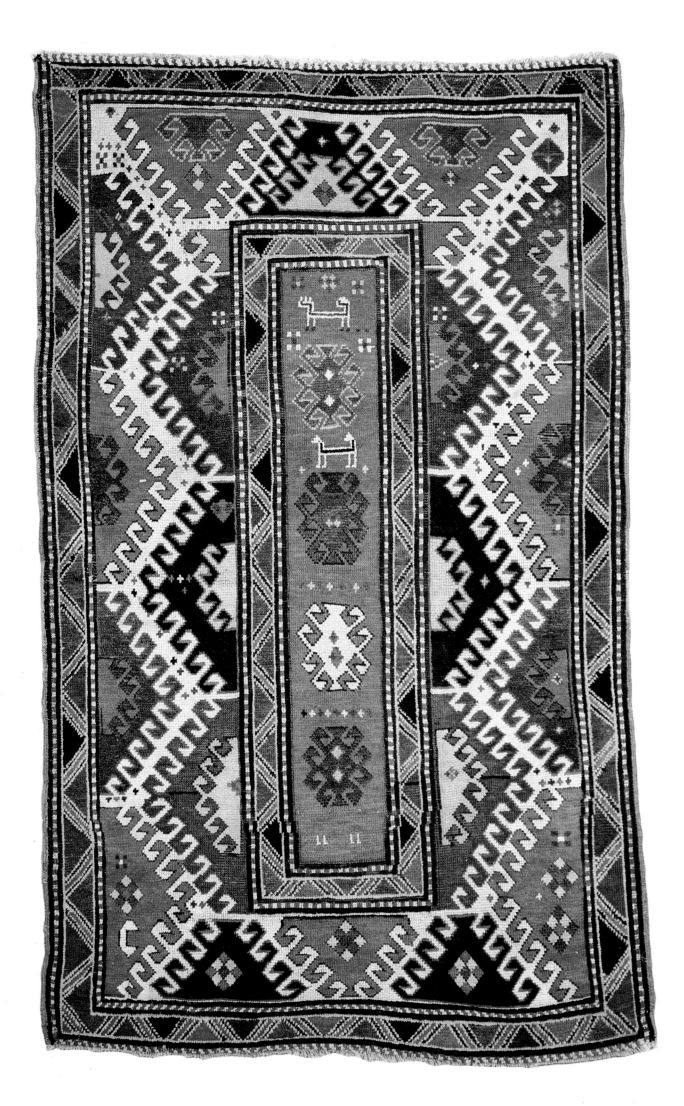

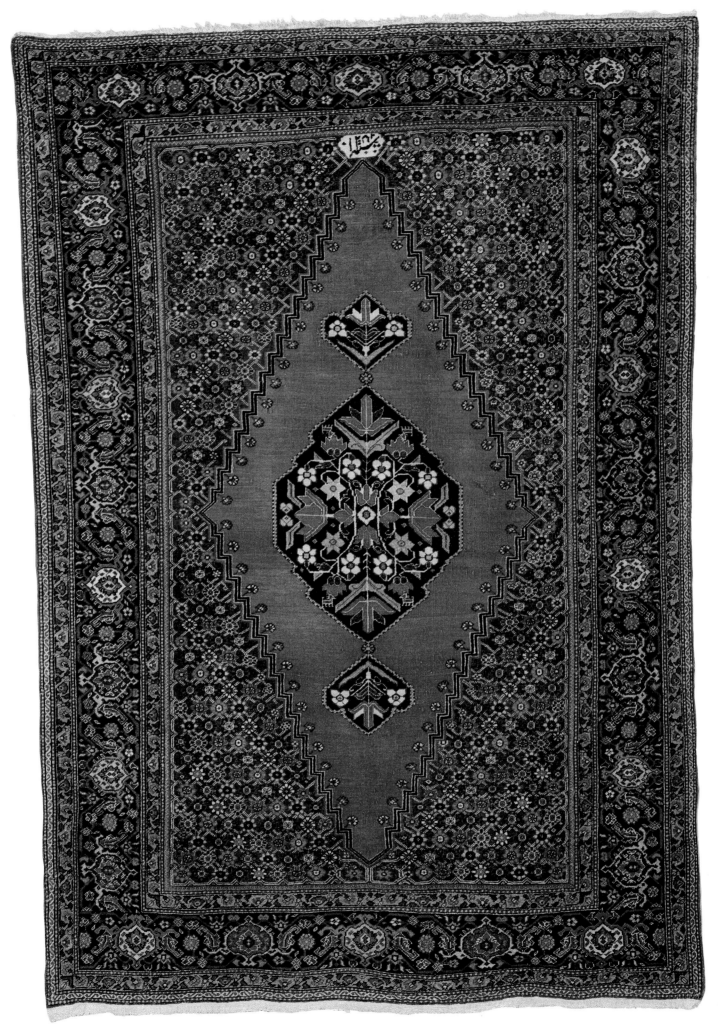

p.116: *Kazak rugs from the Caucasus are noted for their strong individual character and have been given names by Russian scholars according to design and place of origin. This Borchaly design is one of the few in which the border and field are given equal emphasis. Nineteenth century. 221 × 155 cm/ 87 × 61 in.*

PREVIOUS PAGE: *This carpet, a typical product of the Farahan district of central Persia, is dated 1282 (AD 1865). Such carpets were special favourites of the older generation of dealers born in the Middle East. They are now rarely seen and the characteristic Farahan style of weaving seems to have died out around the turn of the century. The design in the main border proceeds in regular rhythm along the sides and ends, but changes abruptly at the corners. This is a typical feature of the cottage industry style. 196 × 130 cm/77 × 51 in.*

BELOW: *For as long as anyone can remember Kurds in the Kelardasht region of northern Persia have been weaving carpets on an upright loom set up against one wall of the house. Both beams are fixed and the warps are kept under tension with wedges. As work proceeds the bench is raised until in the end the weavers are sitting at roof level. 1982.*

RIGHT: *One of the enduring names of the cottage industry in Persia is that of Bijar. Carpets made in the villages around Bijar are the most strongly made and hard-wearing to be found anywhere. Perhaps because they are so indestructible, many Bijar carpets survive from before the great revival of carpet weaving in the last third of the nineteenth century. In spite of the vagaries of changing fashion their strong clear colours and open designs have never been out of fashion. Around 1900. 503 × 351 cm/198 × 138 in.*

who could work practically as fast and more cheaply. Latterly the looms came to be used for specialised orders such as the making of a carpet bearing an insignia to fill a particular space. The last Tomkinson machine-knotted carpets were woven in 1962.

Some products of the cottage industry in Persia are known throughout the world, such as the carpets of Bijar, famous for their clear colours and durability; those of Senneh for their fine workmanship and pastel colours; and the weavings of the settled Baluchis in Khorasan for their dark colours, lovely wool and economical price. Some extremely handsome carpets were made in villages populated by settled people mainly of Bakhtiyari origin. Technical and craft standards in the past were at a high level and have remained so (illus. p.47). They managed in the nineteenth century to make some huge carpets which were never formally designed but followed a style of pattern woven in Jowshaqan, which has been unfailingly popular in Persia for centuries.

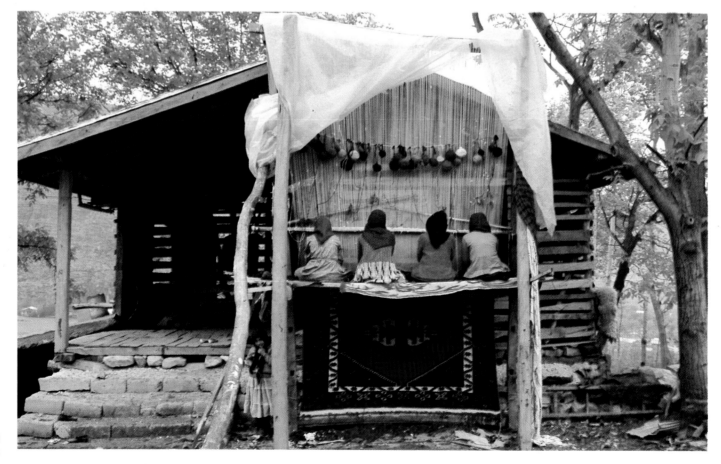

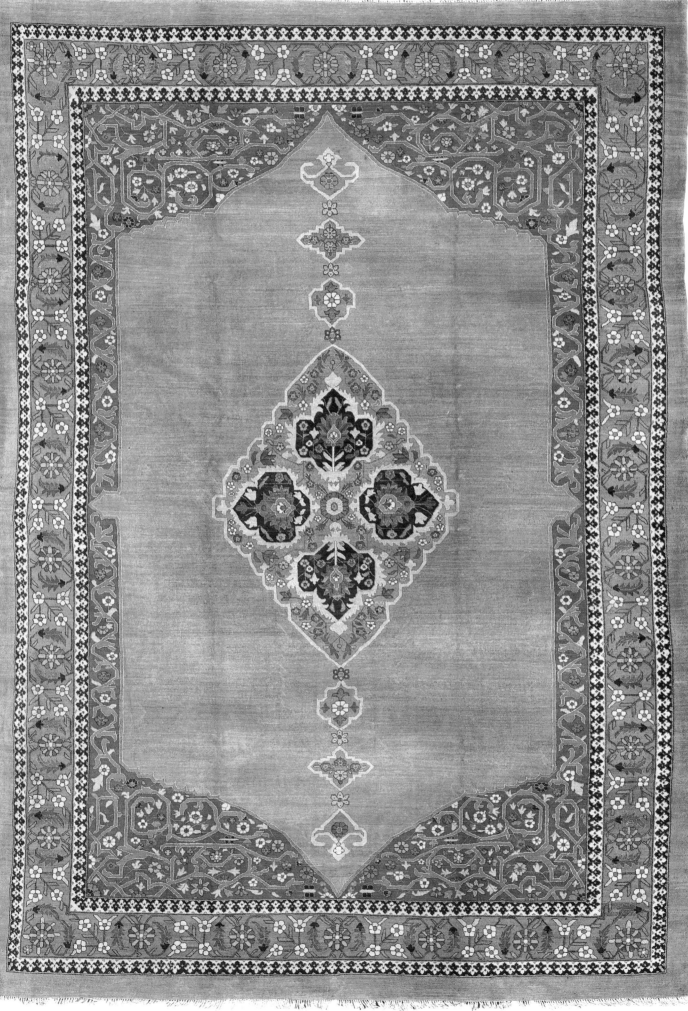

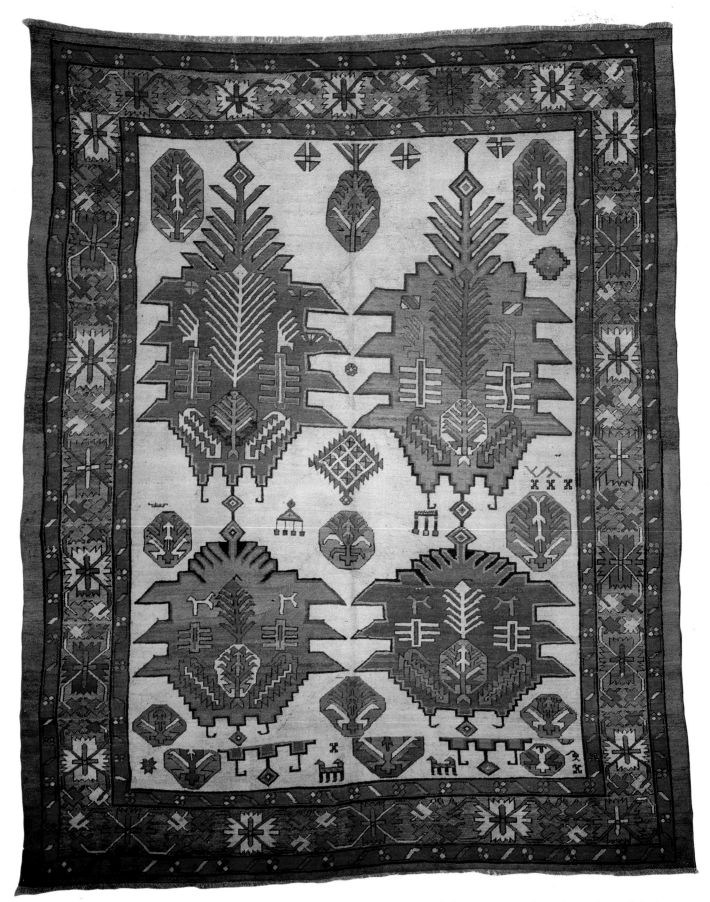

ABOVE: *In the early decades of this century there was a cottage industry in the little village of Bakhshayesh near Heriz in north-west Persia which became renowned for its well made carpets with soft colours and bold patterns. They have an appeal which has not diminished in the light of changing fashions. It is only to be regretted that such rugs have not been made in the last forty years. Nineteenth century. 300 × 235 cm/ 118 × 92½ in.*

RIGHT: *Kurdish weavers are the makers of one of the best known types of all Persian carpets. The town of Senneh, the capital of Persian Kordestan, has become world famous for its fine rugs and carpets, which have a unique construction and colouring. These carpets, the product of one of the most refined cottage industries in Persia, have nothing in common with the Kurdish tribal weavings (p.39) made in the tents and tribal villages of mountainous Kurdestan. This rug with the Vekilli design has the soft colours and typical weave of Senneh work. Nineteenth century. 184 × 130 cm/72½ × 51 in.*

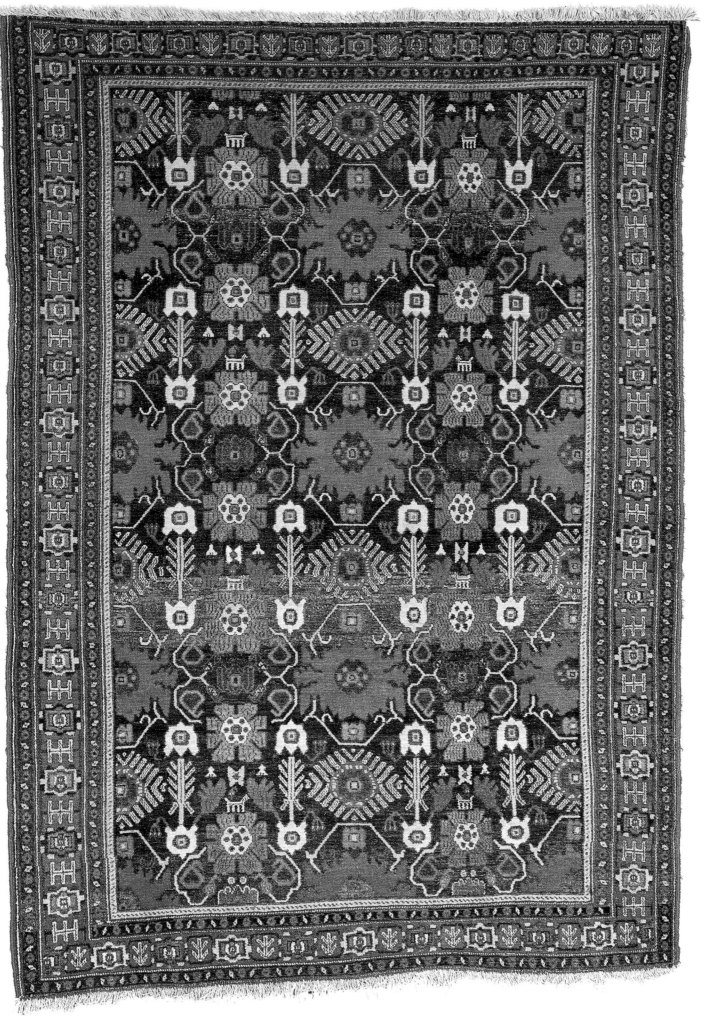

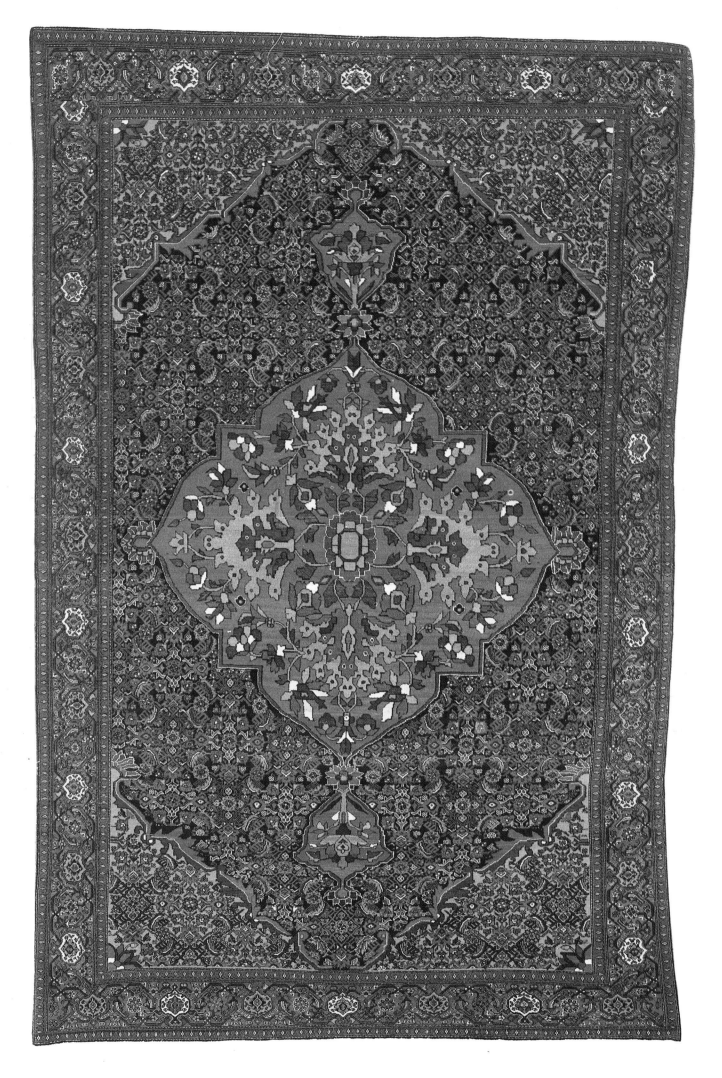

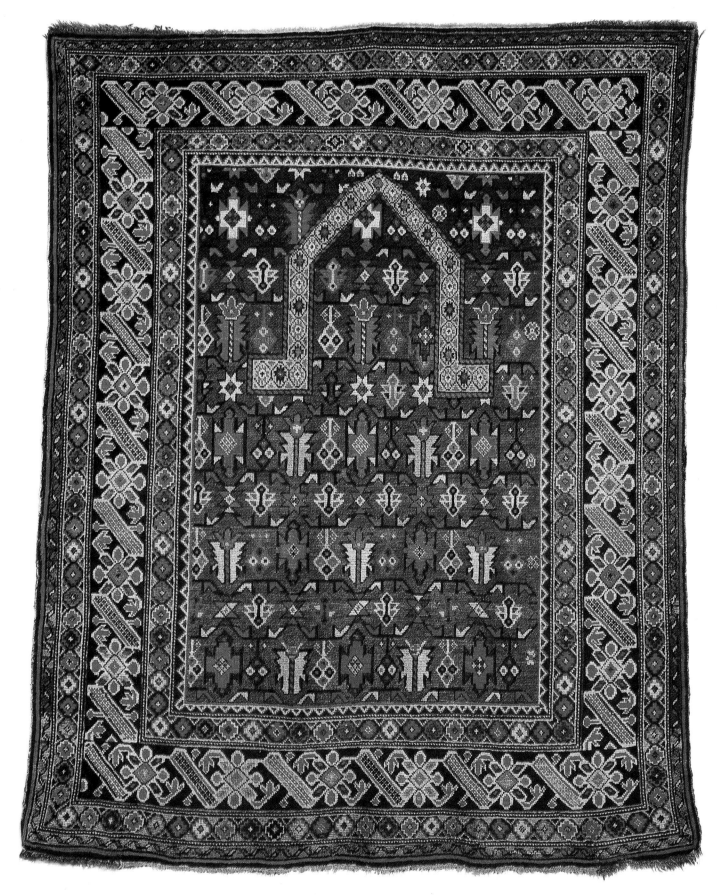

LEFT: *When Persian carpet production revived at the end of the last century some weavings with an established reputation were widely imitated. In this way the small town of Saruk, famous for its well made tightly woven rugs with medallion designs, gave its name to a whole category of well made cottage industry carpets woven in the Arak region. This is one of the originals. Nineteenth century. 208 × 127 cm/82 × 50 in.*

ABOVE: *Used as a prayer rug, the gabled arch is orientated towards Mecca. In practice very few Muslims use such expensive and cumbersome carpets for their prayers, preferring some more simple and practical covering. Great numbers of rugs with a prayer design were made in the Caucasian cottage industry because they were popular with foreign buyers. The design of this example is known as Chichi. Azerbayjan, nineteenth century. 152 × 117 cm/60 × 46 in.*

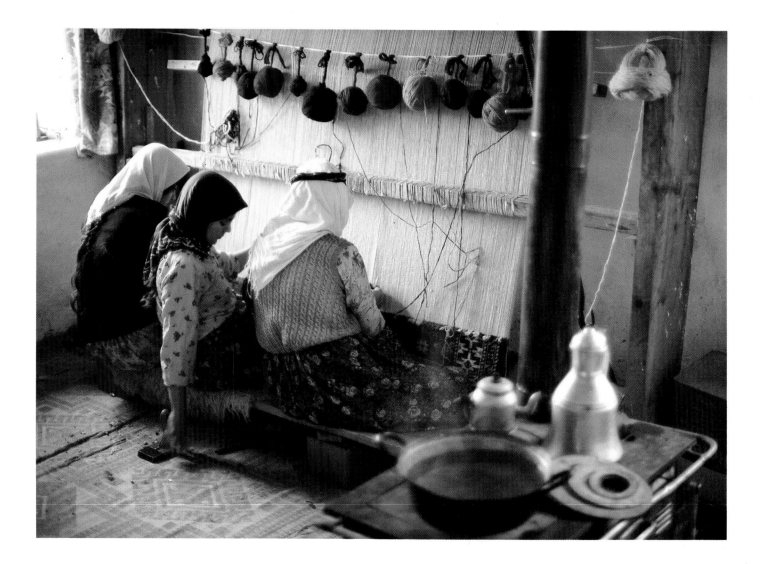

The DOBAG Project

The textile department of the faculty of fine arts at Marmara University, Istanbul, are behind a most interesting social and economic project in the field of carpets. A number of villages in western Turkey are inhabited by settled (formerly Turkmen tribal) people with a long tradition of carpet weaving, certainly brought from central Asia in their westward migration over 500 years ago. Within the last century commercial pressures and synthetic dyes have combined to cause a sad deterioration in the appearance of carpets woven in these villages. The project is to persuade the weavers in these villages to return to using traditional dyes and materials and to assist the villagers within local cottage industries to form marketing cooperatives. The results have been unexpectedly successful. The women have never forgotten their traditional patterns and with a little assistance from carpets borrowed from the local mosque (often dyed with hideous synthetic dyes), they have been able to continue in the manner of 100 years ago. Now it is as if the last century of weaving had never existed. The colours, using only natural dyes, are bright (as they should be) and the patterns astonishing for their traditional consistency. Careful marketing allows weavers to sell at a reasonable price yet obtain more than they were getting for contract work, and as a result standards are rising.

ABOVE: *A carpet with natural dyes being woven in the village of Orselli. The inhabitants of this village are former nomads who settled more than a hundred years ago and have an unbroken weaving tradition going back several centuries. Manisa province, 1986.*

RIGHT: *As soon as natural dyes were reintroduced to a group of villages in western Turkey in the course of the DOBAG project, their rugs began to sell, standards rose and almost-forgotten patterns were seen for the first time in decades. The bright colours come as a surprise to many people accustomed to seeing only chemically bleached, synthetically dyed carpets, but this is how they looked when new a hundred years ago. Sungullu village, Manisa province, 1985. 249 × 151 cm/98 × 59½ in.*

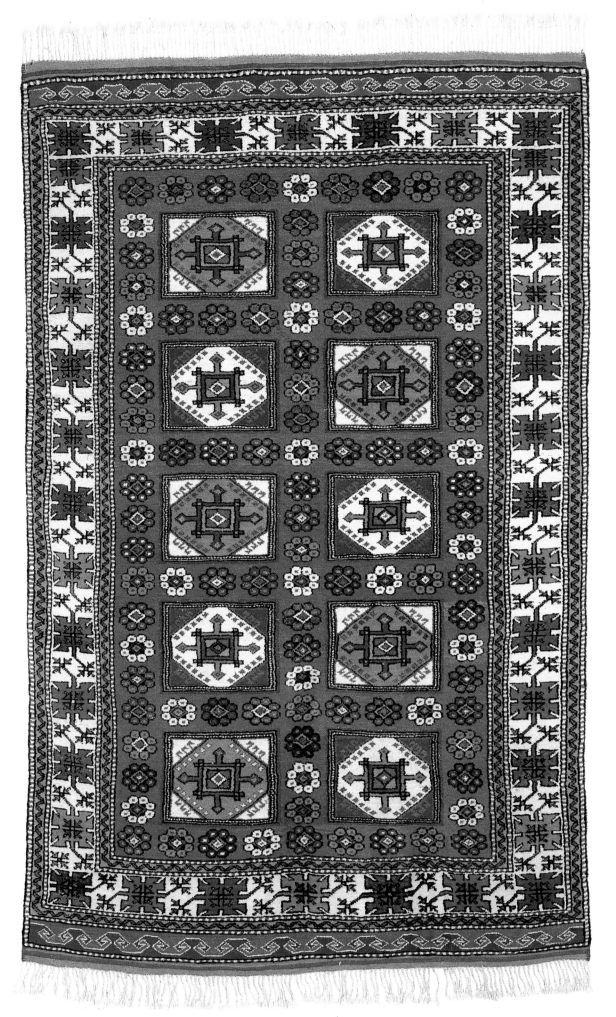

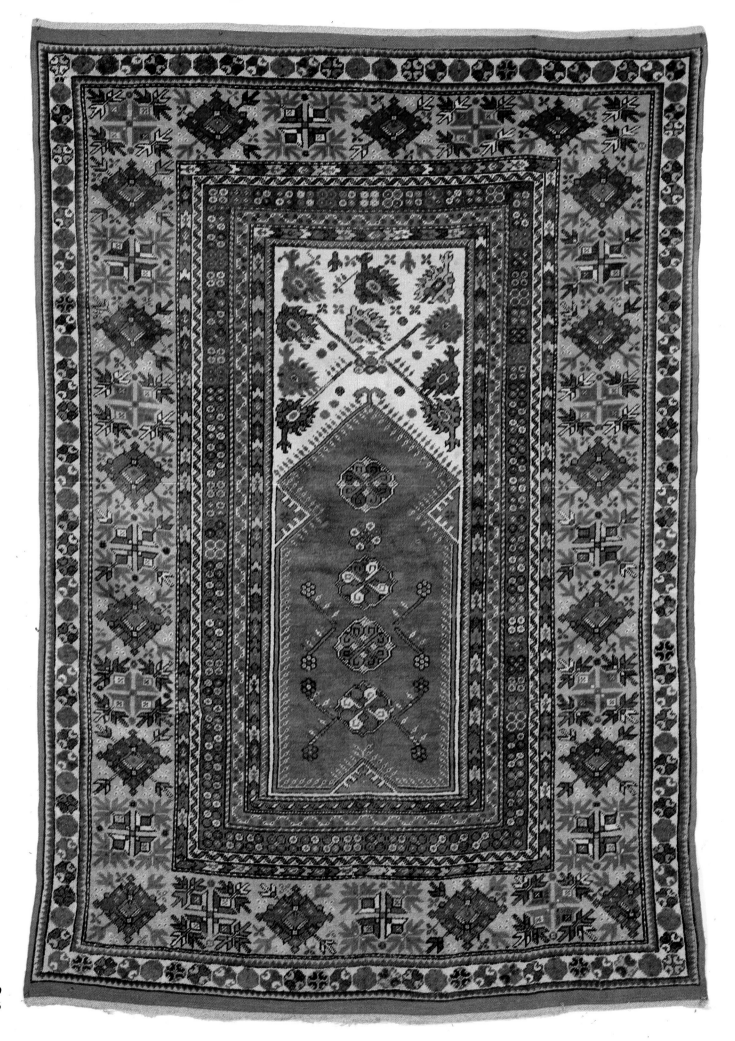

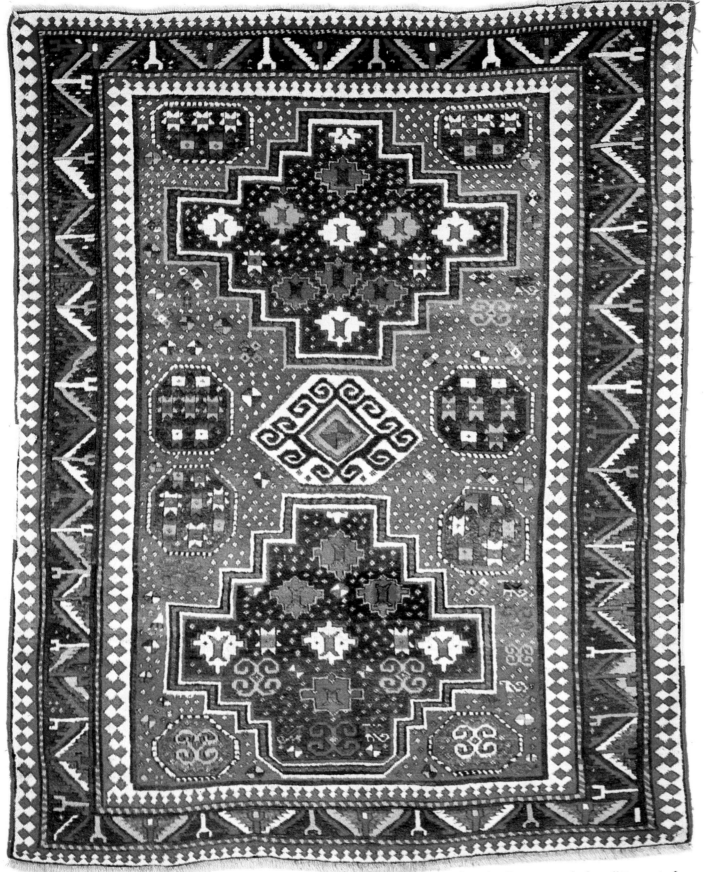

LEFT: *The cottage industry still flourishes in Turkey in the same places as it did in the seventeenth century, and with related patterns. The village of Milas became well known in the nineteenth century for small rugs with lovely colours, particularly prayer rugs, of which this is a typical example.* 175 × 119 cm/69 × 47 in.

ABOVE· *This rug from the Caucasus embodies all the typical features of Kazak work: lustrous wool, long shaggy pile, strong colours and a bold pattern. It has the interesting distinction of having been published in one of the early books on carpets by Mumford in 1900. It also illustrates the 'protective barrier' aspect of the border. The main border has a strong rhythmically alternating pattern and is flanked by two 'guard stripes' with a reciprocally interlocking design. Nineteenth century.* 211 × 165 cm/83 × 65 in.

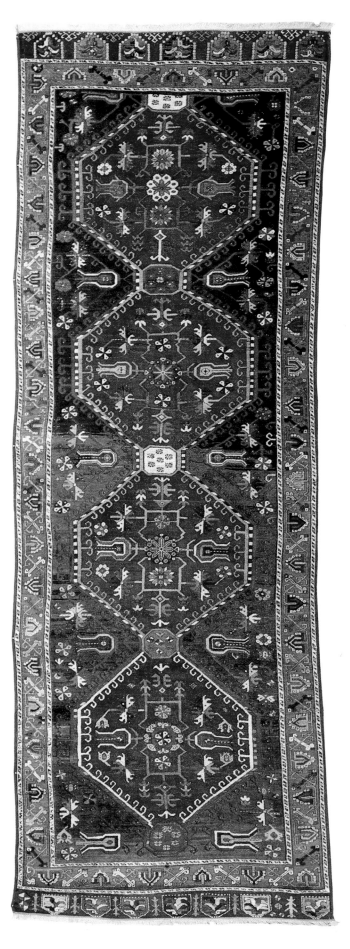

LEFT: *The village of Ladik in central Turkey is best known for its prayer rugs (opposite), but the earlier weavings include a number of rare and attractive long, narrow rugs with a design of conjoined medallions decorated with stylised tulips. Around 1800. 340 × 117 cm/134 × 46 in.*

RIGHT: *The famous prayer rugs of Ladik were produced over a long period extending from the eighteenth century to the twentieth. At first they resembled the prayer rugs designed for the Ottoman court in their layout (p.149), with narrow borders and a broad expanse of plain colour in the field. As time passed the clear area beneath the arch was slowly crowded out with extravagant borders, until at the end it was reduced to a mere patch in the centre (compare p.126 for a similar transformation). Nineteenth century. 190 × 112 cm/75 × 44 in.*

BELOW: *A little-known cottage industry flourished during the nineteenth century in what used to be called Chinese or east Turkestan, now the Sinkiang province of China. There is every indication that the tradition of carpet making in this district is very old. The population speak Uighur, a Turkic language and, although predominantly Muslim, the carpets preserve designs carried over from the Buddhist past of the area. Designs also include rustic interpretations of Chinese patterns such as this enchanting, if rather angular, version of a Chinese paeony scroll pattern. Around 1800. 140 × 92 cm/55 × 36 in.*

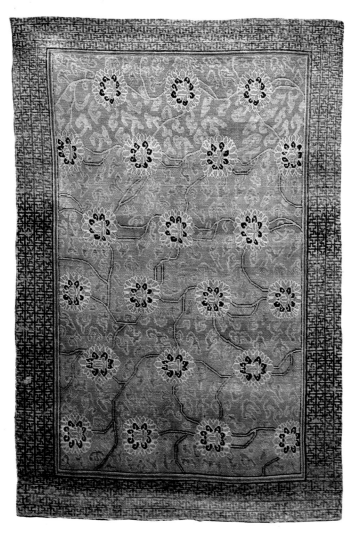

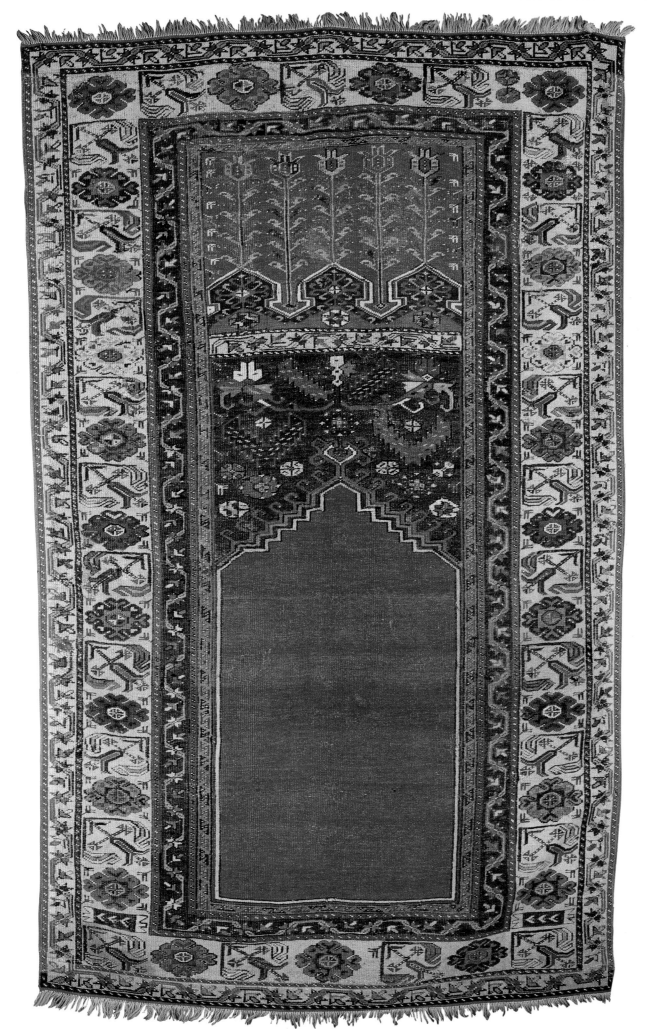

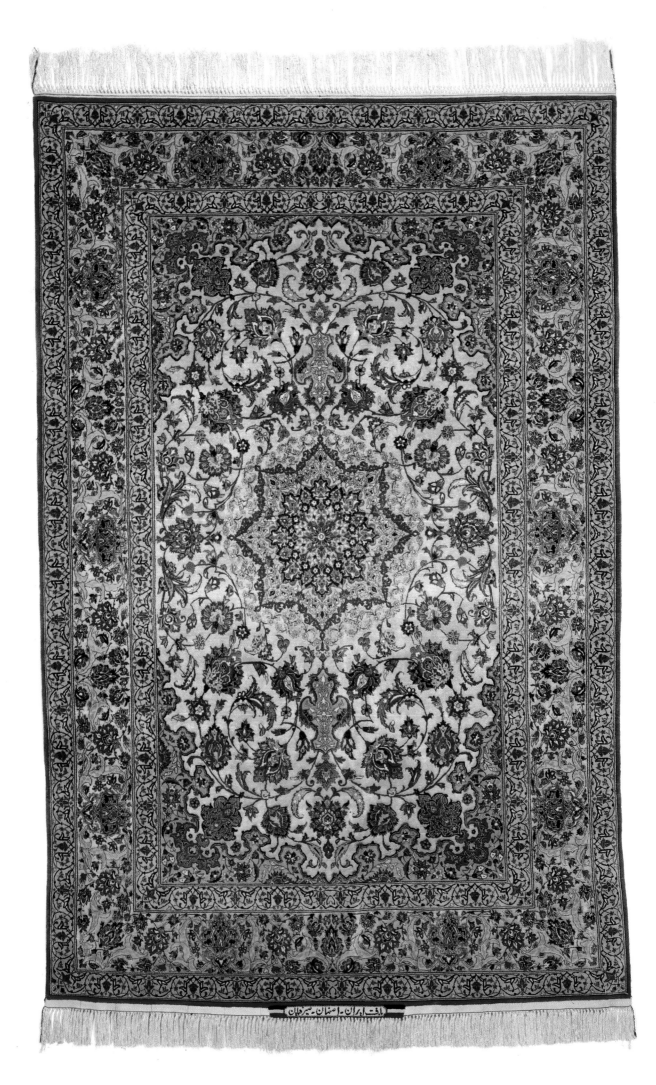

Chapter five

Workshop or town carpets

The workshop carpet is characterised by a balanced overall design (the work of a designer), perfectly graded curves, borders which progress evenly right round the carpet, faultless technique, and the avoidance of great expanses of primary colour. It is the product of advanced technology and a system of specialised production. This recently made example has an inscription knotted within the plain woven band at one end, 'Woven in Iran, Esfahan, by Serafian'. 233 × 149 cm/ 91½ × 58½ in.

The growth of commercial carpets

Tribal and cottage looms are seldom more than 8 feet wide. A carpet can be any length but its width cannot exceed that of the loom. In Persia people adapted the way they furnished their homes to what was available, and instead of having a large carpet covering the whole floor, the custom grew up of having a suite of four carpets in the main room. The traditional long narrow shapes of Persian carpets never found favour in the west and as carpets became more and more a normal part of home furnishing, people asked for much wider carpets for their living rooms. They also wanted colours and patterns which would fit in with their existing décor. These the trade could not easily supply because the massive looms required to make such carpets were beyond the technical resources of the cottage industries. Enterprising merchants therefore set about filling this gap in the market by providing capital for setting up workshops in Persia specifically organised to supply the needs of the western market. This phase, beginning around 1875, has been called the revival period. Carpet production grew rapidly and the export of Persian carpets became a huge business. Europeans also entered the scene to invest in production. The first factory financed and managed by Europeans was founded by Ziegler and Co. of Manchester in 1883.

The mid-nineteenth century had been a period of economic decline in Persia. Some weaving centres appear to have ceased production, but most of the old-established ones were active and were producing rugs, but not in any great quantity. Then suddenly this basically traditional craft, existing at several different levels of technical accomplishment and adjusted to local needs, was subjected to an unprecedented demand for export goods. The demand was met by increased output. During this period thousands of new looms went into production, in the cottage industry and in commercial workshops. The resulting output dominated the market, dwarfing the importance of the tribal rugs. The more remote tribal and village weavers, who normally worked to fill basic domestic needs while aiming to produce a surplus for trade and barter, also experienced the increased demand for carpets. They obligingly wove more rugs, but the increase was commonly accompanied by a decline in standards, although some tribal groups proved remarkably resilient. In the commercial workshops standards, far from declining, improved to reach a high level of technical excellence. But, as the term 'export goods' has come to imply in the larger field of art objects, aesthetic values changed. The commercial carpet industry created a new product which came to occupy a special place in the history of carpet art.

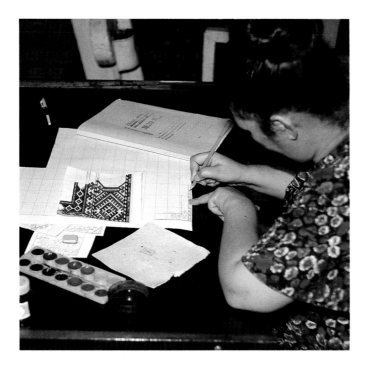

RIGHT: *The south Persian city of Kerman has been an important centre for the production of workshop carpets back to the sixteenth century. Like many other centres Kerman suffered in the troubled times of the nineteenth century and weavers turned their hand to making shawls, a lucrative export business dominated by Kashmir. Shawls finally went out of fashion in the west about the time that demand for carpets was increasing sharply. The presence in the city of looms, skilled weavers and designers, enabled the Kermanis to take immediate advantage of the turn of events, since when skilful designers and the traditionally high standards in the workshops have taken Kerman to a position of world renown. This fine rug woven 'by the order of Hajj Muhammad Ibrahim Kermani' has a shawl design. Around 1900. 224 × 139 cm/88 × 54½ in.*

LEFT: *An artist in the state carpet factory of the Turkmen SSR recording a traditional design on a squared paper cartoon for use by weavers in the factory. Although the designs are taken from traditional tribal carpets, as factory employees the relationship of the weavers to their product is now different from what it was in the past. The steel looms have a mechanical shedding device and craft standards are high. Ashkhabad, 1985.*

BELOW: *In commercial workshops designs are converted to cartoons by drawing them onto squared paper. These are cut into sections, pasted onto cardboard and coloured by hand. In this Rumanian factory cartoons for a European design are being prepared. 1970s.*

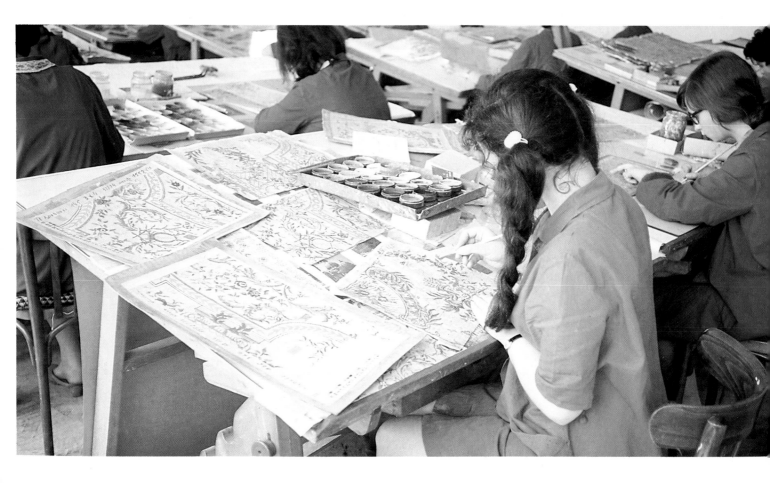

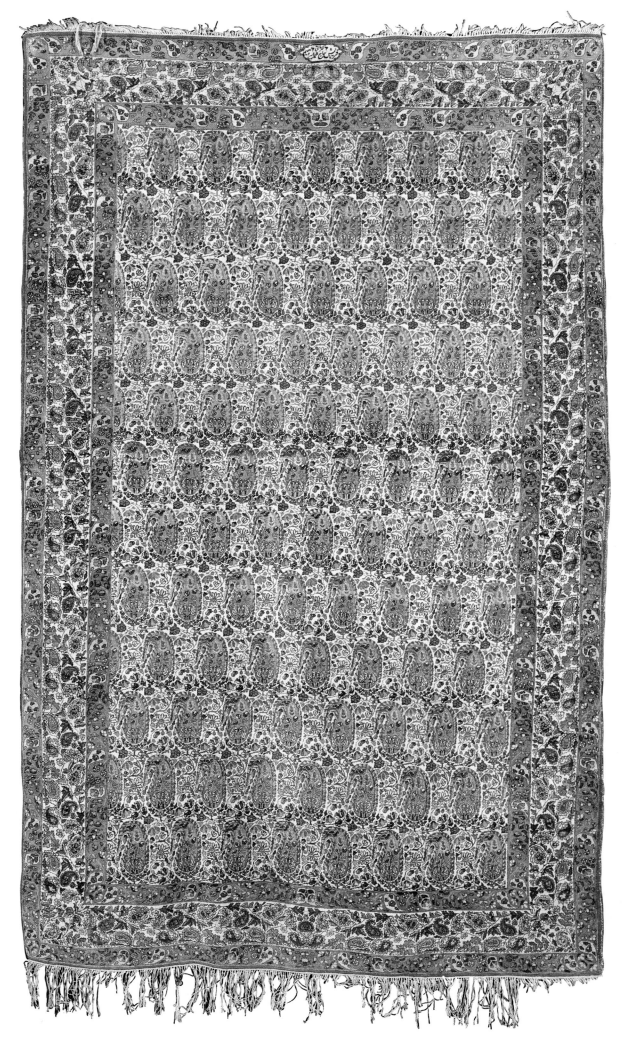

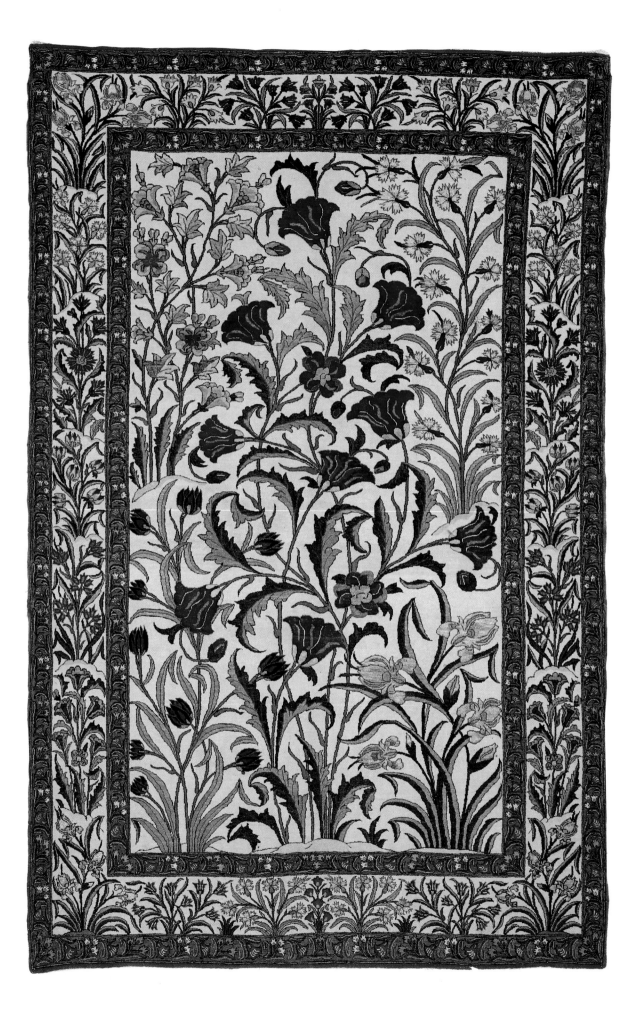

LEFT: *Weaving began in Qom in the 1930s. It soon acquired a high reputation for quality of workmanship and originality of design. In Qom a sort of decentralised workshop system operates in which weavers work at home to standards normally found only in workshops. This rug has a design inspired by seventeenth-century Indian court carpets. It has highlights in silk and is typical of the high quality work associated with Qom. 215 × 137 cm/84½ × 54 in.*

Production

The new system converted carpet making into a production process, which is continued in the same way today. Craftsmen are recruited, trained and employed by the company to work on each stage. These include the purchase of raw materials, sorting, carding and combing, spinning, plying, dyeing, designing, cartoon making, weaving, clipping and washing. Specialisation allows each craft to be developed to a higher level than is possible among the cottage and tribal weavers who do everything themselves apart from the dyeing. It also makes for a much more uniform quality in the finished article. On the other hand the weavers and spinners are no more than employees in a large organisation.

The workshop or town carpet as it is often called is almost by definition woven from a cartoon. The art of the carpet is therefore the art of the designer. The weaver reproduces the design with more or less accuracy according to her skill. Recognising a designed carpet is usually easy. The curves are graceful, flowing and even, the overall composition is perfectly balanced and the design flows evenly all round the border, with a motif neatly and exactly placed in each corner. Sometimes a tribal or cottage weaver will copy a workshop rug, the

Making large carpets of Ushak character at Sparta, Turkey, 1910. This is a type of 'low tech' workshop producing large quantities of coarsely made, crudely patterned carpeting.

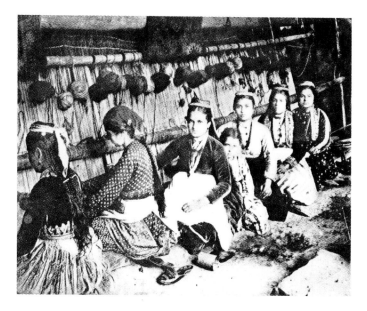

Qashqai weavers, for instance, being excellent copyists (illus. p.93: although an astonishing feat of workmanship, a careful look at the curves and the corners reveal that the finer points were beyond her).

The distinction between a cottage industry and a workshop is not always clear and some overlap does occur. I referred previously to the important weaving centre at Qom, which developed in the 1930s and which has no factory as such, all the looms being in the weavers' houses. The highly skilled weavers work under contract and weave to an exact design supplied to them by the contractor, who also supplies the yarns. The quality control is good and the end product has all the features of a workshop carpet. The carpets of Kashan are known today for their quality and workmanship but in the late nineteenth century, at the start of the revival, all carpets were woven on home-based looms. A glance at these early Kashans reveals the typical features of cottage carpets, clumsy corners and wonky curves in otherwise excellent products. As the weavers became more skilled and were able to reproduce exact patterns the carpets took on more of the character of workshop products.

At the other end of the scale one finds employees working in a factory making large but crude carpets, not woven from a cartoon. An example of this type of work are the 'Sparta' carpets, coarse imitations of earlier Ushak designs made in Isparta, Turkey, in the early decades of this century.

So far we have mainly discussed Persian workshops which, as they were first in the field, held a dominant position for many decades. But it was not long before market demand stimulated others to join in. Workshops for large-scale production were established in Turkey, Pakistan and India, and later in Nepal, Rumania, Russia and Afghanistan; and on a smaller scale in many countries, among them Egypt, Tunisia, Israel, Lebanon, Yugoslavia and Iraq. In China there appears to be no indigenous folk tradition although carpet workshops have been in continuous production for at least three hundred years. With growing demand production was increased and China continues to maintain a huge export trade.

As with any commercial operation the product is governed almost entirely by what will sell. An exception is the occasional carpet made to order. What the public will buy depends on dozens of imponderable factors related to fashion, national prosperity, international politics, war, revolution and so on. A great advantage of the commercial workshops is that they can respond immediately to new fashions or requests from importers overseas, as illustrated by the Art Deco carpet made in China to a design presumably provided by a European (illus. p.142). Market demand was not all from overseas; the pictorial carpets for which Kashan is well known were clearly a Persian fashion. In the absence of specific requests the managers of the workshops, in consultation with the designers, have to make a policy decision on what designs to produce. Today, in the carpet producing countries of the world, there are few truly original schools and none that approaches the quality of work produced by the court designers of four hundred years ago.

RIGHT: *In the workshop the weaver is trained to work knot by knot from a cartoon and execute exactly what the designer specifies. It is thus possible to have any design woven into a carpet. Here the design is a picture drawn in the nineteenth-century Qajar style depicting Alexander the Great and his war with the devil. The work has been executed to a high standard and there is a large colour palette, including some synthetic dyes. Kashan, early twentieth century. 201 × 134 cm/ 79 × 53 in.*

BELOW: *A carpet workshop in the Caucasus. The date may be 1913 but there is some doubt. The weavers are working from large paper cartoons which are in themselves something of an anomaly because they are not designs of the curvilinear type normally associated with workshop carpets. The designer has taken traditional village-style rectilinear designs, normally worked from memory, and 'tidied them up'. The urge to collect and give cartoons of 'improved', traditional, memory-based designs to village weavers seems to be irresistible, and it occurs in every weaving country. However, instead of sustaining and promoting the tradition, as might be hoped, it contributes to its disappearance.*

Since the 1870s Persian designers have continued to produce good work. Some design studios are still active and original and manage to retain a traditional character; Qom carpets are a good example (illus. p.134). Chinese designers have successfully maintained their high standards of former times (illus. p.142). They have also tried their hand with new patterns. The European designs work well and are popular and their new Persian designs, although seemingly uncomfortable in the hands of a people who have nurtured the world's greatest designers, are improving rapidly. The Chinese understand better than anyone the use of space; in contrast Persian design is concerned with pattern and overall surface decoration. Tibetan carpets have designs with a strong individual character and are becoming increasingly popular (illus. p.143). Indian designers have tended to rework old Persian patterns. Apart from the Hereke factory (illus. p.14), few new ideas have come out of Turkey, although some carpets of the highest technical quality have been woven in Kum Kapu, a district in the old quarter of Istanbul, with designs based on classical Persian models (illus. p.150).

Since it is possible to translate more or less any design into a knotted pile carpet, designers today should take up the challenge and, following in the footsteps of a long line of designers before them, should apply themselves to making modern designs suitable for this ancient craft.

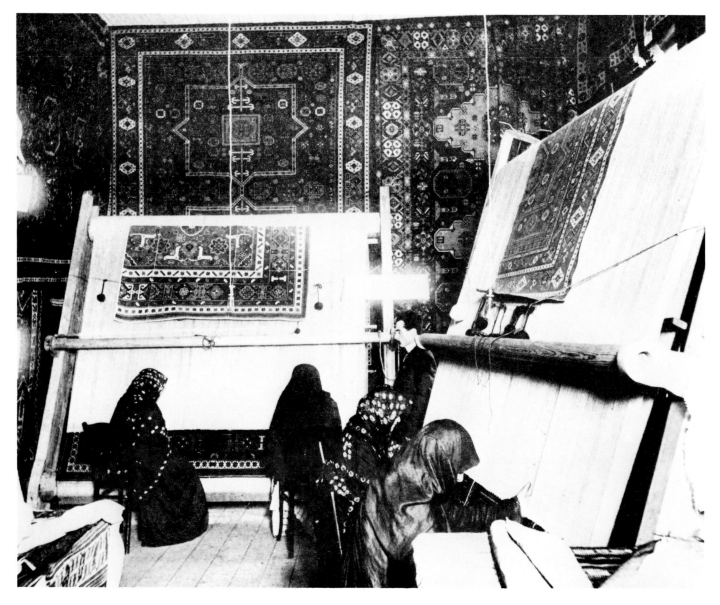

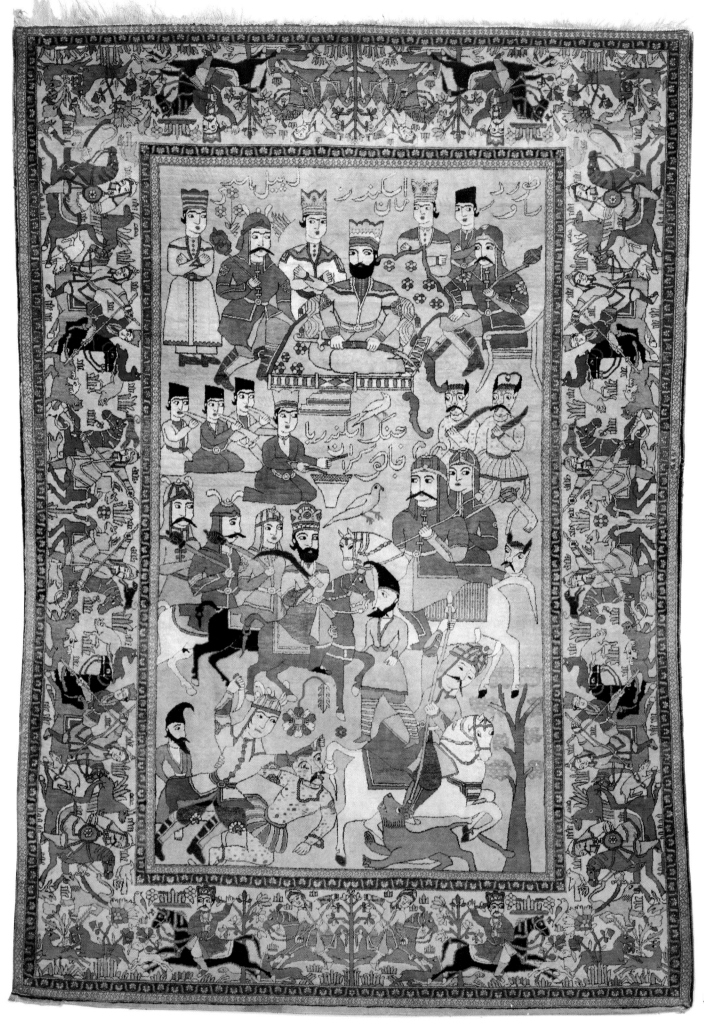

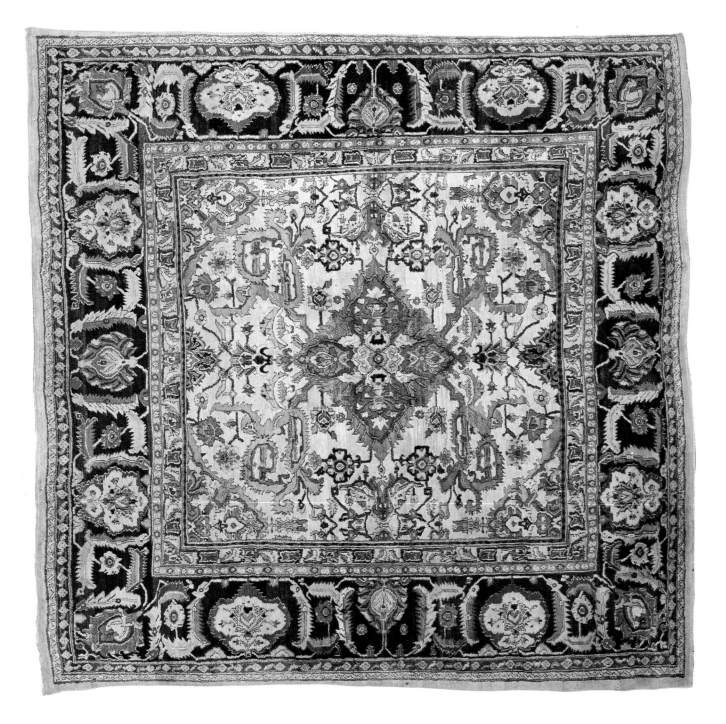

ABOVE: *Not all workshops use cartoons. In India and Pakistan the written-out pattern or talim is used (see p.83). For a carpet of this size the instructions would have been read from the talim by a 'caller' who chants out to the weavers the sequence and number of knots of each colour. Agra, first half of twentieth century.* 309 × 299 cm/121½ × 117½ in.

RIGHT: *Khorasan has been an important centre for the production of Persian workshop carpets from the sixteenth century until today. The carpets of Khorasan are of great interest and beauty but have not received the attention they deserve. The design of this piece derives from court art of the sixteenth century. Although the flowers have become angular and stylised in the manner of the cottage industry (compare p.111), the style is typical of eighteenth-century Khorasan work.* 556 × 287 cm/219 × 113 in.

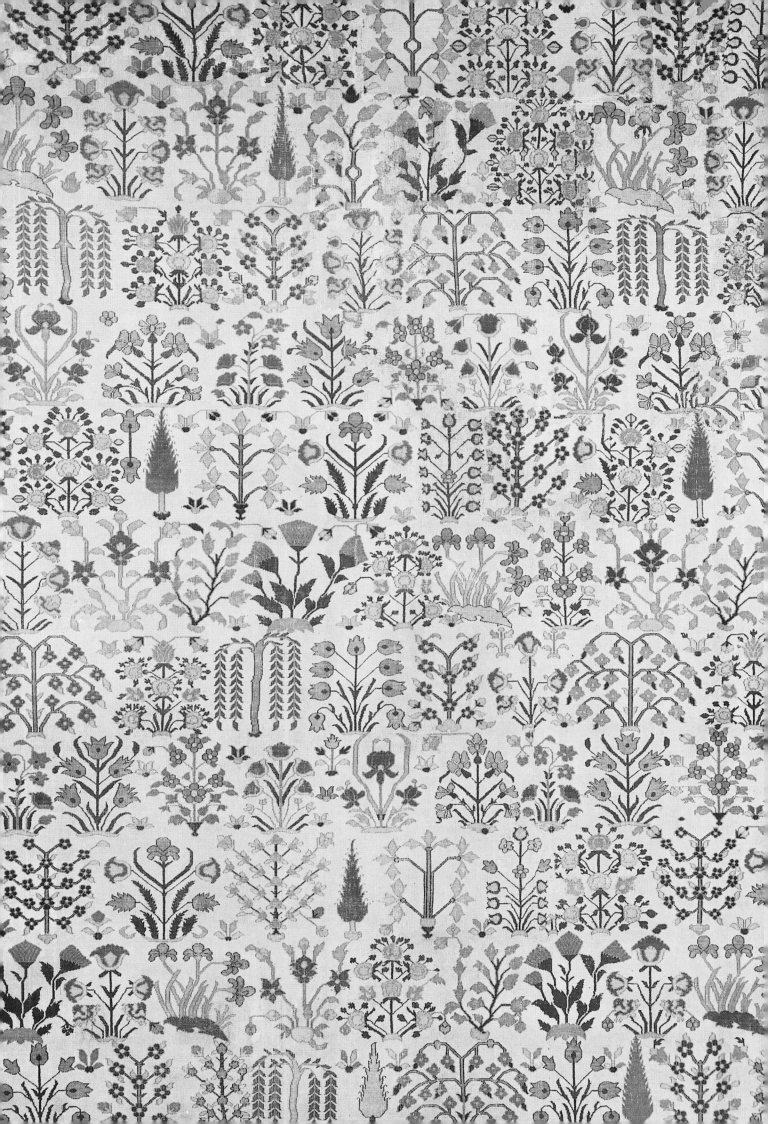

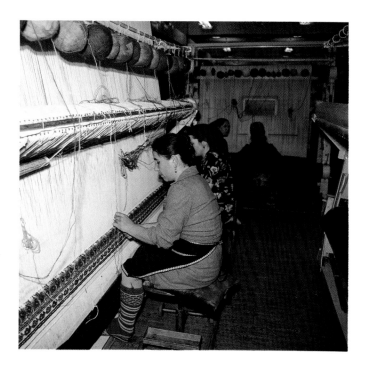

RIGHT: *In the 1920s the production of carpets in China expanded enormously. It is not always appreciated that carpets have been made in Chinese workshops since at least the seventeenth century. Early pieces are as rare as they are interesting. This rather tired example illustrates the Chinese designer's masterly use of space and preference for a perfectly balanced composition. In this respect the aesthetic approach of the Chinese designer is in marked contrast to the Persian approach in which overall surface decoration is important. Eighteenth century or earlier. 211 × 132 cm/83 × 52 in.*

LEFT: *Steel-framed roller beam looms in use in the state carpet factory of the Dagestan ASSR. Derbent, 1988.*

A carpet factory in Rumania, 1970s.

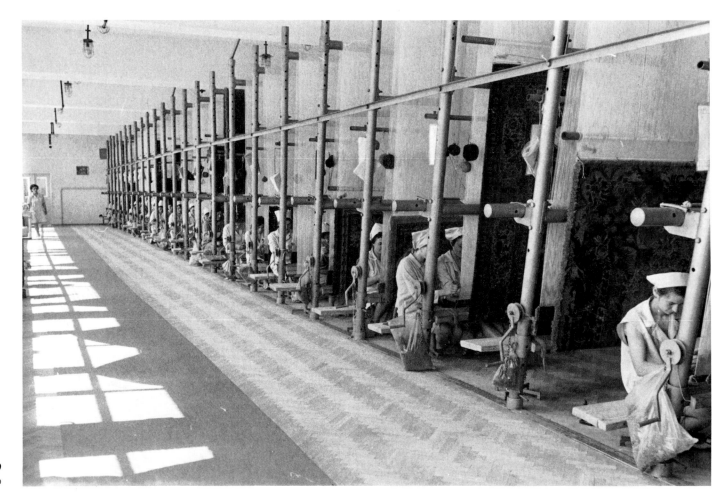

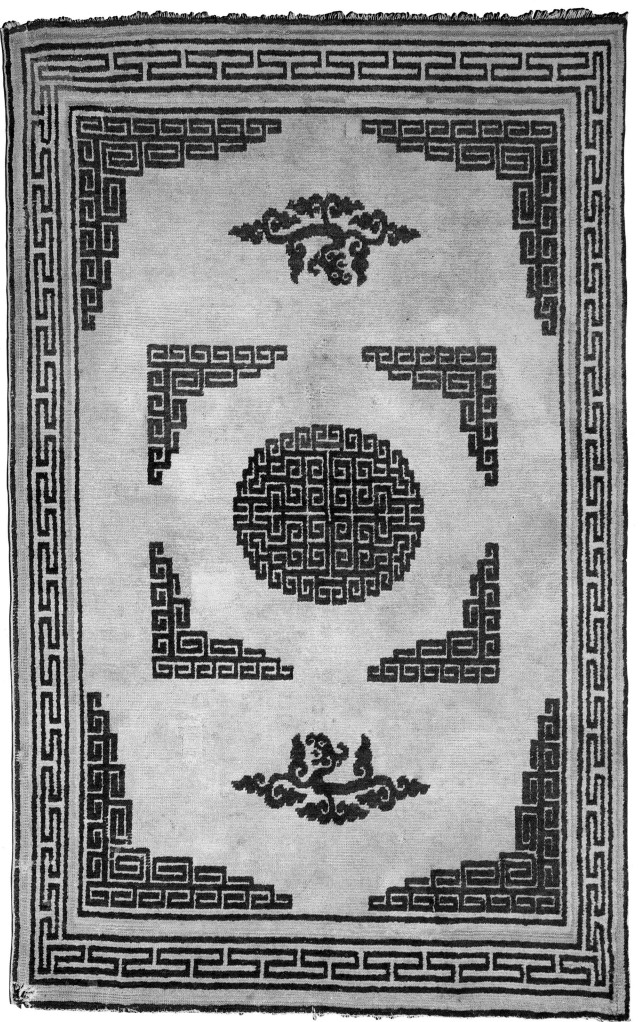

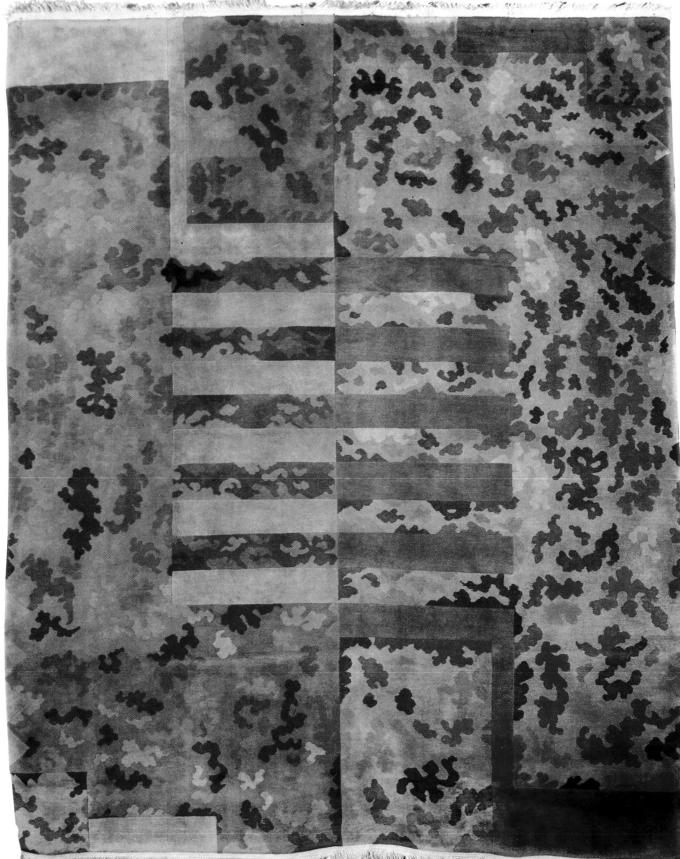

ABOVE: *This carpet stands out from the crowd because of its extraordinary design and colouring. For a brief period Art Deco carpets were woven in China to European designs. This is such a piece and illustrates the point that in a workshop any design can be executed – an outstanding challenge for the modern designer. Around 1930. 298 × 240 cm/117½ × 94½ in.*

RIGHT: *Newcomers to the big league of carpet manufacturers are the workshops in Nepal employing Tibetan refugees. Their carpets are made using a uniquely Tibetan weaving technique with wool of the highest quality. Their designs are original, yet typically Tibetan. They are not expensive and have recently become deservedly popular. 1981. 201 × 146 cm/79 × 57½ in.*

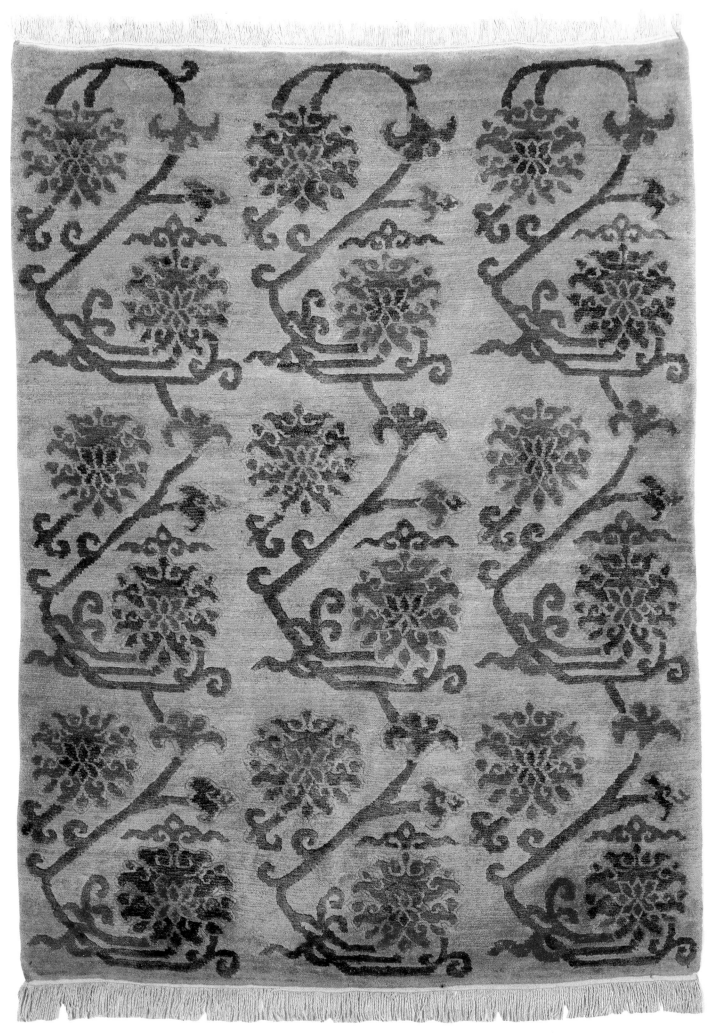

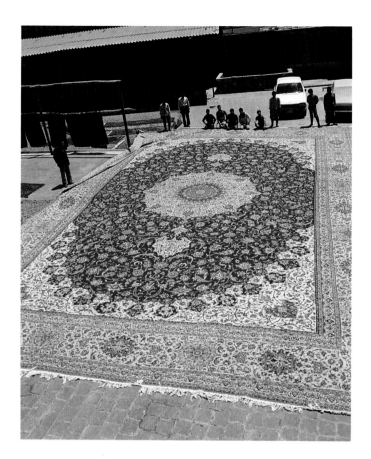

RIGHT: *In the 1920s workshops were established in the Kum Kapu district in the old quarter of Istanbul for the manufacture of carpets of the very highest quality. These found a ready market and are highly prized today. Their designs, as in this example, were often based on sixteenth- and seventeenth-century Persian originals. The luxurious effect of this silk carpet is enhanced by the recessed areas within the main motifs which are brocaded with glittering precious metal filament. Twentieth century. 310 × 210 cm/122 × 82½ in.*

LEFT: *One of the most astonishing developments in workshop production in recent years is the speculation by Persian merchant-entrepreneurs in the production of very large carpets. Each piece requires a huge investment of capital and may take several years to complete. This beautifully designed Nain carpet has an area of four hundred square metres. The largest on record, sold in 1986, was over one thousand square metres, probably the largest piled carpet ever made. Tehran, 1982.*

BELOW: *Turkish women weaving carpets from a cartoon. The workshop is equipped with wide looms which have many technical refinements. As weaving proceeds the carpet is wound onto the lower beam and the warps unwound from the upper. The metal rods are attached to a lever which prevents the upper beam from unwinding and keeps the warps under tension.*

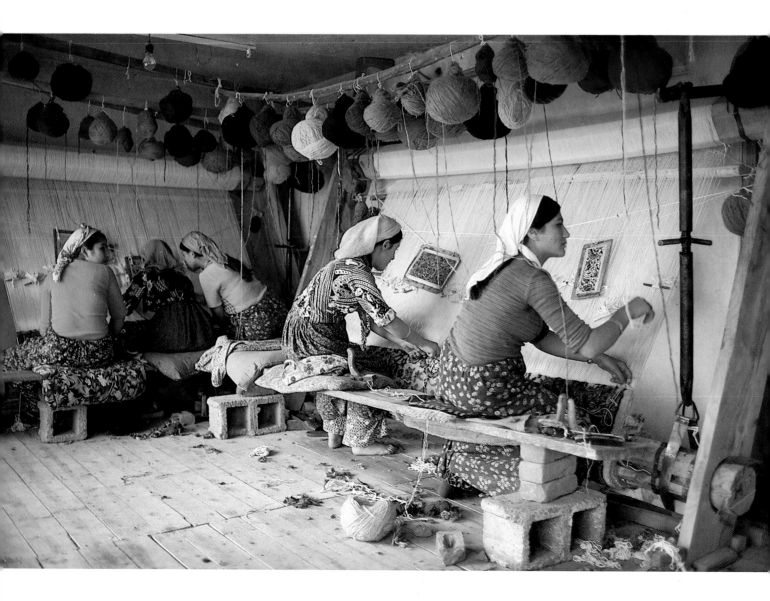

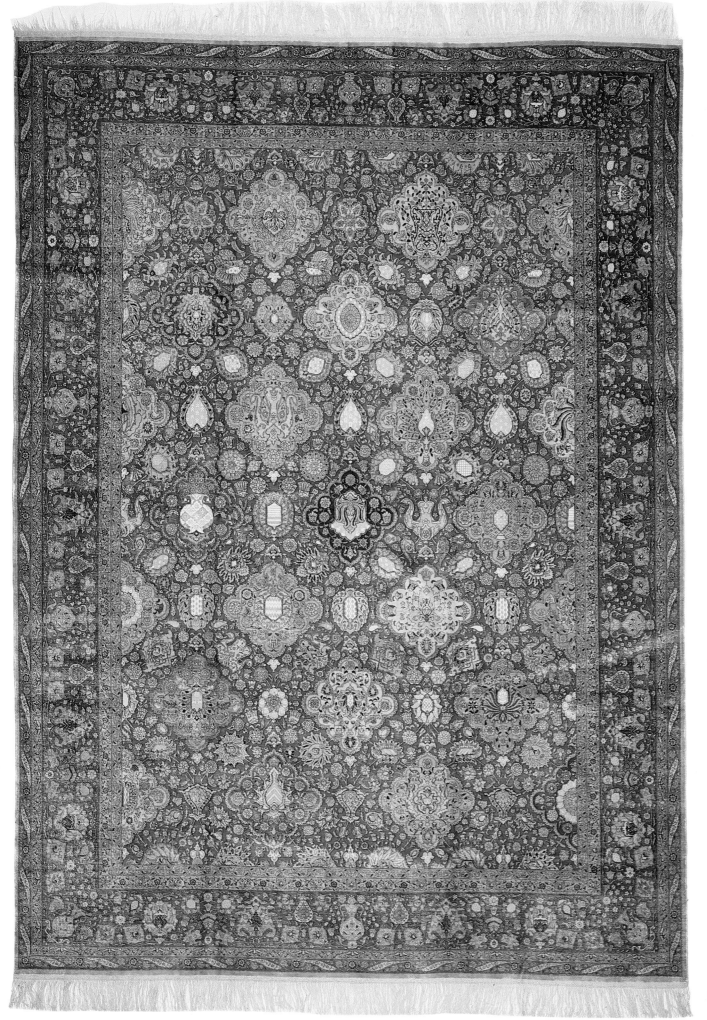

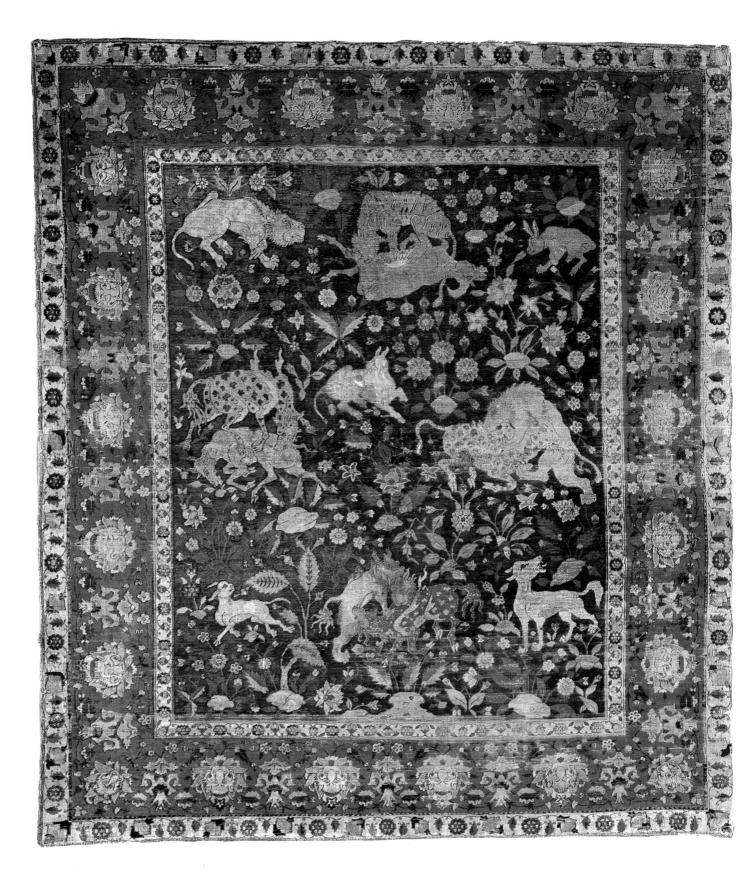

Chapter six

Court carpets

LEFT: *Shah Tahmasp (ruled 1524–76) is believed to have had his carpet workshop in Kashan, the centre of silk weaving in sixteenth-century Persia. Two large silk carpets, one in Boston, the other in Vienna, and a handful of small ones, bear witness to the extraordinary brilliance and technical mastery achieved by the craftsmen of Kashan. This small rug, together with the large carpets, were probably designed by the most talented artists in Shah Tahmasp's court. These court carpets have been a source of inspiration for the designers and weavers of countless other carpets from that day to this (see p.139).* 124 × 109 cm/49 × 43 in.

Background

Court carpets are so important historically that some discussion of them is necessary. In describing the events leading up to the establishment of the commercial workshops in the late nineteenth century, the impression may have been given that they were entirely new. It was only the scale of production which was new; true workshops directed towards the manufacture of large and technically advanced carpets had existed before. They were set up from time to time to serve the needs of the ruling courts, and a number of their remarkable products survive in museums, noble families, churches and the private collections of the wealthy. A brief look at the background to the establishment of these workshops helps towards a broader understanding of carpets as a whole.

Middle Asia has been invaded many times throughout history by the steppe nomads, tent dwelling pastoralists of the vast plains stretching from China to Hungary. The best-known incursion was that of the Mongol horde led by the much-feared Chingis Khan, in the twelfth century. Less well known are the earlier movements of the Turkmen or Turkoman nomads into central Asia beginning in the tenth century. In fact these two groups intermingled and between them had a profound influence on the art and culture of the Middle East. The reason for these huge migrations is not known with any certainty, but it could well have been as a result of competition for resources, or war, in which more easterly tribes forced their neighbours in a westerly direction. In these disturbed times powerful leaders emerged who welded separate tribal units into huge military con-federations. The self-sufficient life-style, high mobility, high-powered bows of special construction and formidable horseback archery, gave the nomads an overwhelming military advantage in the field. Wherever they came, after the phase of destruction, the new conquerors contrived to become great patrons of the arts and learning, and their noble families sired a number of the major dynasties in the history of Asia, among them the Sefavids of Persia, the Ottomans of Turkey, the Mamluks of Egypt and the Mughals of India. ('Mughal' or 'Mogul' is a corruption of the word 'Mongol'.) Even after several generations in power the rulers of these great dynasties never really forgot their tent dwelling past. This is reflected in their liking for tented encampments, the cultivation of the hunt and the architecture of their tombs and palaces, which owe much in form and layout to the tent. It is also reflected in the cultivation of the knotted pile carpet, that very art form which served as the main medium of artistic expression for their ancestors the steppe nomads.

Court styles and their influence

The rulers of the great Islamic courts of the sixteenth and seventeenth centuries were notable for their patronage of the most outstanding artists of the day. An important element of their patronage was the maintenance of a design atelier under the immediate direction of the court. The court artists produced designs in a variety of media including textiles and carpets, setting the pace for new styles and fashions. The carpets therefore, together with ceramics, calligraphy, paintings and so on, form part of the corpus of art produced under the patronage of the dynasty and are named accordingly. As the ruling houses were Muslim, the carpets are, with reason, classified as Islamic art. The workshops themselves were sometimes staffed by craftsmen in the direct employment of the court, but more often they acted as suppliers of goods of a standard and design specified by the royal atelier. In this case working for the court did not preclude the makers from engaging in normal commercial activities; nor did it prevent rival workshops from turning out similar, less expensive items in the same style. For example, a whole gradation of quality from the outstanding to the mediocre is seen in carpets and textiles worked in the Ottoman and Mughal court styles. High fashion then as now was surrounded by its imitators. More imitators copied the imitations and so the style worked its way outwards to towns and villages far from the capital. Women in the rural communities may never have seen the originals, and had no access to luxurious materials, so they copied the new style in the medium they were accustomed to. Velvets were translated into embroidery and knotted pile work (illus. p.20); luxurious carpets with silk foundations were copied using less costly yarns. Inevitably the designs were adapted and corrupted but they lived on to be incorporated into the folk tradition. Here they survive in rustic form centuries after the originals have passed out of fashion.

Some wonderful carpets have survived which are firmly associated with the Mamluk court of Egypt. They are believed to have been woven in Cairo but there are still uncertainties about this. The whole surface is covered in a glorious abstract statement in red, green and blue – there is nothing comparable in the whole Islamic world. The earliest date from the late fifteenth century and they continue through to the seventeenth when the style changed from centralised geometric patterns to overall floral designs using the same colour scheme. The change followed the fashion for floral designs set by the Ottoman court in Turkey. Unlike other works commissioned by the courts, Mamluk carpets had a negligible influence on later weaving. They remain an isolated and mysterious group of high achievement. As a family they have few

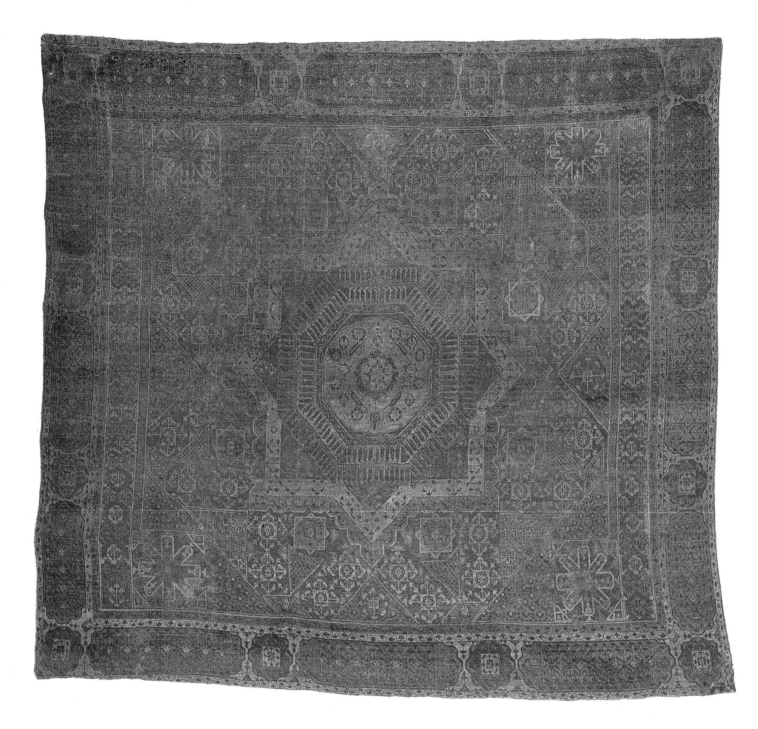

ABOVE: *Perhaps the most marvellous and mysterious of all carpets are those associated with the sixteenth-century rulers of Egypt, the Mamluks. They have strongly centralised designs worked in luminous green and (insect-dyed) red, which seem to radiate an assembly of smaller geometric figures. The pinnacle of achievement of this design school is a silk carpet in the Museum of Art and Industry in Vienna. This small square carpet, contemporary with the silk carpet in Vienna, was first published in 1892 and has survived in remarkable condition. Sixteenth century. 258 × 240 cm/101½ × 94½ in.*

RIGHT: *Carpets produced for the Ottoman court in the sixteenth century were enormously influential. They were copied and recopied in towns and villages throughout the country, some versions even reaching the nomadic encampments. This example, now in the Kuwait National Museum, is made with the finest materials and has been worked from an exact cartoon known to have been used in the making of other court rugs from this period. 172 × 125 cm/67½ × 49 in.*

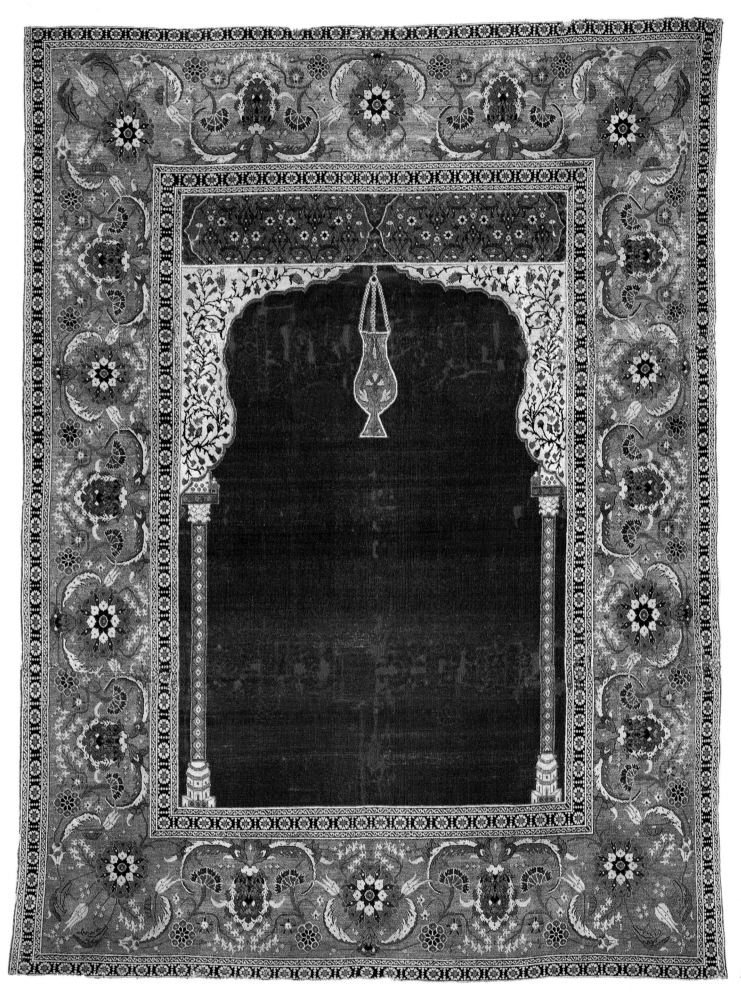

This large silk carpet must have been made in a workshop equipped with technically advanced looms, highly skilled weavers, draughtsmen and cartoon makers. Technical details point to Turkey as the source. Only the workshop at Hereke, patronised by the Ottoman court, or the workshops in the Kum Kapu quarter of Istanbul, were sufficiently advanced to have woven such a piece. As it is a copy of a sixteenth-century carpet in the Museum of Art and Industry in Vienna, which was first published in 1926, it is most likely to have been woven in Istanbul in the 1920s. 617 × 310 cm/243 × 122 in.

known ancestors, descendants or relatives.

In Turkey there was a vigorous domestic tradition even in the fifteenth century. Carpets evidently made in cottage industries were being exported to Europe at this time, as paintings of the period reveal. Against this background a flamboyant new court style developed during the second half of the sixteenth century. Large curving feathery leaves, palmettes, rosettes and tracery are combined into a graceful swirling pattern. Tulips, hyacinths and carnations were added later.

At this time a new prayer rug design was introduced with an architectural theme, featuring arches supported by columns (illus. p.149). The presentation of a space divided by columns is familiar in medieval European art. How and why the architectural theme entered the Islamic prayer rug and the connection, if any, with European art is uncertain. Prayer rugs prior to the Ottoman inter-pretation included the arched form but no columns. The

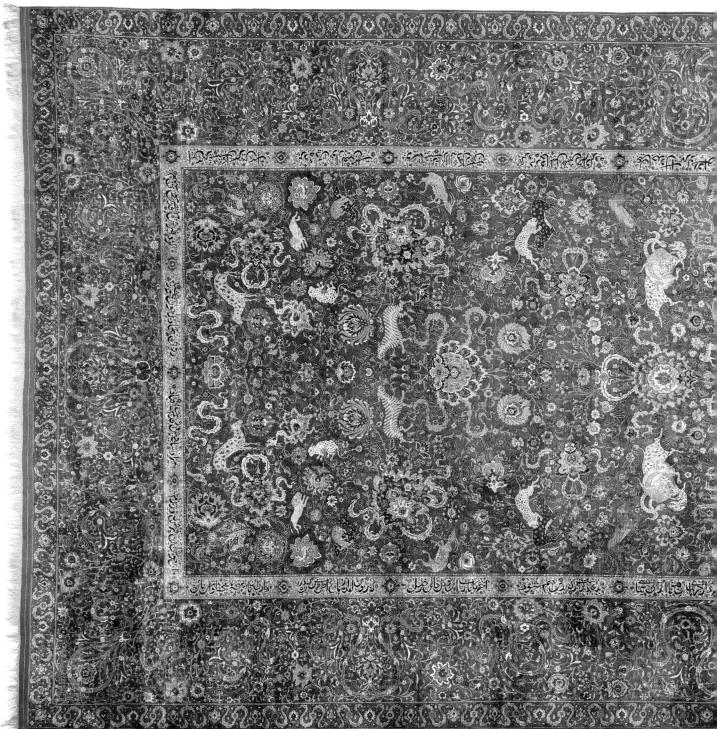

reformulation of the arched prayer design in the late sixteenth century gave Turkish weavers a rich theme which, after three hundred years, can still be found in a great array of different interpretations (illus. pp.4, 126 and 129).

Another style of luxury carpet was supplied to the Ottoman court during the nineteenth century, probably from a factory at Hereke set up in the 1860s.[12] They are extremely finely knotted on a silk foundation with interpretations of sixteenth-century Persian designs. After early difficulties, including a fire, the Hereke factory perfected its lavish carpets. When they appeared in small numbers in the west they were initially mistaken for weavings of the sixteenth century and have often been published as such. With the lapse of the Ottoman dynasty in 1918 Hereke carpets reached a wider public and the factory now produces some of the finest weavings on the market. The possible existence of carpets

made for the Ottoman court between the seventeenth century and the 1860s has been overlooked by scholars and it is still possible that some atypical carpets in the Persian style were made in the eighteenth and early nineteenth centuries. One large silk carpet (illus. p.150) has the character of a piece made for the Ottoman court but is unusual in that its design, instead of being in the Persian manner, has been copied directly from a known sixteenth-century Persian carpet in the Museum of Art and Industry in Vienna. It may therefore have been made in the 1920s after the publication of the Vienna carpet.

Persian court carpets are a study in themselves. Our knowledge of where the surviving court carpets were made is still fragmentary; much of it is scholarly guesswork. The earliest court carpets were probably woven in Tabriz during the Turkoman period in the late fifteenth century. They have a centralised design consisting of a more or less circular medallion of lobed or

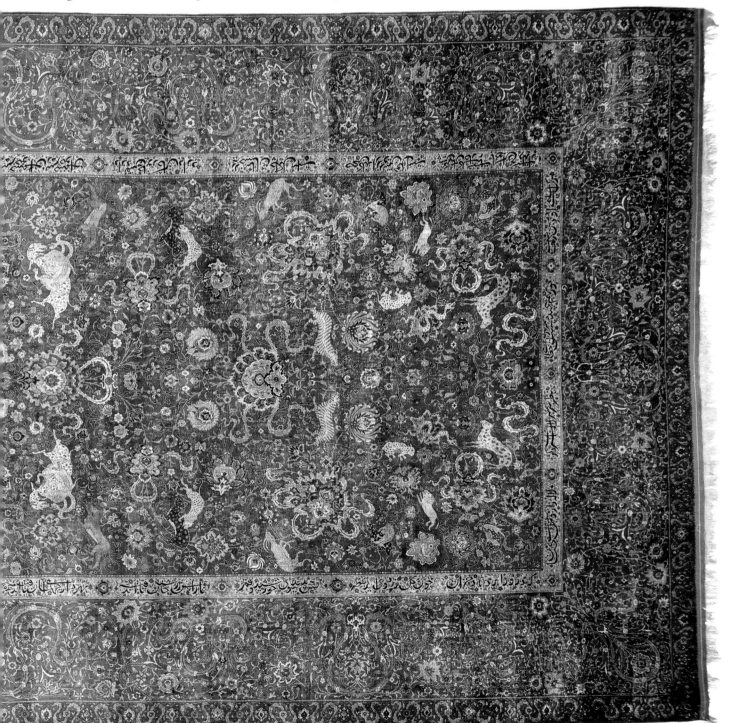

151

crenellated outline placed on a field covered with an endlessly repeating design of branched tracery. The medallion design was the great contribution made by Persia to the world of carpets. It is perhaps best known in the famous Ardebil carpet in the Victoria and Albert Museum, London. Like many artistic ideas, the theme of the central medallion is an old one with ancient religious and metaphysical roots in the art of central Asia. Its ultimate origin is probably in the far east. In Persia it found new expression and has been the subject of innumerable interpretations over the centuries. It continues to this day as the most popular and widely used of all carpet designs.

In the early sixteenth century, under threat of invasion by the Turks, the Sefavid court moved to Qazvin. Carpets with the medallion design probably continued to be woven in Tabriz which was the largest city in Persia and remained the commercial capital for a long time to come. At Qazvin Shah Tahmasp attracted to his court some great miniature painters. The hand of one of his best artists can be recognised in the design of two outstanding carpets, one in the Museum of Art and Industry in Vienna and the other in the Museum of Fine Arts, Boston. Both are made of silk enriched with precious metal filament and they are thought to have been woven in Kashan, the centre of silk weaving in Persia and the probable site of the royal carpet workshop. A group of small carpets, some with a design of fantastic animals in combat and others with variations of the medallion theme are also believed to have been woven in the same workshop. These carpets required enormous resources of money, technical skill and artistic accomplishment and represent the pinnacle of achievement in the art of carpets in Persia. Kashan remained an important centre for the production of fine carpets throughout the sixteenth century and on into the seventeenth.

At the end of the sixteenth century Shah Abbas moved his court to Isfahan and built there a glorious royal capital, endowing it with pavilions, palaces and richly tiled mosques. He also established a carpet workshop for the production of carpets 'of silk and gold'. These were used as an instrument of diplomacy and sent as royal gifts to the rulers of potentially friendly countries. Many have survived in the treasuries of the noble families of Europe. These carpets were intentionally extravagant, even vulgar in their overt luxuriousness, and were clearly designed to impress. They were so popular that European noble families, rich enough to engage in a little game of international one-upmanship, commissioned carpets from Isfahan and ordered the weavers to put the family coat of arms into the design.

In the seventeenth century Kerman was famous for its carpets. Strictly speaking, these were not court carpets, but they were of comparable quality. We know that a carpet was specially ordered and designed for the decoration of the shrine of the Sufi saint, Sheikh Nematollah, at nearby Mahan. There were other centres of excellence in Persia. A design school existed in Khorasan, perhaps in Mashhad and another in Herat (see p.139). In the turbulent times of the eighteenth and early nineteenth centuries carpet-weaving declined and some centres ceased production. When it revived in the 1870s, the old centres of excellence – Tabriz, Kashan, Isfahan and Kerman – soon returned to the forefront.

No workshops capable of producing court quality carpets appear to have been established in the Caucasus. Glorious carpets were made there from the seventeenth century onwards and large numbers exported, but they look like the products of medium technology workshops or the cottage industry.

India has no longstanding indigenous tradition of knotted pile carpets. The first court carpets were made there in the second half of the sixteenth century by craftsmen brought from Persia. At first they had a Persian character, but in the seventeenth century a distinctive Mughal style emerged, and by the middle of the century they had reached an astonishing peak of technical and artistic perfection. Carpets from this period are decorated with realistic flowering plants and lattice designs. The best have a silk foundation and a woollen pile made from the fleece of the mountain goat of Tibet and Ladakh which has the dyeing and wearing properties of wool but the visual and tactile character of silk. The sumptuous effect of those carpets made during the reigns of Shah Jahan and Aurangzeb has never been surpassed.

Under the patronage of the Indian Nawabs carpet workshops continued shakily into the nineteenth century when they were joined by the jail workshops in an expanding commercial production. Contrary to the tradition in most other countries, Indian carpets are woven mainly by men.

Mention should be made here of carpets woven in China for the Ming rulers. The earliest surviving examples date from the sixteenth century. They have a woollen pile and, as might be expected, are designed with motifs having royal associations, such as the five-clawed dragon.

Finally, Muslim Spain was an important carpet centre. Literary references to royal acquisitions go back to the thirteenth century, and the earliest examples date from the fourteenth. From the fifteenth a number of carpets with royal associations survive. They are decorated with the coats of arms of royal families and were presumably specially commissioned. In the sixteenth and seventeenth centuries Spanish carpet designs acquired an increasingly European flavour.

The system of court patronage is best seen as a special development of the relationship between a commercial workshop and its customer. The royal workshops produced the most technically accomplished, sumptuous, and visually prodigious carpets ever made in response to the demands of a customer with limitless funds and an appetite for the best that money could buy.

RIGHT: *Carpets woven for the Mughal court in the sixteenth century were made with Persian-style designs. Soon the court designers developed a uniquely Indian style. In the seventeenth century Indian carpets reached a peak of technical perfection which has never been surpassed. Their designs have remained influential to this day. This eighteenth-century carpet retains many features of those luxurious weavings. The pile is made from the underwool of the mountain goat of Ladakh and Tibet which looks and feels like silk but has the dyeing and wearing properties of wool.* 310 × 180 cm/122 × 71 in.

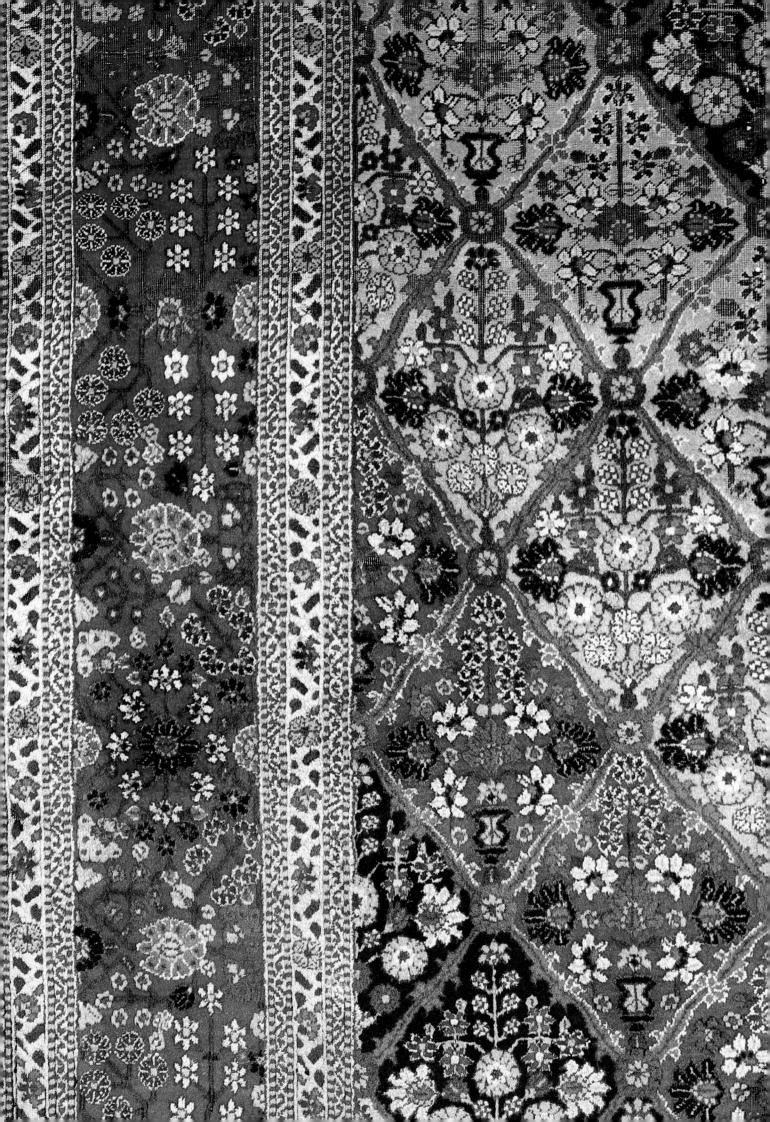

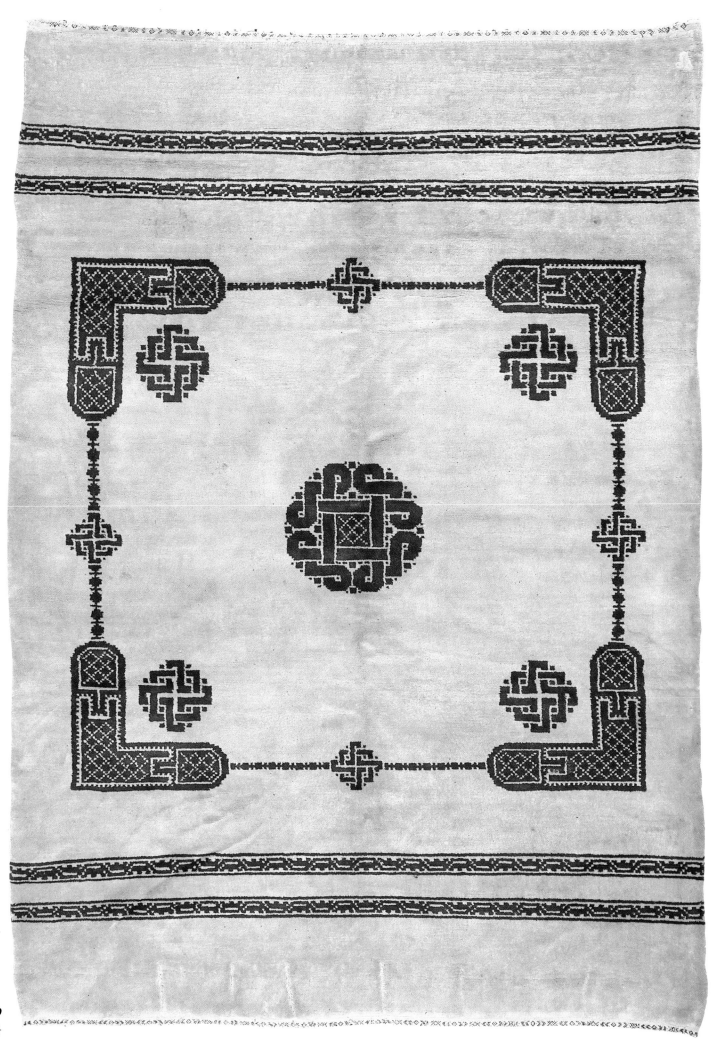

Chapter seven

Symbolism

Of all the questions about carpets the most difficult are those about the meaning of their patterns. In rural communities children learn to weave patterns by imitation in the same way as they learn language or pick up tunes. If you go to a village and ask a weaver the 'meaning' of the designs she uses, she would not be able to tell you. The designs all have nicknames, such as silver plates, ear ring, yellow-head, mouse tail, four fish, boxes, arrows and footprints – terms which are of course descriptive, just as we speak of scrolls, latch hooks, key frets, waves, stars, bird heads and medallions. Such names have no value in determining the root meaning of a design or how it entered their vocabulary – questions the rural weaver would have no more idea about than the man in the street would have about the root meaning of the words he uses.

To understand the 'meaning' of carpet patterns we must know their history and origin. This study is at an early stage. Patterns, like words, have entered the vocabulary of tribal and village ornament from many different sources. The later they entered, the easier it is to identify their source. Let us take as an example the weavings of the Caucasus. During the huge expansion of carpet weaving in the second half of the nineteenth century, many new patterns were introduced. They were copied from local flatweaves, embroideries, Persian and Turkish silks, European textiles and printed matter. An earlier group of designs can be identified as having originated in Persia during the sixteenth century. Although they have undergone many modifications over the centuries, their connection with the original designs is easy to trace. A few designs still used in the Caucasus have their origin in an international Islamic style of the fifteenth century. Take away all these designs and you are left with a residue of even older motifs, the origin of most of which can only be guessed at. Cognate forms can be identified in the weavings of other peoples, such as the Turks and Turkmen, but cannot be said to have originated from them; just as the cognate forms of many basic words reveal the common ancestry of the Indo-European languages. This residue of 'basic' patterns can be thought of as the ancient core of a design vocabulary, linked to the cognate forms of other weaving peoples through common ancestry or ancient contacts. We can imagine how two branches of a tribe became separated; inevitably they were exposed to different influences. Weavers learned new designs which were added to the old, which in turn were slowly altered and forgotten. After many generations the outward appearance of the weavings of the two groups were completely different, but if their core motifs were identified and compared they would be found to be related through a common structure.

LEFT: *The design of this north African carpet is copied from a late Roman ('Coptic') textile. Its design refers to ideas of great antiquity which are present, perhaps unconsciously, in many Asian carpets (see pp.80, 114, 148). It is in effect a model of an ancient concept of the world. The medallion marks the 'centre', a metaphysical centre, which can be anywhere and indeed there are many 'centres'. By putting himself 'in the centre' man is able to make a connection with the upper world, source of light, life and order. The centre is signified by the sun at its zenith, often represented as a tree or a pillar surmounted by a disc or ball. Here it takes the form of an endless knot. Space is indicated by the four cardinal directions, and space-time by the marking of the four corners of the world. In each corner endless knot forms mark the 'four suns' which are the directions of the rising and setting sun at the vernal and autumnal equinoxes. Nineteenth century. 229 × 156 cm/90 × 61½ in.*

In the study of other facets of human life, such as music, religion or ritual, where tradition (in its root meaning of 'handed on') plays an important part, the same is found to be true. New forms do not immediately displace the old but are added to them. The old forms and ideas, continuing alongside the new, are buried without being lost. In this way ancient forms can survive over long periods. For example, Béla Bartók, studying Turkish folk music in the 1930s, found specific musical forms which provided 'irrefutable proof' of identity between the musical traditions of Hungary and Turkey which must date back to the sixth or seventh centuries, a time when the ancestors of the Turks and the ancestors of the Hungarians shared a common nomadic life on the Eurasian steppes.[14] Likewise, worship by Muslims at the stone *Ka'aba* in Mecca by sunwise circumambulation is a ritual form which can be traced back to the bronze age in other parts of Asia.

Carpet scholars are still at the descriptive stage in their studies, recording the vocabulary of motifs in different weaving traditions. The process of unravelling their origin and meaning has barely begun. Current work suggests that the core motifs found in the rural weavings of western and central Asia derive from a pre-Islamic religious iconography of great antiquity, perhaps of Shamanic origin. According to this scheme the world is divided horizontally into three levels: upper, middle (our world), and lower. The upper world, signified by the sun, is the source of outer and inner illumination. Contact with the upper world takes place along a vertical axis, variously represented as a tree, pillar or post at 'the centre of the world' (the axle of the world), hence the sacred tree, or tree of life. Although these motifs are still alive in the spiritual and artistic language of Shamanism, perhaps the most ancient living religion in Asia, they exist as core motifs buried in the religious imagery, iconography and rituals of Hinduism, Judaism, Buddhism, Christianity and Islam, and are easily recognisable in the religions of ancient Greece and India. The most direct way to recover the meaning of these core motifs is to study how the myths, rituals and religion of the ancient and modern peoples of the steppes relate to their artistic language – a task which has hardly begun.

To illustrate the caution that must be exercised in looking for the 'meaning' of designs, a good example is the Turkmen carpet illustrated on p.64. Early books describe the rounded designs as flowers or the footprints of an elephant. Others propose in all seriousness that they represent the rounded tents of the Turkmen, with the grid of connecting lines representing irrigation channels. A more sophisticated idea is that they are tribal emblems depicting totemic birds. All these views share the belief that the designs represent or are pictures of something. This conception is based on our habitual way of thinking and seeing, and bears no relation to the thought processes of the people who wove them. The designs no more represent something than a tune represents an apple, and to try to discover a 'meaning' in that sense is to impose our own thought forms on another culture.

Of course there are recognisable animals, birds, human figures, combs, water jugs – even teapots and samovars – in some carpets, but again we must be careful not to be too hasty in thinking we understand their significance. Can we really understand the meaning of a rug full of animals to a person whose life is bound up with them and whose livelihood depends on them? To give an example, the child on p.50 wears on her head a triangular object made of cloth with something hanging from it. This is an amulet protecting the child from harm. Weavers commonly put amulets into their carpets for protection. They are triangular and usually have comb-like projections from the long edge: see p.17 (left hand side, three rows from the bottom), p.37 (several), p.62 (many), p.64 (top left corner), p.76 (bottom left corner), p.85 (bottom left corner), p.91 (top left corner of inner field), etc. It is important to realise that this design does not represent an amulet, it *is* an amulet – it protects by its presence. In other words the device in the rug has a materiality, it generates a field of force able to interact with other unseen forces and is not merely an intellectual abstraction.

Workshop carpets are a different matter. Their designs cater for and are influenced by an urban and cosmopolitan clientele. Representational themes are common, ranging from gardens through idealised portraits of famous people to copies of French paintings.

Conscious symbolism (in the classical Greek sense of the word) does exist in carpets. In the court art of sixteenth-century Persia, Sufi ideas were deeply influential. The Sufis practised a profound, often ecstatic spirituality, passed on as a living tradition by a direct chain of transmission from teacher to pupil. There were (and are) many brotherhoods in which different techniques and attitudes were taught. Sufi ideas found expression in literature, poetry and the visual arts. The king embodied the kingly virtues and was seen as the 'pole of religion' round which all revolved – a classic example of a core motif retained from ancient times. Several carpets designed by court artists of this period survive, among them the famous hunting carpet in the Museum of Fine Arts, Boston, which is redolent with Sufi imagery. It is designed around a central focus, presumably where the king's throne stood. In the field royal figures on horseback ride through a supernatural landscape engaged in an energetic hunt. One fights a lion with his bare hands, a royal motif dating back two thousand years. The combat can be seen as a symbol of the struggle of man with his lower nature on the path from existence to being: the journey towards the ultimate unity, where 'there remaineth but the face of thy Lord resplendant with Majesty and Bounty'.

Various themes from court carpets of that period, designed with a precise and intentional imagery, have been copied and recopied over the centuries to enter the popular vocabulary, their original meaning forgotten. There they remain like fragments of an ancient parable preserved in a children's story, waiting for the handsome prince to fight his way through the tangled thicket of ignorance and forgetfulness to bestow his awakening kiss upon the one who sleeps.

RIGHT: *This comfortable looking bag has a traditional design in the local style. Madder and indigo are still used to dye the wool. Shavak village, Tunceli province, Turkey.*

'*Because the eye can in a moment encompass the whole surface of a rug it is assumed that it can be seen at a glance. But no worthy piece gives up its meaning so lightly. Its inner beauty is revealed only to a sympathetic and leisurely observation which knows how to read the pattern. The finer examples are often as elaborately composed as a symphony and as sensitively organised as a sonnet. The elements of the design are like notes in a melody or words in a poem: only as they are individually understood, interpreted and assembled is their meaning made plain. In order to see a rug, therefore, it is necessary to sense the quality of each component part, to feel the manifold relations of the parts to each other and to comprehend them all in a harmonious and significant unity. The great carpets are ready to declare their glory, and a wonderful glory it is, to those and only those who will make this effort of attention.*'

A. U. Pope, 1926.

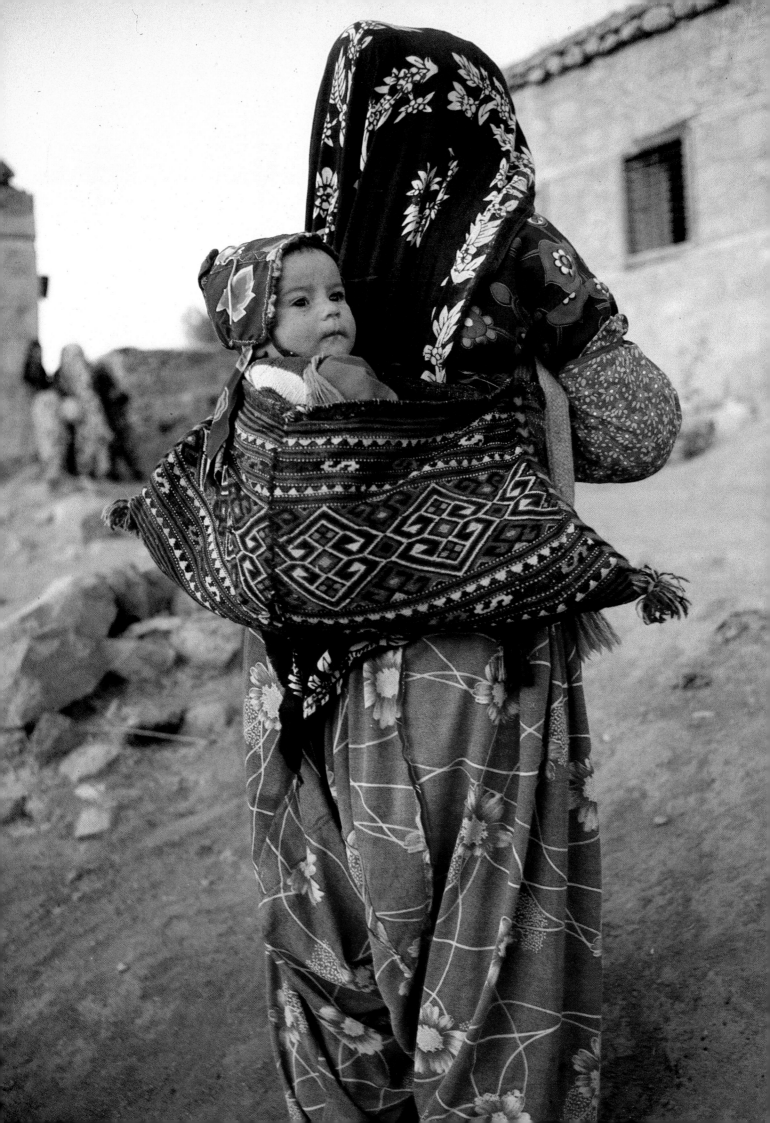

Notes for Buyers and Sellers

For some reason carpet traders have never had a good reputation, though they behave no worse than dealers in other specialised goods such as furs, jewellery and antiques, which are also sold to a public almost completely ignorant of the objects they are buying. At the outset, therefore, it must be clear that the more buyers understand about the product they are buying the fewer problems they are likely to have. These notes describe how carpets are bought and sold and point out some of the difficulties likely to be encountered.

BUYING NEW CARPETS

The organisation of the trade in new carpets is quite complex. In the countries where a free market operates, small traders collect individual pieces from weavers in the towns and villages and sell them to major local dealers who in turn sell to one of the main merchants in the big cities. Foreign buyers, normally large wholesalers, then ship goods in bulk to their warehouses in Europe or the USA. The main warehouses of the international wholesale carpet trade are in New York, London and Hamburg. Retailers and department stores buy from the wholesalers and put them on sale to the public. Some more confident retailers go to the country of origin and buy locally from the main merchants, but the price they get depends on their skill and experience and is not guaranteed to be better than that offered by a European wholesaler who has been buying in bulk for years and knows every aspect of the business. A few small dealers, shopkeepers and boutique owners short-circuit this system by going to the carpet-producing countries and by dint of enthusiasm and hard work find interesting goods at reasonable prices. However, they are often inexperienced in matters of international trade and may have hair-raising experiences with lost goods and incorrect customs documentation.

Whenever and however you buy, four things must be remembered. First, there are no bargains in the new carpet business: if you believe advertisements about clearance sales, urgent liquidations and warehouse prices you are naive. Second, if you are tempted to buy 'for investment', don't. Third, the only valid reason for buying a carpet is because you really like it, and fourth, you are going to spend a long time looking at your purchase, so examine it carefully and choose at leisure.

The department store
The advantages of buying in a department store are that there will be a fairly good choice with no heavy sales pressure and perhaps good credit facilities available. The mark-up is often surprisingly low and many department stores have sales once or twice a year when over three-quarters of their annual turnover can be made. Goods brought in for the occasion are likely to be cheaper because they are often consigned on a sale-or-return basis. This can be a good time to buy if you know what you want.

The high street store
A test of whether your local carpet shop is any good or not is how long it has been in business. The 'established reputation' still seems to be the only guide open to the public, although a firm that announces on its letterhead 'established in 1821' could well have bought the name from a defunct company. These are usually one-man businesses, so if you are thinking of buying from such a store it is worth making several visits, meeting the proprietor and establishing some kind of rapport with him.

Before parting with your money you are strongly advised to agree several things in advance. First, ask if you may take the carpet home and see what it looks like for a few days. The vendor should readily agree to this, be willing to have it insured (on *his* policy), and be prepared to deliver if it is not too far.

Second, ask what happens if you want to bring the carpet back. It is a rare and generous dealer who will offer to return your money and put the carpet back into stock. It is a great aggravation for a dealer to get goods returned, but he will normally agree to take them back for the sake of his reputation. You can expect, however, to be offered goods by way of replacement and you can be sure the dealer will extract some premium to compensate him for the trouble you have caused. Alternatively, he will offer to sell the carpet on your behalf. This second option is extremely unsatisfactory. You have no control over the sale or its terms and the carpet could remain unsold for years. When finally you are completely discouraged the dealer will tell you that a buyer came in the other day and offered half the price you wanted. You will be persuaded to accept and only later will you discover that the buyer was the dealer himself.

Third, ask if he will accept an offer for the piece. Though bargaining is not part of normal shopping tactics in the west, it is always worth a try and you are likely to gain respect rather than derision by doing so.

Fourth, ask about the terms of payment: these days, the terms are as important as the price. See if you can get favourable terms. If not, demand a discount for immediate payment in full.

Boutiques, craft shops and small dealers
It can be great fun to buy from a small shop. The owner will be keen to do business, will probably be short of money and, as likely as not, will be an enthusiast. He will not have a large selection but he may deal in things outside the main stream of commercial goods and have local knowledge of how and where they are made. It is always worth making an offer for something, but do not expect extended payments and do not expect to be greeted with open arms if you take something back.

Fashionable shops in capital cities
There is a street in every big city where the wealthy and fashionable like to shop or be seen shopping. Luxury carpets have now joined jewels, furs and designer clothes. If you have the money, or enjoy shopping in such places because it flatters your ego, then be content when you see the same object on sale for a third of the price elsewhere. The style of business in these locations tends to be aimed at 'oncers' – people who buy once and never return. You are likely to be persuaded by a well groomed salesman that the marvellous silk you are being offered is a great investment. If you knew how large a premium you were paying for your 'investment' – in other words, the difference between what you have to pay and what you could realise from its sale – you would realise that not even your great-grandchildren could make a profit.

Closing-down sales
If you have not come across the closing-down sale you soon will. This new method of selling carpets, now widespread in Europe and the USA, is based on the very simple principle that avarice, cupidity and greed are unfailing sources of positive motivation in human beings.

A short lease is taken in a good central location. A new retail carpet shop opens up, is active, does a bit of advertising and trades for long enough to become known. After a few months a huge advertising campaign is mounted announcing that the shop is closing and that all stock must be cleared at incredibly low prices. The gullible public pours in, believing that this is an opportunity not be be missed, and that the chance to buy a bargain will be one in the eye for that stodgy old trader across the street who has been overcharging people for years.

Needless to say, there are no bargains to be had. You are induced to part with your money because you believe that you are getting a bargain. The trader moves on to the next location and the story is repeated. It is a selling technique based on simple deception and human weakness. The locally established traders feel it is unfair competition and harmful to anyone trying to build up and maintain a business in the long term. Attempts have been made in some countries to make the practice illegal.

Brokers

Another new selling method has emerged in recent years. The theory is good; the practice less so. Brokers offer a service: they will take you round one or more of the main carpet warehouses where tens of thousands of carpets are stored. Normally the general public cannot deal with the wholesaler direct, but thanks to the brokers' special position they can take you anywhere, so an enormous choice is open to you. Since it is a wholesale warehouse you will, in theory, be able to buy for much less than you would have to pay in a department store or retail shop. And for this service you pay nothing, because the broker is paid by the seller in the form of a 'small commission'. As part of the service you are likely to get a heavy sales pitch about how good an investment carpets are.

In practice, however, things are not as they seem. Brokers are tolerated in the main warehouses, and they do take clients more or less anywhere. But looking through stacks of carpets is a time-consuming business and often requires the assistance of two warehouse employees. In the time it takes the broker, the client and the two employees to look through the stacks and choose a single piece, a retailer might have bought a hundred pieces. To compensate for this, the seller gives a 'special' price – a specially *high* price – amounting to something just less than the full retail price elsewhere. This extra mark-up is used automatically for any client a broker brings in because the price must include the broker's 'small commission', which is usually around 30 per cent. Brokers, of course, are interested in making a sale and not in getting the price down – the higher the price the greater their commission.

If you accept that you are unlikely to get any major price advantage and really want the range of choice available in a warehouse, you can get a letter of introduction from a retailer or department store – a long-established practice respected by all parties.

There is a special problem in buying from warehouses. Most of them hold carpets in bond. That is to say, none of the payments normally due when goods enter the country have been made, a device which facilitates the process of re-export. If you remove a carpet from a bonded warehouse without exporting it, all duties and taxes must be paid immediately. So once you have bought a carpet and taken it out of the warehouse, it cannot be put back into bond.

The evidence that new carpets are a 'good investment' is extremely shaky. It is possible to demonstrate that some types of carpet have risen in price between this date and that. The problem is that the premium you have to pay when buying and selling is such a large percentage of the total that the only person who fails to make a profit will probably be you. Buying for investment is probably the worst of all reasons for buying a carpet. Think of the carpets you buy as consumer goods: be pleased when they last for several generations, be delighted when they increase in value, but do not buy in the belief that you will necessarily make a profit whenever you want to cash in.

BUYING OLD AND ANTIQUE CARPETS

Old carpets have no accepted price. How much a piece is worth is a matter of opinion, which is arrived at by weighing up several different things: age, rarity, condition, artistic quality, quality of workmanship, quality of materials, original production cost in labour and materials, and current perception of desirability, i.e. fashion.

Condition

Condition is the most important single factor affecting a carpet's price, and is amenable to some sort of assessment by the non-expert. Old and rare carpets are likely to be both expensive and in distressed condition. It is a matter of fine judgement how much damage and wear is acceptable in an old piece, but if you are looking for 'perfect' antiques they will probably not be antique. Examine the carpet carefully and look for the following.

● **Completeness**   Is the carpet complete? Frequently the side cords are cut off, together with a couple of rows of knots, and a false side cord sewn back. This is an ugly mutilation, happily less common than it used to be. The first parts of a carpet to be worn, chewed or vacuum-cleaned away are the ends and fringes. Carpets are often tidied up by removing the pile back to a convenient line and fraying out the ends into a new fringe. Even worse, the outermost border may be missing altogether. With a false side cord and the ends frayed out, the carpet at first glance *looks* perfect, but missing borders reduce a carpet's value substantially.

● **Cuts**   Has the carpet been shortened or reduced in width? A trader would ask it if has been 'cut'. Long runners are often skilfully reduced in length to fit a particular space and sometimes carpets with repeating patterns are so cunningly altered that it takes an expert eye to detect it. A cut carpet will always have a reduced resale value.

● **Holes and repairs**   Holes are most easily seen by holding the carpet up to a window. It is essential to ask if a carpet has any repairs; an honest dealer will always point them out. It you buy a carpet and then begin to notice repairs that he has failed to mention, this says a lot about his probity. A repaired carpet will be less valuable than a perfect one, but it is a matter of degree. A small re-weave is quite acceptable where there would otherwise be a hole. Some repairers are so skilled in matching wool colours and inserting new yarns that the new parts are practically invisible at first sight.

● **Re-piling**   Has the carpet been re-piled? The treatment of worn areas is problematical. A carpet can be re-piled by inserting new knots into the existing foundation, but true matching of wool and colours is simply not possible. The old technology cannot be repeated: the new wool has a different twist and ply, it is carded and not combed, it is dyed with different dyes and so on. For this reason, there is a move among collectors and connoisseurs to ask for the conservation of old carpets rather than their restoration. Very small areas of re-piling are acceptable, but anything more and the carpet is in danger of becoming over-restored and unsaleable. Re-piling can be difficult to detect at first sight. The easiest way is to run the hand over the surface of the pile which should feel equally smooth all over; re-piled areas feel rough by comparison with the original.

● **Painting**   Often the foundation of a carpet has a lighter colour than the pile. When the carpet becomes worn the foundation shows through in an ugly way. A cheap way to improve the appearance is to tint the offending foundation the colour of the surrounding pile. This used to be done with spirit-based leather dyes or waterproof inks and still is for large areas. Today, 'retouching' with felt-tip pens is common. This process, known to the trade as 'painting', represents the lowest form of assault on a carpet except putting glue on it (see below). Any painting, however little, greatly reduces the value of a carpet. Its presence is an admission that the seller has little respect for a piece. Rather than offer a painted piece to a client, a dealer may prefer to unload it through the salerooms because paint is often missed by the inexperienced. Look especially at the black areas which tend to wear out most quickly.

● **Glue**   Some people, finding a hole in their carpet, repair it by sticking a canvas patch on the back with glue. It is impossible to remove rubber-based glue from a carpet whatever anyone may say, and any carpet with such glue on the back is ruined. Old-fashioned animal glue, however, which sets hard, can be removed with enzyme treatment.

● **Rot**   A carpet exposed to water or damp may have a rotten foundation. There may be nothing to see on the surface but the carpet may have a brittle feel and small cracks or splits visible on the back should arouse suspicion. Some dealers pinch and fold carpets to see if they can make the threads snap but this can be quite destructive to pieces which are not rotten but simply fragile through age.

● **Stains**   There are no rules about stains. Some can be removed by specialists but the discoloration of major areas by urine is impossible to rectify. Stained carpets are best avoided.

● **Wrinkled and misshapen carpets**   Crooked, misshapen and wrinkled carpets and those that will not lie flat on the floor should be avoided altogether. They are constantly being tripped over, the wrinkles get worn and holes appear, and such faults are almost impossible to rectify.

Other factors affecting value

Age alone is no guarantee of value or quality. Age is much more important with tribal and village rugs than workshop rugs. In the 1880s, the break-up of traditional life in many tribal communities, the introduction of synthetic dyes and the increasing demand for saleable goods all conspired to cause a progressive fall in rural craft standards. By contrast, the quality of workshop carpets steadily improved in the first half of the twentieth century. In the absence of specialised knowledge, the simplest and surest guide to the age and artistic quality of rural carpets is their colour. With a good colour sense it is possible to recognise the traditional palette of vegetable dyes without any special training. With this instinctive knowledge alone great strides can be made in picking out the good rugs from the rest.

A discussion of other factors is beyond the scope of these notes except to say that fashion plays a large part in determining the price of carpets. Information about rarity, quality of workmanship and materials can only be learned by observation and experience.

Specialised dealers

Old and antique carpets are mainly handled by specialist dealers. Most learned their trade from their fathers and grandfathers, though a fair number of small businesses have been started up lately by newcomers to the trade. Practically all successful antique carpet businesses are the result of the flare, taste and energy of one person. If you want to buy, take your time, get to know the owner, find out if you like his taste, and don't be pressurised. The dealer is human like you. He will respond to your interest and enthusiasm and is much more likely to give you a good deal if you behave in a decent and straightforward way. If you are arrogant and pretentious, with money, he will make you pay accordingly. A dealer who will not take the trouble to talk to you but always sits in the back office and sends one of his minions to deal with you is best avoided. He is probably looking for 'oncer' business.

Apply the same basic principles as with buying a new carpet. Ask to take the piece home before deciding, make an offer, and ask for favourable terms. Especially ask the dealer about the carpet's faults: like humans, there are no carpets without negative qualities. Again, find out if you can take a piece back and on what conditions.

Interior decorators

If you feel you have arrived at a point where you can afford a decorator to tell you what you ought to be wanting according to the latest canon of fashionable taste, take the trouble to discover the reputation of the person you employ. There are many honest decorators who have the respect of their customers and the trade. When they introduce a customer to a dealer they are normally given a discount of around 10 per cent which they receive as a commission on the sale. However a few have achieved notoriety for their greed and double-dealing. This is the kind of thing that happens. Finding he needs a carpet, the decorator shops around among the dealers – without the client, of course. When he finds something more or less suitable he will ask the price. The price

quoted is agreed between them on condition that it is trebled when the client comes to look at it. The decorator demands a huge commission, say 50 per cent. If the dealer refuses to go along with the deceit, the decorator threatens to take the client elsewhere. Dealers are not happy with this kind of business which they feel puts them in an invidious position.

Regular auctions

Here I refer to established auction houses holding regular catalogue sales; hotel auctions (see below) are something entirely different. It is not sufficiently understood that, except for some heavily advertised sales which attract a lot of interest from the public, most goods at most auctions are bought by dealers with much more knowledge and probably more buying power than you. It follows that you are unlikely to get something really cheap. On the other hand, if you want to buy a piece you are likely to find yourself bidding against the trade. If you are unknown to the dealers, they will stop bidding when they reach the price they have marked in their catalogue, so you will get what you want at a good price.

The problem with buying at auction is that raising your hand to bid is a voluntary act. No one is obliging or persuading you. Once the hammer falls the carpet is yours to pay for and take away. If it needs washing, repairing, does not lie flat on the floor, is too big for the space you had in mind, or has faults you failed to notice, it's your problem. The dealer with his infrastructure of cleaners and repairers is easily able to take care of these things, and he will not have failed to notice that the carpet is crooked, cut, painted or rotten. Here it is worth mentioning that when you buy from a dealer you are paying for his knowledge, expertise and taste – are they not worth something?

Buying at auction can be exciting and you can buy well, but it requires knowledge and sound judgement. Inevitably the motto is *caveat emptor* – buyer beware. There are a few golden rules for buying in auction which even the most experienced ignore at their peril.

First, examine the object carefully before the sale. Do not imagine that your taking an interest in it will suddenly excite everyone in the room. Having examined it you may decide that it is in too poor a condition or not what you wanted. It is too late to have your first careful look back home.

Second, have a clear idea how much you are going to pay before the sale and set a strict limit to your bidding. If you cannot stop your arm bobbing up in the heat of the bidding, you must get someone else to bid for you.

Third, pay for and remove your property as soon as possible after the sale to avoid the risk of damage or loss. The property is technically yours at the fall of the hammer.

If you have a good relationship with a dealer or specialist it is sometimes worth asking him to bid for you on a piece and paying him a commission. If you like and trust him it can be quite rewarding for both parties.

Hotel Auctions

Have you ever seen an advertisement in the newspaper which reads 'By order of the Grand Duchy of Lichtenburg liquidation sale . . .'? The advertisement evokes distant grandeur, accumulated treasures, the urgent need for money, great bargains – and all this on your doorstep. Do you pause to think why the Grand Duchy should be unloading its treasures in your home town and not in Paris or Amsterdam? Not at all, you rush along to the sale to scoop up the bargains. 'Viewing on day of sale only . . .' – never mind, you can't go wrong. You arrive and cannot find anyone to talk to except some clueless secretary who seems to know nothing. The sale begins. One or two people are bidding strongly . . . they seem to know what they are doing. Your piece comes up . . . the auctioneer hypnotises you with his honeyed phrases . . . 'incredibly rare Royal Princess Bukhara made from the underbelly wool of five hundred specially bred sheep reared on the high pastures of Mount Marzipan and dyed by a secret process handed from father to son for seventeen generations . . . I have never seen an example to match the quality and uniqueness of this exceptionally valuable treasure, the heirloom of a noble family . . .' Nervous and flushed with excitement, you start bidding . . . a few more bids and it will be yours . . . to hell with the roof repairs . . . this is the chance of a lifetime. The hammer falls – it's yours. Yes . . . it's more than you thought of paying . . . quite a lot more. Your wife looks pale.

Hotel auctions are a variation on the theme of greed and avarice played to the accompaniment of suggestibility and gullibility. Employees of the company (usually an offshore company) are dotted around the saleroom. Known as 'puffers', they put in bids if things look sluggish, and are even known to whisper encouraging words into the ear of a nervous bidder. Be sure that you will not be allowed to change your mind after the sale, and you will have to live with the results of your folly. The money will be collected with relentless efficiency. Nor will you be able to take your purchase back and exchange it for something else, at least not without the greatest difficulty. The goods offered are usually a mixture of new and semi-old pieces with a few old pieces thrown in. There is usually some 'star' piece with an extravagant description – 'specially made to the order of Prince Korkmaz Osurgan for the harem of the Crystal Palace'. The prices realised at these auctions are sometimes outrageous and their conduct is often confusing in the extreme, with goods coming up in any order and some being auctioned two and three times.

Door-to-door salesmen

Surprising as it may seem, the door-to-door carpet salesman still exists. He is known as a 'clapper' and is likely to be a highly skilled operator. He will not actually come and knock on your door but will probably telephone with some introduction, however tenuous. He concentrates on soft targets – elderly ladies with kind hearts and retired people, often professionals, who are ill equipped to deal with the guiles of the city slicker. He will be presentable, well-spoken and plausible. The clapper often starts as the employee of an established carpet shop, taking goods on approval from the owner and trying to sell them to earn a bit of extra money. A common story is that he has fallen on hard times, in fact very hard times. So much so that he must sell at a loss simply to get enough food for his wife and small baby. He is pathetically grateful when you agree to help him out, and he offers to give you your money back at any time should his fortunes recover a little. He gives the name of the place where he works, hoping and praying that no one will telephone. If for some reason you do want your money back and decide to contact the store, the chances are that he no longer works there. Clappers tend to specialise in a few well-rehearsed routines, some of them so comical that a book should be written about them.

One of the best was developed by a London-based specialist who at one time had so many people chasing him that he had to lie low for a while, so low in fact that he instructed his wife to send out obituary notices. He had a routine for selling rugs with stains. A companion helped to set the stage by keeping guard while the incredibly valuable carpet was being unloaded from the car, in case some artful criminal made a snatch-and-run attack. The buyer was implored to promise never to sell the stained carpet – a treasure of exceptional value and scarcity. Normally such carpets were guarded as imperial heirlooms, but this rarity was given by the Sultan of Turkey to a trusted friend as a special token of affection, and passed by inheritance into a family he knew. It took him three years of negotiation before they would sell it – you can imagine how expensive it was. The carpet was used on the occasion of the defloration of the Sultan's first wife. The stain is the visible evidence of her virginity. The buyer was further begged to promise never to wash the carpet because that would completely destroy its value. ·

Another is the disgruntled driver act. The seller arrives in a car with a carpet for sale, with an appointment of course. The seller orders the driver to carry the carpet into the buyer's house, and gets him to move the carpet from place to place to find where it looks best, speaking to him in a brusque and unfriendly way. Having quoted a price, the seller makes an excuse to leave the room to go to the car or attend to something. While he is away, the driver unburdens his soul, complaining how poorly he is paid and how badly he is treated. He takes the buyer into his confidence, explaining how the seller is a rogue and always asks too much money for his carpets. He, the driver, knows his master's habits and happens to know exactly what was paid for the carpet. He wants to get his own back somehow. He gives a little advice to the sympathetic buyer. 'If you offer him so much [substantially less than the asking price], you could probably buy it. He will get angry saying that it was an unfair offer and he won't be able to stay in business if he sells for so little. But stick to your guns. Tell him it's your final offer.' The buyer is delighted with this advice and makes his offer to the seller on his return exactly as suggested, securing the carpet – thanks to the advice of the disgruntled driver – at what he believes to be a give-away price. Needless to say, the driver is the seller's accomplice.

SELLING

Selling is much more difficult than buying. There can be little doubt that this fact lies behind the suspicion in the public mind about the carpet trade as a whole. If members of the general public knew that they could cash in their purchase at any time and get a good return, they would buy confidently and the trade would flourish. Unfortunately it is not so. The public has the greatest difficulty in finding out the value of the things they own and certain unfair practices conspire to depress prices in the salerooms.

Selling to dealers

If you have an old carpet and want to sell it, what do you do? If you take it to a dealer he will quite rightly ask you what you want for it. You do not know. You took it to him in the hope that he would tell you what it was worth. The dealer has been bitten by this problem too many times. If he offers you the real value, which will probably be higher than you expected, you will become suspicious that really it is worth much more. You will take it to another dealer who buys it by offering just a little more than the first dealer. The first dealer is therefore made into a fool for telling the truth. If he offers you a fraction of the value to avoid arousing your suspicions and you later find out it is worth much more, he is branded as a rogue. It is an insoluble problem, so dealers learn to force the seller to state what price they want.

The only real way to find the value is to seek out the most competent expert, probably a dealer, and ask for an insurance valuation, for which you must pay. State clearly and unequivocally that you are not selling the piece and have no intention of doing so. Get a certificate in writing giving the age, description and valuation of the piece. If you are still in doubt, get a second valuation and pay a second time – it can be well worth it. If there is any hint of a sale in the air, human nature being what it is, the whole exercise could be invalidated.

After a decent lapse of time, go to a dealer and offer the carpet for sale. If he tells you it is very nice and attractive, it means he does not like it and will only buy if it is very cheap. If he paces round it flicking the corners over with his foot telling you how poor it is, how it is crooked, will cost thousands to put into saleable condition, and how this and that is wrong with the design and colour, then he wants it. When he asks the price, quote him double the insurance valuation and see what happens. If it is buyable at that price he will not let you out of the shop until he has bought it, though he will use all sorts of tactics to reduce the price. He will ridicule you and make an absurd counter-offer, repeating the sorry catalogue of its failings. If you agree to sell, do not leave it in the shop until you have been paid, even if he says he wants to show it to his restorer for an estimate of the repairs. If you do, you are likely to find it has been hawked round the trade in your absence. If you refuse the price he offers, he may suggest selling it on your behalf. Do not be tempted to give your rug on sale-or-return. Be prepared to take it out of the shop and ponder the day's encounter in the quiet of your home – there is nothing to lose. You can try again somewhere else: if you are really asking too much it will soon become apparent, but if you ask too little you cannot bargain upwards. Remember, however, that as a matter of habit a dealer will never pay the asking price because it is part of dealer lore that a seller will not be satisfied unless the buyer puts up a good fight. A trick dealers sometimes play on a specially greedy colleague who wants to sell something is to accept the first asking price and write out a cheque immediately. The seller, convinced that he has sold too cheaply, will torture himself thinking about the money he could have made.

Selling at auction

The auction ought to be the best way of selling. Indeed it often is, but there are hidden problems. In theory, the auctioneer acts as the agent for the seller. He advises on valuation, the reserve to place on the article, catalogues it, informs the buying public, and puts it up for sale using a system of open competitive bidding. For his services, he charges a percentage commission on the selling price.

The introduction of the buyer's premium whereby the auction house makes a charge on the buyer as well as the seller reflects the reality of the auctioneer's position. In practice, the auctioneer is not so much on the seller's side as on his own side. Auctioneers know only too well that most goods are bought by dealers. If an auction house makes too great an effort to go over the dealers' heads directly to the end buyer, it will risk upsetting its main clients. Except for a few high-profile sales in the big auction houses, the efforts of most auctioneers are geared to feeding the trade. They would rather sell something cheap than risk not making a sale at all, so when you take your piece in to be sold you are likely to be persuaded to accept a very low reserve.

If the auction really represented the free market this would not matter, because competition would ensure a satisfactory price. Unfortunately the bidding is all too often not governed by the rules of the free market economy, because of a widespread practice among dealers known as the 'ring' in Europe and the 'pool' in the USA. Since most of the buyers are dealers they know each other, and before the sale they agree among themselves not to bid against one another on certain items. These items are bought by the ring or pool as cheaply as possible. After the sale they hold a second secret auction, known as the 'knock-out',

according to certain arcane rules and procedures. Making agreements not to bid against each other (as opposed to forming partnerships for joint purchase) is illegal, but impossible to eradicate.

So who are the winners and the losers in this game? The clear loser is the seller, who receives a fraction of the price paid by the person in the ring who finally gets the carpet. The auctioneer loses, because he gets a reduced commission from both buyer and seller. In theory, the dealer wins because he gets the carpet cheap and the amount the seller should have got is shared out among his colleagues. He does not need to worry that what was bought at auction for a hundred will be sold for a thousand, because the piece will probably be exported and no one will know. In fact, however, the gain is only a short-term one. The rings keep the market permanently depressed, making it difficult for sellers to get a fair price for their goods. This in turn undermines confidence and destroys the home market. It is astonishing how few dealers seem to understand this or, if they do, have the courage of their convictions. Some of the blame must lie with the auction houses for their failure to take the slightest risk on the seller's behalf, setting the reserve too low in their eagerness to make a sale, and occasionally for their plain ignorance.

Auctioneers have a particularly unpleasant practice known as the 'bought-in commission'. If for any reason your property is unsold, they claim the right to charge you a commission which can be half the normal selling commission on the price reached during the auction. This is manifestly unfair. The auctioneer, of course, has expenses, but the cost of cataloguing and handling something worth a thousand is *not* a hundred times as much as something worth ten. Another twist is that some auction houses only charge a bought-in commission if you insist on a reserve higher than the one they recommend. The one they suggest will be so low that it virtually guarantees a sale.

Unsold lots should be subject to a fixed handling charge to be agreed before the sale. Never agree to a bought-in commission. If the auction house insists, go elsewhere.

The last sting is insurance. Auctioneers' rates are high and virtually amount to an additional commission. Try to get your goods insured on your own policy.

If, after reading this directory of difficulties, you feel that the carpet trade is a dangerous jungle, remember that the best and quickest way to learn is to go out and buy. Regard your first mistakes as your tuition fees in the school of life and then go on to enjoy this vast and fascinating world.

Glossary

ABRASH

A word of Turkish origin normally used to describe the colour of a horse; it means dappled, speckled or mottled. The term has long been used in the trade to describe the small variations in hue and saturation found within a single colour in a carpet. It applies to two distinct phenomena. The first is caused by the crude technology of the tribal and village dyer which, combined with variations in yarn diameter, makes small variations in the colour of yarn dyed as a single batch. In the carpet this appears as a mottling which gives the colour an attractive life; an absolutely uniform colour, by comparison, appears dull and dead. The second is the abrupt change occurring at the point where one batch of wool finishes and another, not quite matching, begins: a distinct horizontal line is visible at the junction between the two batches. Carpet collectors, who are chiefly interested in village and nomad carpets, enjoy both kinds of abrash and will accept variations in colour of a degree that many merchants would consider a serious fault. The more sophisticated the carpet the less

acceptable these variations are, and noticeable batch changes in an urban carpet can reduce its value considerably.

AFSHAR

Also Avshar; a Turkic-speaking nomadic and partly settled tribal group in Southern Persia with summer pastures in the mountains south and west of Kerman; they are weavers of excellent piled and pileless rugs traded in and around Shahr-e Babak and Sa'idabad (Sirjan). Smaller groups exist in Khorasan, north-west Persia and Turkey. The picture is confused in Turkey by the tendency of nineteenth-century travellers to call any nomads Avshar.

ARDABIL

Burial place of the fourteenth-century Sufi Sheikh, Safi ad-Din, who gave his name to the Safavid dynasty (1499–1722). Its first ruler, Shah Ismail (1457–1524), a direct descendant of the Sheikh, had his tomb built close by. 'The Ardabil Carpet', one of the treasures of Islamic art in the Victoria and Albert Museum, London, and its pair in the Los Angeles County Museum of Art, are said to have come from the shrine of Sheikh Safi at Ardabil. Doubt remains about this both because the carpets are too large to fit in the shrine and because of the mercenary intrigue and concealment that surrounded the second carpet when the first was sold to the Victoria and Albert Museum in 1893.

The term 'Ardabil' is also used in the trade to describe the design of a carpet with a central medallion and sixteen pendants on a field with swirling foliate tracery.

BAKHTIYARI

A nomadic group in southern Persia migrating between the central Zagros mountains and the low-lying areas around Ahvaz; in common with the LURS they speak a Persian dialect with archaic features. They are also settled in numerous villages in a wide area east of the mountains around Shahr Kord, known as the Chahar Mahal.

BALUCH

Also Beluch, Balooch, Beludj; black-tent nomads inhabiting east Persia, west Pakistan and south Afghanistan with small numbers in western Afghanistan and Turkmenia. They speak a language related to Persian. Numerous villages of settled Baluchis in Persian Khorasan are the main source of commercial Baluch weavings, though confusion reigns over the distinction between them and the weavings of the Aimaq and Timuri tribes of eastern Afghanistan.

BUKHARA

For centuries a centre of Muslim learning and spirituality, and the principal trading point for Turkmen tribal carpets; many Turkmen carpets as a result have erroneously been called 'Bukhara' though carpets were probably produced there commercially as well.

CARDING

A process in the preparation of fibres for spinning, by drawing them repeatedly across rows of small metal teeth set into paired wooden implements, one held in each hand. The aim is to clean the wool and randomise the fibres. Yarn spun from carded wool traps more air than combed yarn, is warmer, softer to the touch, less smooth and less shiny (compare COMBING).

CHI CHI

An uncomfortable term that has become attached to an easily recognisable type of Caucasian carpet. Chi Chi carpets are finely knotted, have distinctive colours and designs and were most likely made in the coastal plain of Azerbayjan near Kuba. The usual explanation is that the name is a corruption of the word Chechen, an ethno-linguistic term referring to people living in Daghestan and Checheno-Ingush. It is highly unlikely, however, that these carpets were woven either in Daghestan or by Chechen people. Other possible explanations of the name are that it derives from the Turkish word *chichek*, flower or flower pattern; that it results from a syllabic repetition common in colloquial Turkish, and that it is a geographical term referring to a region just below the junction of the Kura and Arax rivers.

COMBING

A process in the preparation of wool for spinning in which the fibres are drawn repeatedly through the metal teeth of a large comb, usually held between the knees. The aim is to render the fibres more or less parallel. Objects woven with yarn spun from combed wool have a smooth, hard, lustrous surface. The process is equivalent to the production of a worsted yarn. Though time-consuming it gives a result that cannot be achieved by mechanical means (compare CARDING).

ERSARI

Also Arsari; a large Turkmen tribal group practising agriculture and herding, distributed along the Amu Darya valley and in north-west Afghanistan. They began to settle 400 years ago, but the Afghan Ersaris were still using tents in the 1970s. A major movement to Afghanistan occurred in the 1920s. The Amu Darya Ersaris produced a mixture of objects, some made for the tent and others of a distinctly urban character made for the market place.

FLAT WEAVE

A loose term used to describe any pileless weaving, for example a KILIM, VERNEH or a SOUMAK.

GABEH

A Lori word used to describe fairly coarse, long-piled rugs made by nomads of the central Zagros mountains for use in the tent. They are decorated with bold abstract patterns or naive designs and used to be considered too crude to be worth trading but recently their artistic value has been recognised.

GUL

A term of disputed origin and significance. At its most basic it is a crude transliteration of the word for flower (Persian) or roundel (Turkish). In practice it is used to describe the discrete ornaments arranged in an endless repeat pattern used by Turkmen weavers to decorate their carpets, bags and other weavings. From material surviving from the nineteenth century, it is possible to say that each tribe had its own weaving style in which certain colours and guls were used in an easily recognisable combination. It is tempting to associate particular designs or guls with certain tribes as heraldic devices or tribal emblems, but this idea does not bear critical examination. It seems that most of the designs are used by most of the tribes and that several of them are of considerable antiquity. Over the years the various tribes have modified common patterns in different ways to produce a variety of closely related ornaments.

KARAKOYUNLU

Also known as the 'black sheep Turkoman', a tribal group of Turkmen origin with an important place in the history of Azerbayjan, Persia and Turkey. Their descendants, consisting of a few dozen families, are still fully nomadic in the central and western Taurus region of Turkey.

KASHKULI

A sub-tribe of the nomadic QASHQAI with summer pastures in the central Zagros mountains of south Persia. They are of Persian appearance, speak a Turkish dialect and are famous for the quality of their weavings.

KAZAK

In origin a tribal name, now a town, river and district in the extreme west of the Azerbayjan SSR, noted for its coarse, long-pile carpets with shiny wool and vigorous designs, some closely related to patterns found in Turkish carpets. Little has been written on the ethnology of the region. The weavers were Turkic nomads, now settled, who came to the region at the time of the great westward migration of Turks in the eleventh century.

KAZAKH

The name given to the people of Kazakhstan in 1936, more correctly Kazak. It originated as a derisory term in the fifteenth century, when a group split from the Uzbeks who called them Qazak or freebooters. Today they are the largest group of felt-tent nomads, known for their felts and reed screens; they are not strong in piled carpets.

KILIM

Also Kelim (Turkish forms), and Gelim, Gilim, Gileem and Geleem (Persian forms); a pileless smooth-surfaced weaving in which the pattern is formed by the wefts which completely conceal the warps.

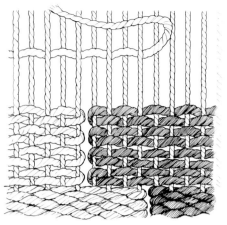

Kilim technique. A weaving with vertical gaps where one colour finishes and the other begins is a slit tapestry. To minimise weakness, vertical lines are replaced by a series of steps.

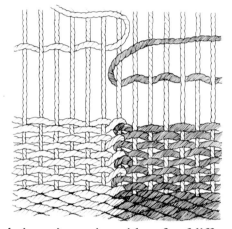

Kilim technique. A weaving with wefts of different colour returning around the same warp is a dovetail or shared warp tapestry – one of several methods of avoiding gaps between adjacent colours.

KIRGHIZ

An ethno-linguistic term used to describe a people of east Asiatic appearance, speaking a Turkic language, living in the Kirghiz SSR, Tajik SSR, western and north-western Sinkiang and north-east Afghanistan. They are classical felt-tent nomads who make felts, reed screens and some carpets. Their origin is debated, though their westward migration is well documented. Among the Kirghiz, fair complexions and striking blue-grey or green eyes are not uncommon.

KNOTTED PILE

A type of weaving in which tufts of wool forming the pile are wrapped around one or more (usually two) warps to project at right angles to the plane of the weaving. They are 'tied' individually, a transverse row at a time, and are held in place by ground wefts. The process is to be distinguished from the making of hooked rugs in which tufts of wool are poked into a pre-existing loosely woven fabric. In carpet weaving, knots can only be inserted as weaving proceeds and not afterwards. The 'knots' are not true knots though they do encircle one or more of the wefts to form a highly durable fabric. The pile 'knots' cannot be pulled out as they can be when the tufts of pile are simply looped round the warps.

There are three basic types of knot: the Persian, Senneh, open or asymmetrical knot; the Turkish, Ghiordes, closed or symmetrical knot; and the Spanish or single warp knot. The Persian knot is well suited to fine, detailed work and is found in all court carpets, almost all urban workshop carpets and some Persian village carpets; it is also used by some tribal groups in Persia and

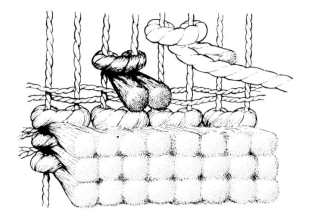

Weaver's eye view of the Turkish knot.

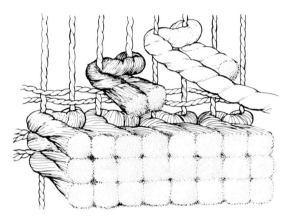

Weaver's eye view of the Persian knot, one of several variations.

neighbouring countries. The Turkish knot makes for a more durable fabric and is used throughout Turkey and the Caucasus, by most tribal weavers outside Persia, some Persian tribal weavers and in many villages in northern and western Persia.

KURD

A people of Indo-European origin speaking a Persian dialect with archaic features, though some tribes in contact with Turkish-speaking communities have adopted Turkish. They have lived in a region of eastern Turkey, north Iraq, and Iranian Kordestan for thousands of years. They are also to be found in north Iran, Khorasan, Azerbayjan SSR, Armenian SSR and Georgia. Most are settled farmers but there are large communities of black-tent nomads. Between them they produce a great variety of piled and pileless weavings.

LOOM

A structure for keeping WARPS under tension with a device for creating a shed to facilitate the passage of the WEFTS (see SHEDDING DEVICE). In carpet weaving the loom is a rectangular frame with the warp stretched between two transverse beams. Among nomads and in some villages, the frame rests on the ground (horizontal loom). The shedding system consists of a fixed heddle rod and a moving shed stick. Warp tension is maintained by wedges, and the weaver advances from one end to the other as weaving proceeds. To save space, this simple loom system can be fixed upright (as in Kelardasht): as work proceeds, the weavers raise their bench ever higher. In many villages a different warping system is used so that the weavers do not have to move upwards as they work. The warps are not attached to each beam, but wound continuously round both. When the line of work is uncomfortably high, the wedges keeping the beams under tension are taken out and the entire warp system is moved round like a roller towel. With work at the right height the wedges are then

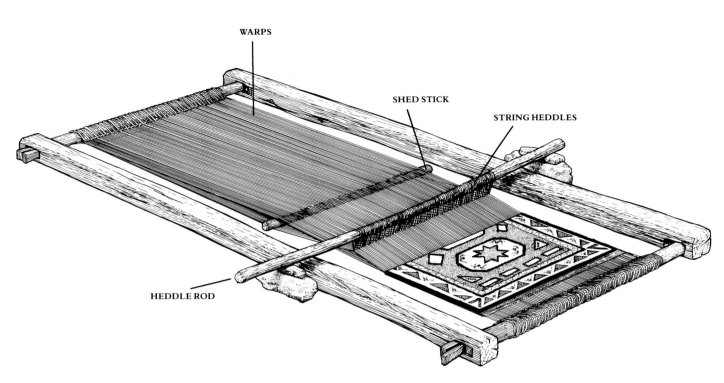

WARPS

SHED STICK

STRING HEDDLES

HEDDLE ROD

The horizontal loom is a simple frame resting on the ground. The weaver moves as work proceeds.

replaced. Even more convenient is the 'roller-beam loom' in which both beams rotate independently. At the start the warps, which may be long enough for several carpets, are rolled up on to the upper beam. As weaving progresses, the warps are gradually unrolled from the upper beam and wound on to the lower. A refinement found in the most advanced workshops is a shedding device with two moving heddle rods.

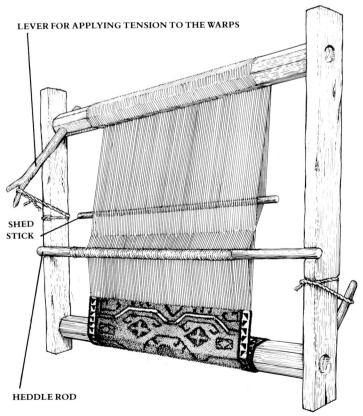

LEVER FOR APPLYING TENSION TO THE WARPS

SHED STICK

HEDDLE ROD

The 'roller-beam loom' allows the warps to be unrolled from the upper beam onto the lower so that the point of work can be adjusted to suit the weaver.

LUR

(Adjective: Lori), a tribe of black-tent nomads and settled villagers, long established in the northern and central Zagros mountains of south Persia, politically and linguistically linked to the BAKHTIYARI. They make interesting piled and pileless weavings.

MAMLUK

Also Mameluk, Mameluke; the name of a Muslim dynasty which ruled in Cairo from 1250 to 1517. The name derives from the Arabic word for slave because the line was founded by Turkmen slaves who siezed power in a palace coup. There is clear evidence linking a group of carpets to the Mamluk court but no agreement as to where they were made, because their decorative style cannot be related to other known Mamluk works of art.

MONGOL

An ethno-linguistic term referring to a people living today in Mongolia, southern Siberia, Inner Mongolia, the Dzungarian region of Sinkiang, and the Chinghai region of north-eastern Tibet. Historically they were at the centre of the last major confrontation between the world of the steppe nomads and the world of the cultivators and city-dwellers. Their effect on the material, artistic and spiritual culture of Asia was enormous, whereas their linguistic and genetic influence was minimal because they were absorbed by the peoples they conquered. Today there are still large numbers of nomadic herders living in felt tents in Mongolia. Weaving is not part of their culture.

MORDANT

From the Latin for 'to bite', the term describes a substance used to prepare wool or silk for dyeing. The mordant attaches to receptor sites on the surface of protein fibres and makes a chemical bridge between the dyestuff and the fibre. The commonest mordants are alum (potassium aluminium sulphate) and iron sulphate. Madder and the yellow plant dyes require a mordant, whereas indigo does not.

MUGHAL

Also Mogul, Moghul; an Indian dynasty which ruled from Delhi and Agra between 1526 and 1858. The name derives from the word Mongol because its founder Babur was, remotely, of Mongol descent.

NOMAD

The most superficial definition refers to people who roam about in search of pasture. In the context of carpet weaving, the nomads encountered have a highly ordered life governed by constraints not apparent to the casual observer. In essence, the nomad obtains his livelihood by combining two sets of marginal land. In the Eurasian steppes, nomads move north in the summer and south in the winter. In middle Asia, Turkey, Persia, Afghanistan, Tajikistan and Kirghizia, changes in altitude replace the north–south movement: in winter, nomads descend from the mountains to low-lying areas. If the nomadic cycle is broken by closure of migration routes or loss of the use of one of the pastures, animals die of starvation and the people rapidly become impoverished. A point often missed is that successful nomadism requires a fairly high level of material culture. Though stock-breeding is the principal livelihood of nomads they will use any available means of sustenance including hunting, fishing, food-gathering and agriculture.

OTTOMAN

Also Osmanli; a Turkish dynasty (c.1290–1924) which ruled from Bursa (Brusa) and Constantinople (Istanbul), named after its founder Osman. The Turks gradually encroached on the Greek-speaking world of agricultural Byzantium, opening the doors to a massive immigration of nomadic pastoralists with an economy based on sheep, horses and camels. Ottoman Turkish cultural achievement and military power was at its height in the sixteenth century when they conquered large parts of the Arab-speaking world and extended their rule to the Balkans. The fear engendered by their incursions into Europe remains in the folk memory of western Christendom.

PLAIN WEAVE

Used here to describe a weave in which the warp and weft are of equal tension and spacing. On the surface the warp and weft are equally visible.

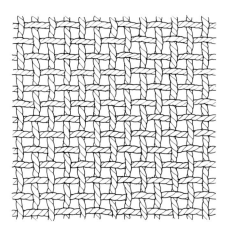

Plain weave.

PILE

See KNOTTED PILE.

PLYING

The process of twisting together two or more strands of yarn to make a thicker one. The resultant twist is usually in a direction opposite to that of the component yarns. In the village and tribal context, most warps, wefts and pile yarns are two-ply, which means that two strands of spun wool have been plied together. For urban and court carpets mechanical devices have been used from the sixteenth century onwards to produce yarns with three, four, six, ten or more strands plied together.

QAJAR

Originally a Turkic tribal name, it is also the title of a dynasty which ruled Persia from 1796 to 1925. It is named after its founder, Aga Mohammed Khan Qajar.

QASHQAI

Also Qashga'i, Qashgai, Kashgai; a political confederation of nomadic tribes in southern Persia officially disbanded in 1956. They speak a Turkish dialect, use black goat-hair tents and migrate between the coastal plain of the Bushehr province near Borazjan, Ahram and Khormuj, where they have their winter quarters, to the central Zagros mountains in the Shiraz province, north-west of Shiraz and east of Abadeh. There are six main sub-tribes: Shesh Boluki, Kashkuli Bozorg, Amaleh, Derrehshuri, Farsi Madan, and Kashkuli Kuchek. They are known for the quality of their weaving, though many of the carpets and KILIMS sold in the Shiraz bazaar are the work of settled villagers.

SACHIKARA

A Turkish-speaking tribe of black-tent nomads with summer quarters in the eastern Taurus mountains of Turkey.

SARIKECHILI

A Turkish-speaking tribe of black-tent nomads in the eastern and central Taurus mountains of southern Turkey. They often migrate to their winter quarters in the south in company with the SACHIKARA.

SALOR

A Turkmen tribe famed for the weaving skills of its women. The tribe was virtually annihilated as an independent entity by a series of military defeats in the mid nineteenth century.

SARYK

A Turkmen tribe most recently situated in the valley of the Murghab river south of Merv (Mary). They are best known for their rather ugly carpets made in quantity for the market place around 1900, though their earliest pieces are among the loveliest Turkmen weavings.

SEFAVID

Also Safavid; a Persian dynasty which ruled from Tabriz, Qazvin and then Esfahan from 1506 to 1722, founded by Shaikh Safi of ARDABIL. Two great Shahs, Tahmasp and Abbas, were enlightened partrons of the arts who enriched Persia with many fine buildings and a legacy of artistic treasures.

SHAHSAVAN

Also Shahsevan; a political confederation of Turkic-speaking tribes formed in the sixteenth century. They were once powerful but a succession of political misfortunes has reduced them to a few scattered families. They migrate from the Moghan plain on the border with the Azerbayjan SSR to summer pastures on the slopes of mount Savalan. They use a distinctive type of low circular felt-covered tent which lacks the supporting trellis wall of the Turkmen, Kazakh, Kirghiz and Mongol tent. They are prolific and skilled weavers specialising in flat-woven functional objects. There is evidence that they once wove piled rugs about which little is known.

SHEDDING DEVICE

To facilitate the insertion of the WEFTS, weavers used a device for raising and lowering alternate WARPS. In tent and home this consists of strings (heddles) looped around alternate warps and attached to a fixed stout pole (heddle rod) at the front of the loom, and another movable stout pole (shed stick) separating the other set of alternate warps. The opening between the pairs of warps through which the weft threads are passed is the shed, and the mechanism for achieving it is the shedding device. In workshops, especially in India and Pakistan, the single, fixed heddle rod gives way to a system with two heddle rods which are raised and lowered alternately to create the shed and counter shed.

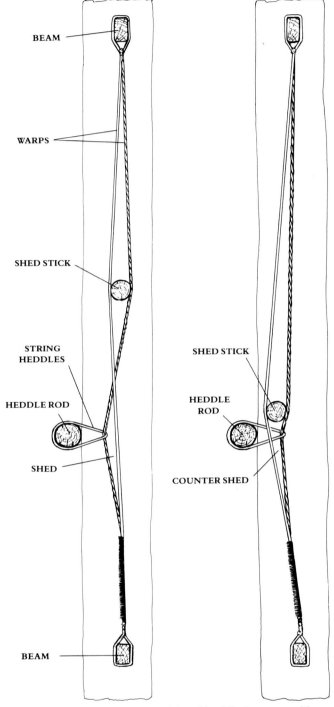

BEAM

WARPS

SHED STICK

STRING HEDDLES

HEDDLE ROD

SHED

BEAM

SHED STICK

HEDDLE ROD

COUNTER SHED

The shedding device of a typical fixed heddle loom used by rural weavers. A permanent shed is formed by string heddles looped around a fixed heddle rod. The counter shed is created by moving the shed stick towards the heddle rod.

SOUMAK

Also Sumak, Sumakh, Soumakh, Sumach; a term of disputed origin. The most plausible derivation is from the town of Shemakha, former trading centre and capital of the Shirvan province of the eastern Caucasus. Other suggestions are: a derivation from the Turkic word *sekmek*, to skip or run in a series of jumps (referring to the weaving process), and from the name of plants of the genus *Rhus* used for dyeing, especially dyer's sumach. It has come to mean two things: a type of domestic floor covering

produced all over the eastern Caucasus worked in a technique of weft wrapping and, by extension, the technique of weft wrapping itself, and any object made by this technique. Thus 'a soumak' is understood to be a rug worked in soumak technique, normally an east Caucasian weaving. Similarly, 'an Afshar soumak' refers to a rug woven in soumak technique by a member of the Afshar tribe, while 'a soumak bag' simply means a bag woven in soumak technique. See also WEFT WRAPPING.

SPINNING

The process whereby a continuous thread is formed by twisting fibres together. The twist may be imparted by the rotation of a weighted rod (spindle) suspended from the thread or resting on the ground. Alternatively, the rod may be attached to a rotating wheel driven by hand (spinning wheel) or a machine.

TALIM

Also Ta'lim; a weaving programme written in a special notation that specifies the colour, the number of warps to be covered by that colour, and their sequence. The system is first recorded as having been used for the weaving of Kashmir shawls. After the collapse of the shawl industry in 1877 it was adapted for the design and weaving of piled carpets. Today it is widely used in Pakistan and parts of India, especially Kashmir.

TEKKE

The dominant Turkmen tribe in the second half of the nineteenth century, makers of a great variety of refined weavings. Their carpets, eagerly collected by Europeans, were baptised 'Royal Bukhara' by merchants wishing to enhance their appeal.

TIE-DYEING

A method of forming patterns on a textile by manipulation of the dyeing process rather than the weaving process. In the dye bath, dye is prevented from coming into contact with the yarn or fabric by tying up or wrapping parts of it so tightly that the dye cannot penetrate. In Persia and central Asia spectacular silk textiles (ikats) are made by wrapping the warps before dyeing. Their designs have sometimes been copied by carpet weavers.

TRIBE

The huge literature on this subject suggests that no simple definition is possible. In theory, the members of a tribe claim descent from a common ancestor and are thus linked by ties of kinship. In practice, a theoretical consanguinity is insufficient to hold fairly large groups of human beings together for any length of time and the 'common ancestor' story is often a retrospective invention to justify a situation that already exists. The forces that bind a tribe together are many, including common language and life-style, but the most powerful cohesive force seems to be a political one. Historically, the tribes discussed in this context thrive on strong leadership, which calls forth powerful loyalties and removes the weakening effect of internal conflict over access to limited resources. It is, of course, wrong to confuse tribal with nomadic, but all the nomadic groups discussed here have or have had a tribal organisation.

TURKMEN

Also Turkoman, Turkman; an ethno-linguistic term referring to people speaking a Turkic language living in what used to be called Russian Turkestan (especially in the region now called the Turkmen SSR), in north-eastern Iran and north Afghanistan, with refugee groups in Pakistan and east Iran. There are also Turkmen living in north Iraq and many people in Turkey still call themselves Turkmen centuries after their migration westwards from Turkestan. In the nineteenth century they were divided into several tribes including the SALOR, TEKKE, SARYK, ERSARI, YOMUT, Chodor, Kizil Ayak, Goklen, and Nukhurli. They were outstanding weavers and the carpets they made for sale were traded in Merv, Bukhara and Khiva.

UZBEG

Also Uzbek; formerly a tribal name referring to a people claiming MONGOL descent but speaking a Turkic language. Nomadic groups of tribal Uzbegs still exist in remote regions, but the great majority of the people who call themselves Uzbegs today are farmers and city-dwellers in the Uzbeg SSR, the result of intermingling over five centuries of immigrant Turko-Mongolian people with indigenous Indo-European people. They have adopted the Turkic language, which distinguishes them from the Tajiks, descendants of the indigenous Indo-European population who have retained their Iranian language.

VERNEH

A term of uncertain origin used for a particular type of weaving worked in SOUMAK technique on a plain woven ground with a design of squares containing fantastic birds. They are probably the work of the SHAHSAVAN tribe.

WARP

The longitudinal threads fixed to the loom before weaving begins, which form a basic part of the structure. The established convention is that the term 'the warp' refers to all the threads collectively. However, in carpet literature a single thread is not called 'an end' as it is in other textile literature but 'a warp', and collectively the threads are called 'the warps'.

WASHING

A euphemism for the chemical treatment of woollen carpets which tones down the colours, dulls the whites, makes the pile glossy and gives them a soft and supple texture. The process in some respects imitates the effect of ageing and undoubtedly makes carpets more saleable, but the changes are irreversible and the process is not favoured by purists who believe that carpets should be allowed to age naturally.

WEFT

Also woof; the threads which are added in succession to the WARP, crossing at right angles in the direction of the width of the fabric. In piled carpets they are invisible on the surface; in KILIMS the wefts are the only threads visible.

WEFT WRAPPING

A weaving technique in which coloured WEFTS are wrapped around the WARPS to form the pattern. The basic fabric is built up on a loom with ground wefts as in any other type of simple weaving. The pattern wefts are wrapped as weaving proceeds – for example, over four warps and back under two; over four, back under two and so on – and hide the ground wefts. Weft wrapping is commonly mistaken for embroidery but the process is quite different.

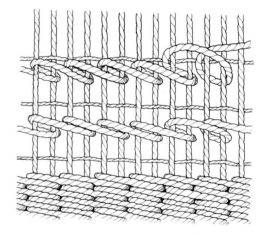

Weft wrapping, one of several variations. Only the coloured pattern wefts are visible on the surface; the structural or ground wefts are hidden inside.

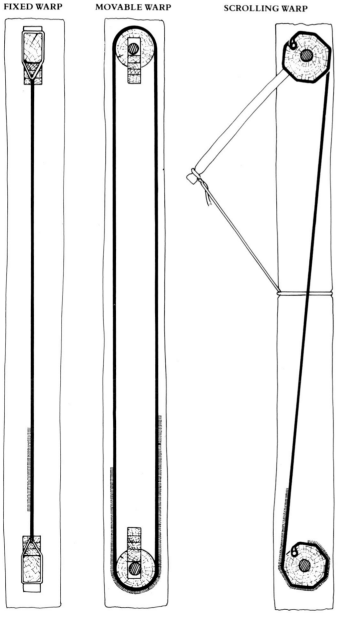

FIXED WARP   **MOVABLE WARP**   **SCROLLING WARP**

YOMUT

A Turkmen tribe found in both Russian Turkestan and north-east Persia. They are farmers, semi-nomads and nomads and in remote regions still retain much of their ancient life-style.

YUNCU

A formerly nomadic tribal group found in the Balikesir region of western Turkey. They weave unusual KILIMS and some piled carpets.

YURUK

Also Yoruk; a term used in Turkey for nomad. Apart from the Kurdish-speaking tribes, most of the nomads in Turkey are of central Asian Turkmen origin and some still call themselves Turkmen. However, over the centuries frequent clashes between central government and the nomadic tribes, formerly the Turkmen and recently the Kurdish-speaking tribes, have caused many nomads to deny their specific tribal origin, preferring to be called simply nomads. Most carpets called 'Yuruk' in the market place are made by Kurdish-speaking people in eastern Turkey.

Three basic warp systems used in carpet weaving.

Notes

1. Bill Holm, *Northwest Coast Indian Art, an Analysis of Form*, University of Washington, Seattle and London, 1965.
2. My favourite is the 'Gapylyk tribe', in Jack Franses, *Tribal Rugs from Afghanistan and Turkestan*, London, 1973, p.7. The term 'Gapylyk', an English transliteration of the Russian version of the Turkmen name of a lambrequin hung over the doorway inside the tent, was not recognised as the name of an object and was assumed to be a tribal name.
3. Technically, indigosulphonic acid, a light blue-green dye obtained from indigo by treatment with sulphuric acid, was the first synthetic dye. It came into use in the 1840s but the major development in synthetic dyes was in the 1870s and 1880s.
4. In technical achievement the Pazyryk carpet can be compared to a product of the cottage industry. It has no corner solutions and was not worked from a cartoon. It consists of a system of repeats with variations that would be within the competence of a highly skilled tribal weaver.
5. The revised dating of the so-called Seljuk carpets has been well and forcefully argued long ago by A. Geijer in *Ars Orientalis*, V, Michigan, 1963, but her views have largely been ignored and the carpets continue to be published as 'Seljuk'. They are typical cottage industry products based on the design of costly silks from China, just as the two seventeenth-century Turkish fragments in this book are based on silk velvet or brocade designs made for the Ottoman court.
6. See Serare Yetkin, *Early Turkish Carpets*, Istanbul, 1981, plate 76.
7. See S.I. Rudenko, *Frozen Tombs of Siberia, the Pazyryk Burials of Iron Age Horsemen*, London, 1970.
8. See Belkis Acar, in A. Landreau et al., *Yoruk*, Museum of Art, Carnegie Institute, Pittsburg, 1978, p.27.
9. Not Uzbeg but the work of nomadic Arabs: T.J. Barfield, *The Central Asian Arabs of Afghanistan*, Austin, Texas, 1981, and personal communication.
10. Sometimes weaving standards are retained while dyeing standards fall. Very few people in middle Asia still use the full range of natural dyes.
11. See note 3.
12. In the eighteenth and nineteenth centuries the Ottoman rulers maintained active, luxurious courts and built magnificent baroque palaces. It would be surprising if they did not also patronise carpet workshops, but where these were prior to 1860 and what they made is still being worked out.
13. Béla Bartók, *Turkish Folk Music from Asia Minor*, Princeton University Press, 1976.
14. See R. Ettinghausen, 'The Boston Hunting Carpet in Historical Perspective', *Boston Museum Bulletin*, LXIX, No. 95, 1971; also S.v.R. Cammann, 'Symbolic Meanings in Oriental Rug Patterns', *Textile Museum Journal*, III, No. 3, 1972.

Acknowledgements and Picture Credits

This book is the result of the collaboration of many parties and the author wishes to express his gratitude to those who have allowed their property to be illustrated, those who have lent photographs and those who have provided photographs of pieces (indicated by square brackets) which are also credited under the owners' names.

Al Sabah Collection, Dar al Athar al Islamiyya, Kuwait National Museum: 149; Apadana Carpets: 134; Atlantic Bay Carpets: 121; Robert Attenborough: 123; Avakian Oriental Carpets: 114, 115; Nathan and Joseph Azizolahoff: 24; Barbican Art Gallery, Corporation of London: 36 (top); May Beattie: 56 (top), 66 (bottom), 70 (bottom); Gordon Begg Collection: 80; David Black: 4, 9 (top), 13, 62, [69], 75, 93, [113], [116], 117, [123], [126]; Yussef and Benyamin Bolour: 43; Eric Bradley Collection: 116; Christie, Manson and Woods: 34, 138; Christie's International, New York: 106, 139; Simon Crosby: 37, 96; Cyrus Carpets: 7, 14, 131; Dinolevi: 142; Lord Dufferin: 69, 113; Eskenazi (Milan): 10, 83 (right), 84–85, 120, 128 (left); Fairman Carpets: 137; Robert Franses: 133; Joss Graham: 2–3, 54 (top); Richard Hall: 72, 87; Dr J.C. Hardy: 99 (top); State Hermitage Museum, Leningrad: 66 (top); Eberhart Herrmann: [49]; Heskia: 40 (bottom); Julian Homer: 104; Jenny Housego: 78 (bottom), 108; Alan Hutchison Library (André Singer, Charlie Nairn, Sue Errington): title page, 30 (top), 51, 52 (right), 53, 65, 77, 81 (both), 83 (left), 92 (bottom), 100 (bottom); Alexander Juran & Co.: 79; Nasrollah Kasraian: 86; Keir Collection: 33, 107; L. Kelaty Ltd: 8, 41, 98, 145, 150; Khalili Gallery: 27; D.W. Kinebanian: 68; Fritz Langauer: 5, 94; Joseph Lavian (London): 35, 47; Musée du Louvre: 146; Clive Loveless: [80]; Roy Macey: 59 (both), 132 (bottom), 140 (bottom); Mathaf Gallery: 36; Roland and Sabrina Michaud: 50, 63, 144 (bottom); Paul Nels: 154; OCM Ltd: 143; Jane Oundjian: 85 (top); Nick Oundjian & London Oriental Carpets Ltd: 17, 29, 45; P & O Carpets Ltd: 111; Jorg Pfeiffer: 54 (bottom left), 58; Josephine Powell: 15 (bottom), 19 (bottom left and right), 52 (left), 54 (bottom right), 55, 82 (top), 89, 95 (bottom), 157; Clive Rogers: 46; Galerie Sailer: 28, 112, 148; Rug Shop: 101; Nicholas Salgo: 88 (top); Jennifer Scarce: 9 (bottom); Shaikh and Sons: 109; Stella Snead and Joss Graham: 60; Sotheby Parke Bernet, New York: 23, 25, 119; Suffolk Collection, Rangers House: 32; Textile Gallery: [15 (top)], 18; Thornborough Galleries: 12, 22, 78 (top); Jon Thompson: 19 (top), 57, [66 (top)], 67, 70 (top), 82 (bottom), [88 (top)], 88 (bottom), 124, 132 (top), 140 (top), 144 (top); Wher Collection: 20, 49, 76, 103, 105, 128 (right), 153; Niel Winterbottom: 73; Marshall Wolf: 129; Georgie Wolton: 74, 197; Richard Wright: 126; A. Zadah: 39, 42, 61, 110; Private Collections: 11, 21, 26, 30 (bottom), 31, 38 (bottom), 64, 71, 90 (both), 91, 92 (top), 95 (top), 99 (bottom), 100 (top), 125, 127, 141; Other sources: 38 (top), 40 (top), 44, 48, 135, 136.

Thanks are also due to all those who gave their help and support at the time of the original project: Mrs H. Andrews, Mr and Mrs Paul Beck, J.L. Arditti, Arky and Ginger Robbins, Simon Boosey, and Moutafian and Co. There are many others who have helped in innumerable different ways, in particular: Michael Franses, David Black and Clive Loveless for the hours of work they put in on my behalf; Christopher Weston and John Fisher for their efforts; Malcolm Ward for his meticulous, attentive work and many helpful suggestions for the improvement of the text; Jo Darrah, André Singer, Jorg Pfeiffer and Roy Macey for their generosity in lending valuable original photographic material; and Eileen Graham, John Mills, Alistair Duncan, William Ruprecht, Jennifer Scarce, Eberhart Herrmann, Joss Graham, Peter Johnson, David Khalili, Mary Jo Otsea, William Robinson, Anthony Thompson and Keith Wayne who have all put themselves out on my behalf; Peter John Gates for photography; Tig Sutton for the illustrations in the Glossary; Tim Aspden of the Department of Geography, University College, London, for the maps; Peter Bausback and Robert Chenciner who were not thanked as they should have been previously; and John Hoole, Curator of the Barbican Art Gallery, for his unfailing courtesy and patience.

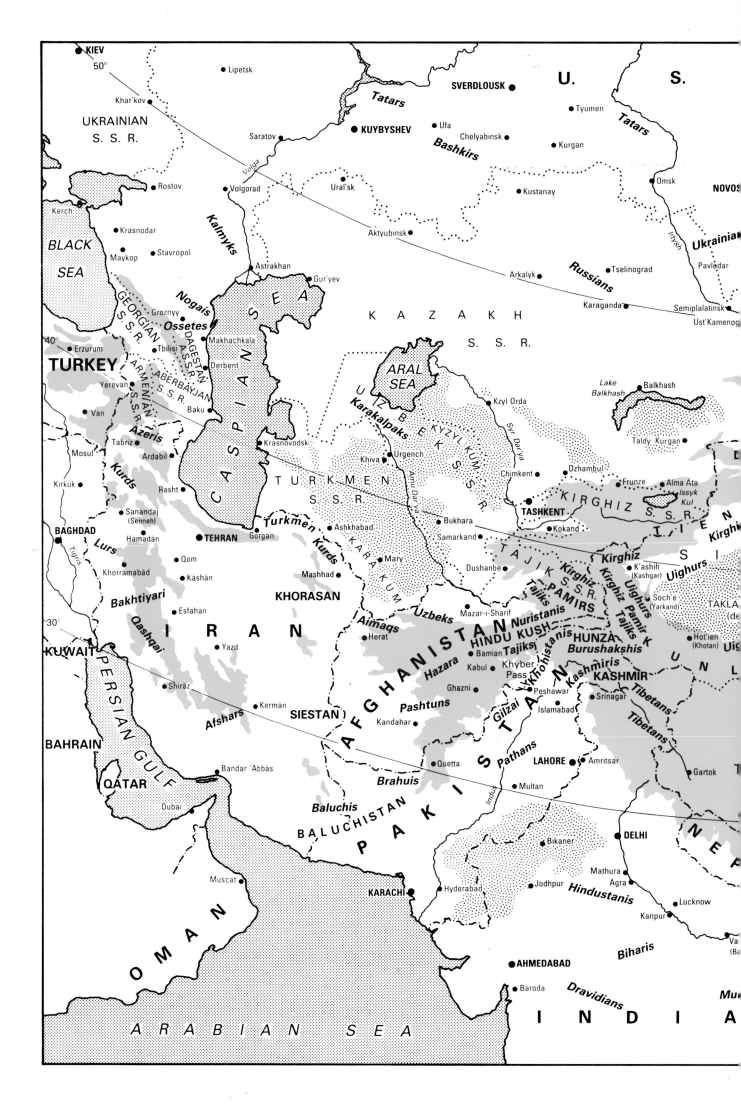

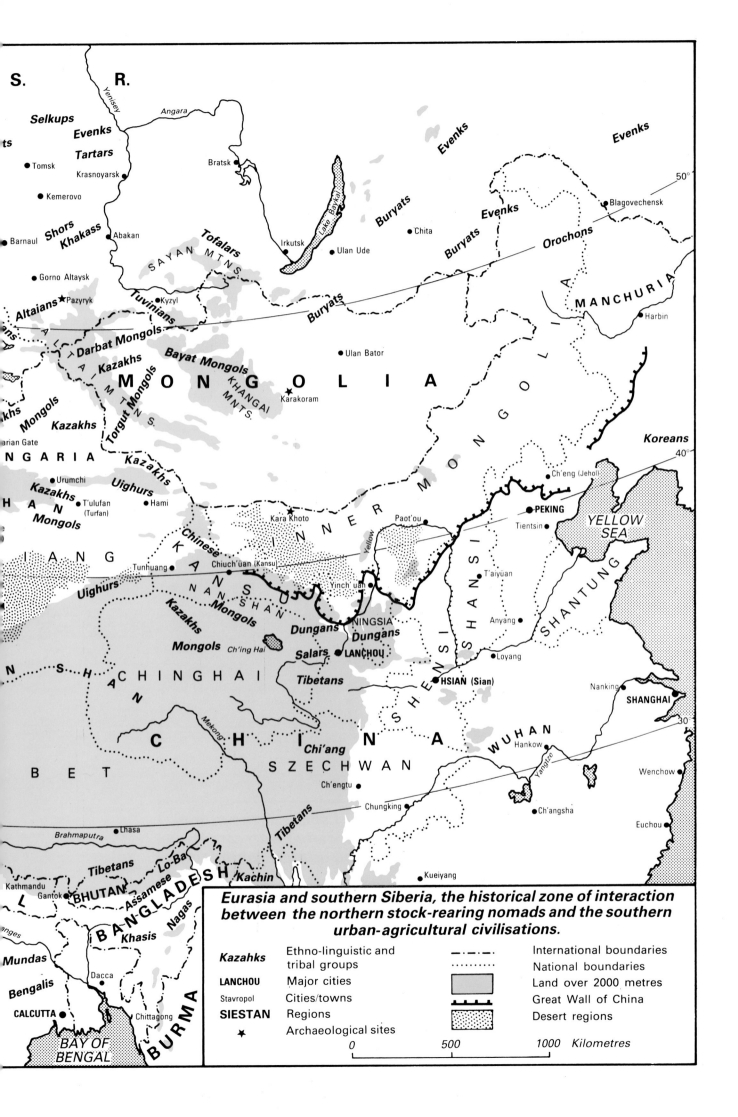

S. R.

Selkups
Evenks
Tartars
• Tomsk
Krasnoyarsk
• Kemerovo
Shors
Khakass
• Barnaul
• Gorno Altaysk
Altaians ★ Pazyryk
Tuvinians
Darbat Mongols
Kazakhs
Bayat Mongols
Torgut Mongols
Mongols
Kazakhs
Kazakhs
NGARIA
Kazakhs
• Urumchi
Kazakhs
Uighurs
• T'ulufan (Turfan)
• Hami
Mongols
IANG
Uighurs
Chinese
• Tunhuang
NAN SHAN
Kazakhs
Mongols
Mongols
Ch'ing Hai
N SHAN
CHINGHAI
BET
Chi'ang
Mekong
Tibetans
Brahmaputra
Lhasa
L
Tibetans
Lo-Ba
Kachin
Kathmandu
Gantok
BHUTAN
Assamese
Nagas
BANGLADESH
Khasis
Mundas
Bengalis
Dacca
CALCUTTA •
Chittagong
BAY OF BENGAL
BURMA

Yenisey
Angara
• Bratsk
Lake Baykal
Irkutsk
• Ulan Ude
Buryats
Evenks
Evenks
• Chita
Buryats
Evenks
Orochons
MANCHURIA
• Blagovechensk
• Harbin
Koreans
50°

SAYAN MTNS
Tofalars
• Kyzyl
KHANGAI MNTS.
KHANGAI MNTS.
Karakoram ★
• Ulan Bator
MONGOLIA
INNER MONGOLIA

Kara Khoto
Chiuch'üan (Kansu)
Paot'ou
Yellow
Yinch'uan
NINGSIA
Dungans
Dungans
Salars
LANCHOU
HSIAN (Sian)
SHENSI
SHANSI
• T'aiyuan
• Anyang
• Loyang
Ch'eng (Jehol)
PEKING
Tientsin
YELLOW SEA
SHANTUNG
40°

Nanking
SHANGHAI
30°

CHINA
SZECHWAN
• Ch'engtu
Chungking
Tibetans
WUHAN
Hankow
Yangtze
• Ch'angsha
Wenchow
Euchou
• Kueiyang

Eurasia and southern Siberia, the historical zone of interaction between the northern stock-rearing nomads and the southern urban-agricultural civilisations.

Kazahks	Ethno-linguistic and tribal groups	–·–·–·	International boundaries
LANCHOU	Major cities	·········	National boundaries
Stavropol	Cities/towns	▨	Land over 2000 metres
SIESTAN	Regions	▙▟	Great Wall of China
★	Archaeological sites	▒	Desert regions

0   500   1000   Kilometres

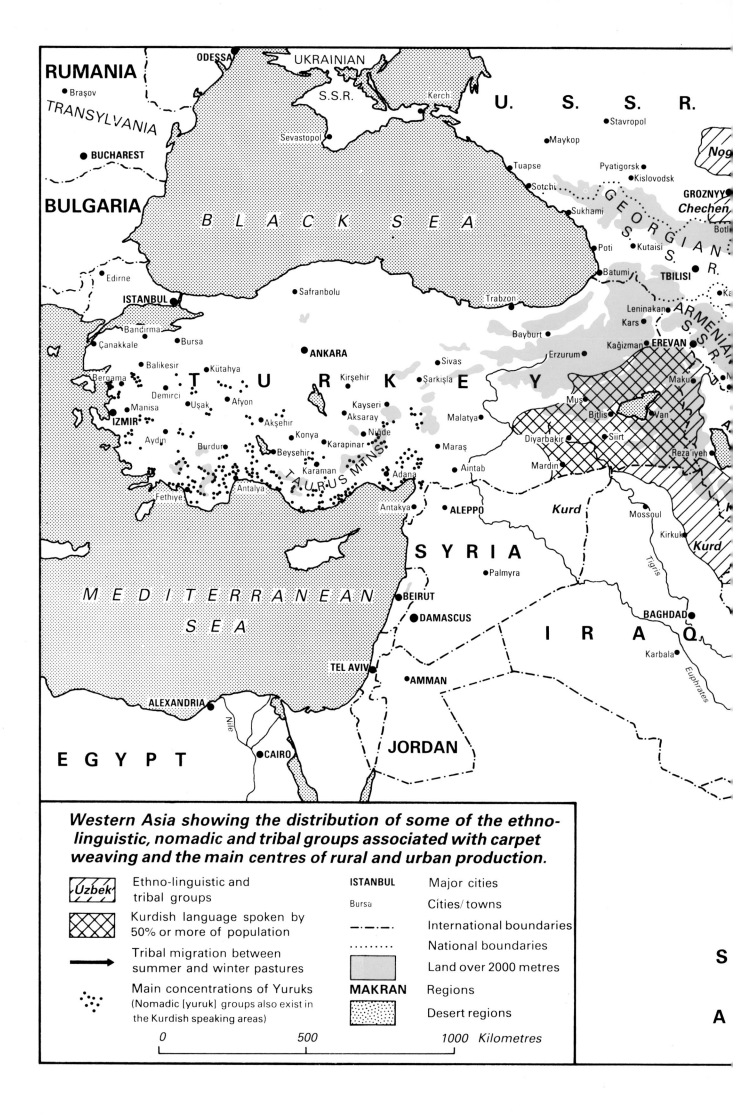

RUMANIA

TRANSYLVANIA

● Braşov

● **BUCHAREST**

BULGARIA

ODESSA

UKRAINIAN
S.S.R.

Kerch

Sevastopol

U. S. S. R.

● Stavropol

● Maykop

Pyatigorsk
● Kislovodsk

Tuapse

Sotchi

B L A C K S E A

Sukhami

GEORGIAN S.

GROZNYY
Chechen

Botl

Noga

Poti   Kutaisi

Batumi   **TBILISI**

Ka

Leninakan
Kars   *ARMENIAN S.S.R.*

Edirne

ISTANBUL

Safranbolu

Trabzon

Bayburt

Erzurum

Kağizman ● **EREVAN**

Bandirma

Çanakkale

● Bursa

T   U   R

ANKARA

Kütahya

Kirşehir

Sivas

Şarkişla

Maku

Muş

Bitlis   Van

● Balikesir

Bergama

Demirci

Uşak   Afyon

Manisa

IZMIR

Aydin

Akşehir

K   E   Y

Kayseri

Aksaray

Malatya

Diyarbakir   Siirt

Mardin

Reza'iyeh

Burdur

Beyşehir

Konya

Karapinar

Niğde

Maraş

Aintab

Kurd

Mossoul

Kirkuk   *Kurd*

Fethiye

Antalya

TAURUS MTNS

Karaman

Adana

Antakya

● **ALEPPO**

Tigris

M E D I T E R R A N E A N

S E A

BEIRUT

DAMASCUS

S Y R I A

● Palmyra

BAGHDAD

TEL AVIV

AMMAN

I R A Q

Karbala

Euphrates

ALEXANDRIA

Nile

E G Y P T

● **CAIRO**

JORDAN

S

A

Western Asia showing the distribution of some of the ethno-linguistic, nomadic and tribal groups associated with carpet weaving and the main centres of rural and urban production.

Uzbek — Ethno-linguistic and tribal groups	**ISTANBUL** — Major cities
— Kurdish language spoken by 50% or more of population	Bursa — Cities/towns
→ Tribal migration between summer and winter pastures	—·—·— International boundaries
⋰ Main concentrations of Yuruks (Nomadic [yuruk] groups also exist in the Kurdish speaking areas)	·········· National boundaries
	Land over 2000 metres
	MAKRAN Regions
	Desert regions

0   500   1000 Kilometres

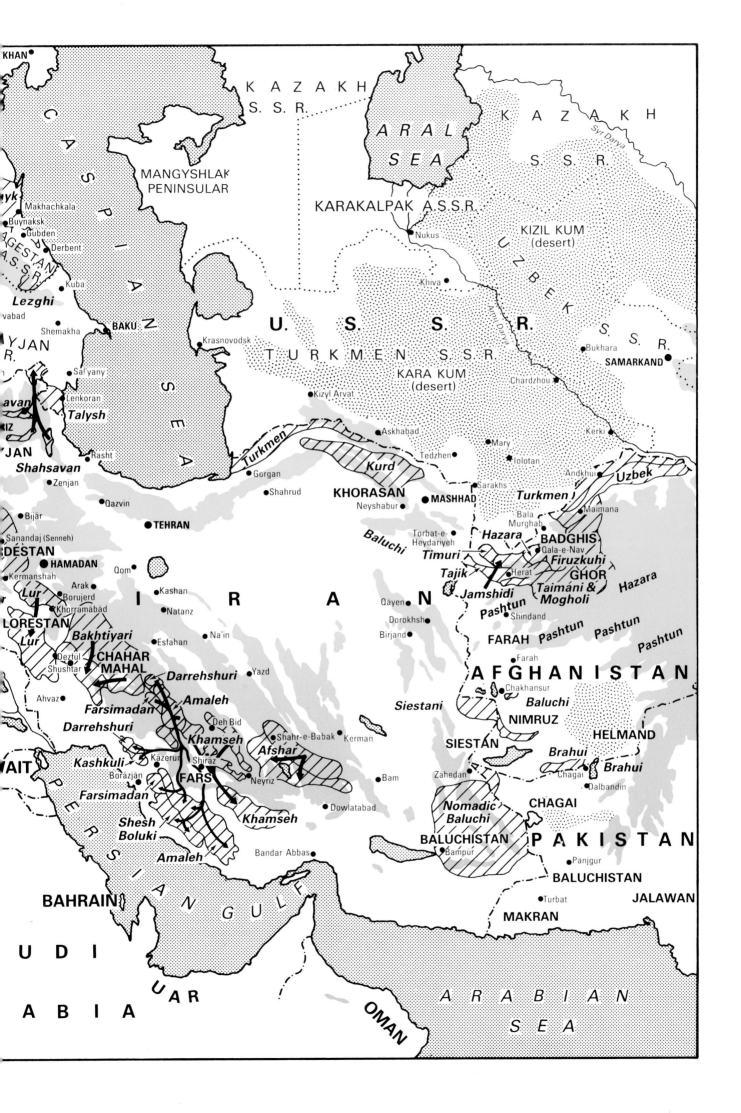

Further Reading

This short annotated bibliography is a strictly personal guide to the publications which I feel have something to offer – doubtless many favourites will be found to be missing. They have been selected for four things. The first is an intelligent and readable text, not simply a copy of what others have written, rearranged a little. The second is good colour illustrations: ideally carpets should be illustrated in colour which makes for expensive books. Many scholarly works are poorly illustrated, however, and of the numerous books published by dealers with excellent illustrations, few have readable texts. The third is artistic understanding: like musicality, some people have it and others do not. Those in the middle get along by learning all they can and watching others, never quite understanding what is going on. In spite of the many exhibition catalogues and dealer publications in which aesthetic considerations predominate, a surprising number of books reveal a basic lack of artistic understanding. The fourth is availability, which includes consideration of the price. This is a hopeless problem because books are being published and going out of print all the time. As soon as they do, their price soars out of sight, and no list stays up-to-date for more than a few months. Some books which are expensive and unlikely to be reprinted have been included here, although they are likely to be found only in libraries.

GENERAL

Bennett, I. (ed.), *Rugs & Carpets of the World*, London, 1981. Broad scope, lots of text and numerous moderate quality pictures per dollar. Better on classical than tribal and village rugs. Approach statistical and taxonomic, rarely riveting.

Black, David (ed.), *The Macmillan Atlas of Rugs and Carpets*, New York, 1985. A multi-author book with essays of varying quality. Good ideas and material but colour only adequate.

Denny, W., *Oriental Rugs*, Cooper Hewitt Museum, New York, 1979. All-time best-seller with a lively intelligent text and a good mix of illustrations.

Dilley, A.U. (rev. edn. by Dimand, M.S.), *Oriental Rugs and Carpets, a Comprehensive Study*, Lippincott, New York, 1959. Well written with much dealer lore, now outdated. Mainly black-and-white illustrations.

Dimand, M. and Mailey, J., *Oriental Rugs in the Metropolitan Museum of Art*, New York, 1973. A handbook of the huge holdings of the Islamic department. Good general introduction. Mainly black-and-white illustrations.

Eiland, M.L., *Oriental Rugs. A Comprehensive Guide*, Boston and New York, 1976. Intelligent, readable text with a sense of history. Little feeling for artistic aspects.

Eskenazi, John J., *L'Arte del Tappeto Orientale*, Mondàdori, Milan, 1983. In Italian. Well researched and meticulous. The best general selection of collectable rugs available (over 350 illustrated in colour). Colour printing only adequate.

Grote-Hasenbalg, W., *Der Orientteppich, seine Geschichte und seine Kultur*, Berlin, 1922 (3 volumes with over 140 colour plates). English edition available as *Masterpieces of Oriental Rugs* (3 volumes, 120 colour plates). Written by a dealer with a great eye. A collection of highly desirable pieces. Accurate colour.

Hubel, R.G., *The Book of Carpets*, London, 1971. Intelligently written with good technical understanding. Mostly black-and-white illustrations. Weak on artistic insight.

Kendrick, A.F., and Tattersall, C.E.C., *Handwoven Carpets Oriental and European*, London, 1922; reprinted New York, 1973. Mainly poor black-and-white plates. Useful as a reference work on historical and later pieces.

General Catalogues

Butterweck, Engel, et al., *Antique Oriental Carpets from Austrian Collections*, Society for Textile Art Research, Vienna, 1986. A catalogue of 200 collector pieces. Excellent colour.

Ettinghausen, R. (et al.), *Prayer Rugs*, Textile Museum, Washington, 1974. Good colour and some interesting essays.

Herrmann, Eberhart, *Seltene Orientteppiche*. A series of sale catalogues of collector pieces published in Munich annually since 1978. Consistently the best colour printing around.

Islamic Carpets from the Joseph V. McMullan Collection, Hayward Gallery, London, 1972. Lovely plates reprinted from the following book which is now rare. Emphasis on court and historical pieces.

McMullan, Joseph V., *Islamic Carpets*, New York, 1965. A catalogue of one of the great collections. He began with classical and historical pieces and ended with village and tribal. Wonderful colour.

Spuhler, F., König, H., and Volkmann M., *Old Eastern Carpets, Masterpieces in German Private Collections*, vol. 1, Callwey, München, 1978; vol. 2 (by M. Volkmann), 1985. Two catalogues of collector pieces. First-class colour.

SPECIFIC TOPICS

China

It is hard to recommend any of the books on Chinese rugs.

Baluch

Konieczny, M.G., *Textiles of Baluchistan*, British Museum, London, 1979. A valuable monograph, and primary source of information on the flatweaves of the Baluchis of Pakistan. Mostly black-and-white illustrations.

Caucasus

Schürmann, U., *Caucasian Rugs*, Allen and Unwin, London, n.d. Basically a catalogue. Ahead of its time. Attributions often intuitive rather than technically based. Treated with biblical reverence in some quarters. Good colour.

Tschebull, R., *Kazak*, Near Eastern Research Center and New York Rug Society, 1971. Exhibition catalogue. Good colour.

Court carpets and carpet history

Beattie, M.H., *Carpets of Central Persia*, World of Islam Publishing, 1976. Exhibition catalogue and monograph on the early carpets of Kirman. A mine of information. Mainly black-and-white plates.

Bode, W. von, Kühnel, E. (trans. Ellis), *Antique Rugs from the Near East*, Klinkhardt and Biermann, Braunschweig, 1955. Classic text. Mainly black-and-white illustrations.

Erdmann, K. (trans. Ellis), *Oriental Carpets*, Zwemmer, London, 1960. Classic text. Mainly black-and-white illustrations.

Erdmann, K. (trans. Beattie and Herzog), *Seven Hundred Years of Oriental Carpets*, Faber and Faber, London, 1970. A collection of monographic essays. Mainly black-and-white plates.

King, Donald (et al.), *The Eastern Carpet in the Western World*, Arts Council, London, 1983. Exhibition catalogue of court and historical carpets with black-and-white and indifferent colour illustrations. A sound summary of current thought on carpet history and court carpet production from the fifteenth to the seventeenth centuries.

Mills, J., *Carpets in Pictures*, National Gallery, London, 1975. A useful small monograph showing how European artists provide a framework for dating old carpets.

East Turkestan (Sinkiang)

Bidder, H., *Carpets from Eastern Turkestan*, Zwemmer, New York and London, 1964. A classic monograph with good colour plates.

Flatweaves

Cootner, C., *Flatwoven Textiles*, The Jenkins Collection, Textile Museum, Washington D.C., 1981. Material mixed, colour good. New ground covered on methodology in the description of flatwoven structures.

Landreau, A.N. and Pickering, W.R., *From the Bosphorus to Samarkand: Flat Woven Rugs*, Textile Museum, Washington D.C., 1969. Catalogue of the exhibition which first aroused interest in flatwoven textiles, many of them nomadic artefacts, which were poorly understood at the time. Mainly black-and-white plates.

Petsopoulos, Yanni, *Kilims: The Art of Tapestry Weaving in Anatolia, the Caucasus and Persia*, New York, 1979. A book written at the start of a phase of intense interest in kilims. Thoughtful text, many illustrations. Needs revision in the light of new knowledge.

Persia

Allgrove, Joan (et al.), *The Qashqa'i of Iran*, Whitworth Art Gallery, Manchester, 1976. Exhibition catalogue, with black-and-white and adequate colour illustrations. Intelligent text with ethnological approach.

Edwards, C., *The Persian Carpet*, Duckworth, London, 1953. An indispensible source book on carpet weaving in Persia in the 1930s and '40s, reprinted several times. Mostly black-and-white illustrations and very expensive for what you get.

Housego, J., *Tribal Rugs, an Introduction to the Weaving of the Tribes of Iran*, Scorpion Publications, London, 1978. An attractive small book based on personal knowledge and extensive travel in Iran. Intelligent text, mixture of black-and-white and adequate colour.

Opie, James, *Tribal Rugs of Southern Persia*, 1981. A sound attempt to chart little-known area of carpets. Good colour, lively enjoyable text by widely travelled dealer.

Tanavoli, Parviz, *Lion Rugs*, Basel, 1985. Exhibition catalogue by artist, sculptor and carpet-lover. Intelligent and interesting presentation, an invitation to look with new eyes at unusual material.

Technique

Tattersall, C.E.C., *Notes on Carpet Knotting and Weaving*, Victoria and Albert Museum, London, 1961. Useful and inexpensive.

Tibet

Denwood, P., *The Tibetan Carpet*, Aris and Phillips, Warminster, 1974. An elegant monograph not strong on colour illustrations.

Turkey

Bruggemann, W. and Bohmer, H. (trans. Herzog and Holmes), *Rugs of Anatolia*, Munich, 1983. A fundamental contribution to the study of Turkish carpets. Covers new ground on dyes and colours. Broad approach based on local knowledge; scientific rather than aesthetic. Good colour.

Landreau, Anthony N. (ed.), *Yoruk: the Nomadic Weaving Tradition of the Middle East*, Carnegie Institute, Pittsburgh, 1978. Exhibition catalogue with mixed black-and-white and adequate colour illustrations. Some interesting essays on felt and aspects of nomadic culture.

Turkmen

Azadi, S. (trans. Pinner), *Turkoman Carpets and the Ethnographic Significance of their Ornaments*, 1975. A serious work with good basic information. Adequate colour illustrations. Approach ethnological rather than artistic. Over-enthusiastic in early dating of many pieces.

Loges, W., *Turkoman Tribal Rugs*, New Jersey, 1980. Good colour illustrations. Dry taxonomic style.

Mackie, L. and Thompson, J. (eds.), *Turkmen*, Textile Museum, Washington D.C., 1980. A catalogue of old Turkmen pieces in US collections with essays on Turkmen history, life, culture and weaving. Colour illustrations plentiful but only of adequate quality.

Schürmann, U., *Central Asian Rugs*, London, 1969. Examples chosen by a dealer with a good eye and flare. Many attributions intuitive and no longer accepted. Thoughtful essays by H. König. Good colour.

Newspapers and periodicals

Decorative Rug Magazine. Published six times a year in New Hampshire, USA. New colour magazine focusing on the wholesale trade and decorators rather than collectors.

Hali. Published in London four to six times a year: glossy, about 200 pages – half of them advertising (interesting in themselves) – and good colour. A remarkable special-interest magazine centred on old carpets with broad coverage of textiles and related fields. Heavily supported by antique carpet trade. Approach object-orientated with bias towards aesthetic aspects; becoming more general. A good medium for keeping abreast of current exhibitions, ideas, books, auctions, etc.

Heimtex. Published monthly in German. Mainly for the trade in textiles for interior furnishing and decorating, including carpets. Some useful articles.

Oriental Rug Review. Published in New Hampshire, USA, six times a year. Changed from newspaper format to a 56-page colour magazine. Started as a review of the auctions, catering for small group of dealers and collectors. Approach parochial, sometimes serious, often whimsical.

Index